Law and Justice
in the Reagan Administration

William French Smith, official Department of Justice portrait by Robert Bruce Williams, 1983.

LAW AND JUSTICE
IN THE
REAGAN ADMINISTRATION
THE MEMOIRS OF AN ATTORNEY GENERAL

William French Smith

HOOVER INSTITUTION PRESS
Stanford University
Stanford, California

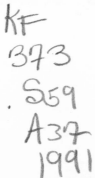
Sketch of Attorney General's Entrance to the U.S. Department of Justice Building appears courtesy of the U.S. Department of Justice.

Photos selected and captions written by Jean Smith and Myra Tankersley.

The Hoover Institution on War, Revolution and Peace, founded at Stanford University in 1919 by President Herbert Hoover, is an interdisciplinary research center for advanced study on domestic and international affairs in the twentieth century. The views expressed in its publications are entirely those of the authors and do not necessarily reflect the views of the staff, officers, or Board of Overseers of the Hoover Institution.

Hoover Institution Press Publication 409

First printing, 1991
97 96 95 94 93 92 91   9 8 7 6 5 4 3 2 1
Simultaneous first paperback printing, 1991
97 96 95 94 93 92 91   9 8 7 6 5 4 3 2 1
Manufactured in the United States of America
Printed on acid-free paper

Library of Congress Cataloging-in-Publication Data

Smith, William French. 1917–
   Law and justice in the Reagan administration : the memoirs of an attorney general / William French Smith
          p.   cm. — (Hoover Press publication ; 409)
   Includes index.
   ISBN 0-8179-9171-9 (hardcover). — ISBN 0-8179-9172-7 (paper)
   . 1. Smith, William French, 1917–   . 2. Attorneys general—United States—Biography. 3. United States—Politics and government—1981–1989. I. Title.
KF373.S59A37   1991
353.5'092—dc20
[B]   91-32376
                                                                  CIP

CONTENTS

FOREWORD

For more than two decades, Nancy's and my life was enriched—
yes, blessed—by the friendship of William French Smith. It was
the mid-1960s when I first met Bill. I was immediately impressed
by his intelligence, his grace, and his wisdom. When he spoke,
he made sense; and when he spoke, I listened. He had a gift for
clear, reasoned thinking, and I came to rely on his advice more
and more. I always knew I could count on Bill for wise counsel,
and he never let me down.

And he never let his country down—even though it meant
leaving family and friends behind. Bill and his wife, Jean, came
to Washington in 1981 so that he could serve as our nation's attorney general.

Let me point something out right here about my strong belief
regarding my choice of appointees for positions in my administration. I did not want applicants for such positions. I wanted capable
and successful individuals who did not seek or want government
jobs. I was willing to persuade them to serve their country, and I
let them know they could terminate their service whenever they
wanted to return to their businesses or professions.

Bill was a magnificent head of the Justice Department. He was
always honest, always fair, always careful, and always motivated
by a desire to do what was indisputably the right thing. He served
his country with dedication and distinction.

It was a source of the greatest comfort for me to have such a
friend from home at the cabinet table. My job included the selection
and appointment of federal judges nationwide, and U.S. Attor-

neys. That job was made easy and foolproof by William French Smith.

When I was coming to the end of my first term in office, Bill told me he was retiring from the Justice Department—but his loyalty never stopped. At my request, he served as chairman of the Board of Trustees of the Ronald Reagan Presidential Foundation, which has created the Ronald Reagan Presidential Library and Center for Public Affairs. It has been completed and, to me, it will always be a monument to him. Bill didn't live to see it completed. His death was a shock to all of us who knew him because he told no one of his illness—and that, too, was typical of William French Smith.

God bless you, Bill. Rest in peace, old friend.

RONALD REAGAN
June 1991

ACKNOWLEDGMENTS

My husband was never a man to waste time. In the first few years following his resignation as attorney general of the United States and his return to the private practice of law with Gibson, Dunn & Crutcher in Los Angeles, he took advantage of his many long airplane flights to and from California and the East Coast (where he sat on a wide variety of boards, both public and private) to record his recollections of the highlights of his tenure as head of the Department of Justice. These writings filled four volumes (more than six hundred typewritten pages).

In 1989, Bill began collaborating with John Greenya, a Washington-based author and journalist, on those volumes, as well as on material from John's numerous interviews with Bill. At the time of his death, on October 29, 1990, Bill had read and approved virtually all of the final manuscript.

When I learned that the Hoover Institution Press wished to go ahead with the publication of Bill's memoirs, I turned to a few of Bill's colleagues—Theodore B. Olson, Robert A. McConnell, and Kenneth W. Starr, members of the "Bill Smith team" at the Department of Justice—and Myra Tankersley, his confidential assistant at the Department of Justice and at Gibson, Dunn & Crutcher. Along with William Bradford Reynolds, former head of the Civil Rights Division at the Department of Justice, these kind, loyal friends provided the advice and counsel that helped pull the book together. Thus, although the memoirs are truly Bill's own, they are also, in the fashion of a good legal brief, a team effort for which, on Bill's behalf, I thank each member. Their support, patience, and dedication is a generous tribute to Bill.

My appreciation also goes to numerous others for their assistance and support: former President Ronald Reagan, Margaret Martin Brock, Henry Salvatori, Gerold Camarillo Dunn, Jr., and, of course, John Greenya, to name a few.

JEAN WEBB SMITH
July 1991

PREFACE

When I read, in early 1990, that the Ambassador Hotel in Los Angeles had been sold to Donald Trump, I reacted with mixed emotions. It was not that I had anything against the ubiquitous Mr. Trump, or any of his associates; it was just that the new report said they would be tearing down the hotel to make room for an expanded, modern structure.

Even though the hotel had been closed for several years, and the chances some buyer might choose to renovate it were slim to none, I was sorry to read that the notices of its death were no longer premature. I would miss the old Ambassador, for it held so much rich history, both for me and for the nation.

On the negative side, the Ambassador was the site of Sirhan Sirhan's murderous shooting of Robert Kennedy.

For me, however, the hotel was a happy place. It was the location for many interesting and important meetings—personal, professional, and political.

Some of the political memories are of the mixed variety. I remember, for example, hearing Richard Nixon give a speech at the Ambassador that probably cost him his 1962 bid for the California governorship. In that speech, Nixon, denying his own political instincts and accepting the counsel of his advisors, publicly disavowed support from the far right wing of his own party.

The next example of a significant event that took place in the Ambassador also involved politics but, happily, this one also had a positive personal side. It was November 1964, I had just remarried, and Jean, my new bride, and I were staying at the hotel. We were about to leave for our honeymoon in Mexico, but as it was election night we decided to drop in at a gathering of Republicans—my lifelong party. They were holding a "wake" for the historic pasting they'd taken in the presidential election between Lyndon Johnson and Barry Goldwater.

When I moved from my native New England to Los Angeles, and joined the law firm of Gibson, Dunn & Crutcher, right after World War II, I became quite active in politics, in the speech and debate arenas, but I had gradually lost interest as my law career blossomed. In the early 1960s the embers rekindled, for some reason, and once again I started taking a more active part.

The gathering was decidedly glum. There was a lot of talk about how bad the immediate future looked for the Republican Party, an outlook I understood but was not quite ready to share.

On our way out of the Ambassador that night, Jean and I strolled into a nearby room where we found a good-sized contingent of the party faithful listening intently to a tall man with an easy smile—and an easily recognizable face. It was the actor, Ronald Reagan.

"Everyone tells you," Reagan said, "that 'these are the times that try men's souls'; well," he added, in the same words that had just come to my mind, "*all times* are the times that try men's souls."

I listened a while longer, and found myself impressed not only by Reagan's simple yet effective way of expressing himself, but also by his obvious sincerity. His thesis was that as far as conservative republicanism was concerned, the 1964 election was not a crushing defeat but only a temporary setback. Conservatism, he said, was a healthy political idea whose time had not yet come.

As we were leaving, Jean asked me why I was shaking my head. "It's just that everybody here tonight," I replied, "is crying the blues—except for Ronald Reagan, who claims things are actually looking up. You heard him. He says he's been speaking around the country for a couple of years now, and he thinks people really believe in the conservative message. He believes it's only a matter of time before they win national office."

"I heard him speak once," Jean said. "He was wonderful, and I certainly agreed with what he said."

I replied, "He's as bright as he is sincere. There's an awful lot of substance to the man. Tonight was the first time I've seen him in a political setting, but I know there's already been talk of running him for the Republican nomination for governor in 1966. And the people who are doing the talking, many of whom are good friends of ours, are quite serious. If he does run, I have a feeling it would be great fun to watch."

"I'll say this," Jean replied. "I'd hate to be the fellow running against him!"

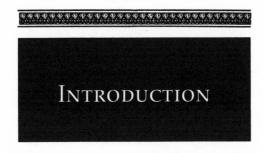

INTRODUCTION

The Reagan wave crashed down on the American political beach
... [giving it] the political power to change America and so change
the world.

Martin Anderson
Revolution, 1988

All of us who followed the Reagan wave ashore came to Washington with what can indeed be called revolutionary zeal. Our banner, held so high by Ronald Reagan, was a new and different philosophy of governing that we intended to put into practice as quickly as we could.

We believed that the federal government was too big, too Washington-centered, and too intrusive, and we planned to do something about it.

Take business, for example. We held the philosophical position that "bigness" was not *necessarily* "badness." And we planned to do something about that.

Or civil rights. We had no quarrel whatsoever with the laws that had been passed to overcome two centuries of discrimination, but we did have objections, from the standpoint of effectiveness, to some of the *remedies*—in particular busing and quotas.

Or take judicial activism, for another example. There was quite a bit of concern that in recent years activist judges had been turning their philosophical point of view into a movement. We were determined to return the courts to their proper constitutional role of interpreting the laws as passed by Congress, not usurping that function.

And then there was, of course, that massive juggernaut known as federal spending. Most of all, we were determined to slow that rate, while at the same time getting the government off the backs of the people, as Ronald Reagan so often promised during his campaign.

There were many other areas in which we intended to apply the tempering force of conservative ideology: The federal law-enforcement effort badly needed reinvigoration; violent crime, drug trafficking, and organized crime all were out of control. Immigration reform was critical, federal criminal law required overhauling, our counterintelligence effort needed reevaluation, terrorism had to be deterred, and a new balance was needed in dealing with environmental problems.

Before going any further, it occurs to me that I should say something about who this "we" is that I have been mentioning. Who were these people who came ashore with me—some running, some stumbling, all eager—as part of the first wave to hit the shore on that invasion now known as the Reagan Revolution?

So far as the cabinet was concerned, only Cap Weinberger (the secretary of defense) and I were from California, but the president's immediate White House staff included longtime associates Edwin Meese and Michael Deaver. All of us, from cabinet rank through the top Schedule C and other White House posts, were true believers. Some may have been more Conservative, with a capital C, and others less so, but we all knew that Ronald Reagan had come to Washington to make a difference, to streamline the ship of state for its return to traditional values.

Interestingly, I think that few of us, back in January 1981, could have sat down and written an essay succinctly identifying those values, or even outlining our exact goals. Yet we all knew what those goals and values were because they were embodied in Ronald Reagan's decade and a half as a public officeholder.

Essentially, we held in common four tenets, four beliefs that made up our basic philosophy. The first is that whether one is speaking of the political or the economic sector, ultimate responsibility should lie with the smallest entity capable of making final decisions. By that I mean that no matter if we are considering such seemingly disparate issues as national defense and local school districts, it is still wise to have the smallest entity that can make a decision do so. Doing so provides a better method of trial and error to see what works. Another significant advantage is that it maximizes citizen participation and provides added incentive for having, whenever possible, states and localities make the decisions that directly affect them.

The second tenet, which is related to what I have just spelled out, is that when it comes to getting things done, emphasis should be on the private sector, not the government. The third is that the best way to secure peace is to maintain a strong national defense; and the fourth tenet is that our democratic system requires that laws be made by our representatives, who are elected by the people themselves, and not by judges, who are appointed.

Those were—and are—our common beliefs. That they never needed to be codified is a testament to the similarity of our minds and our attitudes toward governing and toward the people of the United States. (The closest thing to a codification is "The Speech," Ronald Reagan's stirring address to the Republican National Convention in 1964.)

My main focus, the prism through which I viewed the goals and the accomplishments of the Reagan Revolution, will be the Department of Justice, which I headed, as Ronald Reagan's first attorney general, from January 1981 to February 1985—longer than all but nine of my 73 predecessors.

I intend this book to provide an inside look at the DOJ, the Department of Justice, an institution I believe to be one of the most powerful in Washington *and* one of the least understood.

By late 1980, when Ronald Reagan asked me to become attorney general, I had already turned down a number of governmental or judicial posts, some of them quite important (including an indirect offer to be attorney general *immediately preceding Watergate*). But when the president of the United States himself asks you to be his top legal officer, it is not, as the saying goes, the kind of offer you can refuse.

I have been a lawyer for almost fifty years, and I can say without any hesitation that the capstone of my legal career is the fact that I served for over four years as the attorney general of the United States.

Government service is immensely rewarding. During my years

in Washington, it was the rare person I met who was not motivated by, or received deep satisfaction from, his or her service to the public. Nonetheless, you pay a price for it, because you are exposed to the negative side of human nature as well as to the good.

Routinely, you will witness blatant and enduring hypocrisy, irrational behavior, small-mindedness, ruthlessness, and even betrayal (even though everyone is, theoretically, on the same side). You should also routinely expect that your achievements will not be recognized, or, if they are, will be chalked up to good luck or evil intent. Your faults will be magnified, satirized, and distorted. Public service, indeed!

The obvious question is, why do it? Why accept a government post and subject yourself to all of this? Well, in fact many people simply do not. But the answer, for those who do, is that there is no other experience to match that of public service in the nation's capital.

Washington is the center of activity where the vital decisions that affect the lives and interests of just about everybody are made. It is the hub of the most effective (though possibly the least efficient) system of government yet devised by mankind. And it is the gathering place of the best and the brightest. It is stimulating and immensely exciting. All told, public service in Washington, D.C., is an unparalleled experience.

In this book I have attempted to describe the experiences one is exposed to by accepting government service at a high level. These include the myriad problems and frustrations that surround one and must be dealt with, plus a cross-section of the excitements, fascinations, and pleasures, along with the satisfaction that stems from designing and implementing new policies and procedures.

If there is an overall theme to this book it is that all of this experience—the joy of working with talented, dedicated, and fascinating people, both in and out of government, as well as the exhilaration that comes from public service—is part and parcel of the fact that *we made a difference*.

Finally, I should add that while the book will concentrate on the record—the minuses as well as the pluses—of the Reagan administration, it will also be a picture of the man himself. It has been my pleasure to have known Ronald Reagan in several capacities—

as his personal attorney, and as co-regent of the University of California during his tenure as governor, as his attorney general in Washington, and as a friend—since the early 1960s. We are comfortable with one another, and with one another's views, the latter being, I believe, one of the main reasons why Ronald Reagan asked me to be his attorney general.

Perhaps some of my observations will shed light on this seemingly simple man who has had, and will continue to have, such a profound effect on America—and the world.

WILLIAM FRENCH SMITH
Los Angeles
September 1990

Law and Justice
in the Reagan Administration

1

ENTERING PUBLIC SERVICE

I T WAS UNITED FLIGHT 106, AND I WAS ON THE "FINAL" TRIP to D.C., having crisscrossed the country numerous times in the process of closing down a law practice and a home in Southern California, and entering the vastly different world of D.C. Over Flagstaff, I was approached by a reporter who asked if I had said, at a recent gathering, that "I do not even know where the DOJ building is in D.C." Surprised by the question, I fogged up the response.

A few nights before, friends had hosted a going-away party for Jean and me at Chasen's in Los Angeles. The affair was in a private room, and in addition to the nostalgia of good and old friends, it was notable because we had been presented with an original poster of the movie *Mr. Smith Goes to Washington*. On the poster, the heads of the two stars—Jimmy Stewart and Jean Arthur—had been covered over by photos of Jean and me. Adding an especially happy note was the presence at our party of Jimmy Stewart himself, with his wife, Gloria.

During the evening's toasts, I had told a facetious story which in fact included the line that I did not even know where the DOJ building was in D.C. Except for the waiters and other staff people, all the people there were close and trusted friends. My attempt at humor had been repeated, either with joviality by friends or purloined from context and passed on by others. Whatever the case, this was my first exposure to the "press leak"—something that would become a way of life in my new circumstances.

❖　　❖　　❖

It was Thanksgiving weekend in Palm Springs when I received *the* telephone call, the one from the president-elect asking me to become his attorney general. In a sense, I had expected such a call, but the anticipation was far removed from the reality of receiving the call that I knew would change my life, and Jean's. As I've said, however, the president-elect's question was one that a person could only answer in the affirmative.

There followed the most hectic period of my life. What to do with the house that we had lived in for so many years? Where and how to live in D.C.? How to prepare for the panoply of subjects, a wide spectrum indeed, that I would be confronted with during the confirmation hearings in the Senate? I also had to become knowledgeable about the host of pending matters at the Department of Justice, finding, interviewing, and selecting the many officials needed to populate the DOJ and replace all the presidential appointees, a task akin to taking over AT&T with all its top executives suddenly gone.

In addition, I was chairman of the Presidential Appointments Committee, which was charged with finding, investigating, screening, and recommending candidates for cabinet-level positions, which was close to a full-time job in itself. I had also received a letter from Chief Justice Warren Burger inviting me to attend and to speak to a variety of different groups and events, all of them important.

Although these were "invitations," it was clear from the context that the new attorney general was in fact expected to do all these things. A host of other invitations arrived daily, requesting my presence at and participation in governmental, legal, embassy, social, media, and other events.

Although my tasks were all intertwined, the first order of business was to prepare for the confirmation hearings. In this I had already enlisted the aid of Kenneth W. Starr, a talented young lawyer who had just been selected to be the newest partner in my firm's Washington office. Ken, a former clerk to Chief Justice Burger, later became counselor to the attorney general, in effect the chief-of-staff position. Thereafter, he was appointed to the U.S. Court of Appeals for the District of Columbia Circuit, and in 1990 was named solicitor general of the United States.

A major activity largely unknown to the public is the transition organization. This effort is put together long before the election is held. Each principal activity has its own transition team made up of people very knowledgeable in that area. The function of each team is to know the workings of that agency and the matters before it that require immediate attention. In the case of the Department of Justice, considering the scope of its responsibilities, this was a large assignment.

The DOJ transition team was headed by Richard Wiley, a former chairman of the FCC and prominent D.C. attorney and, as I was later to learn, a dedicated tennis player. Eight other members made up the team. Each was responsible for briefing the new attorney general on the various segments of his new responsibilities, on pending issues, and on the high-profile areas certain to arise in the confirmation hearings.

I immediately set about putting my business and domestic affairs in order in anticipation of total disruption of an otherwise very pleasant life. Pending legal matters had to be transferred to others, and my clients so informed and satisfied. The accumulation of a third of a century had to be dealt with and stored. Stoically, Jean undertook the vast task of packing, moving, and storing, and otherwise deciding what to do with possessions accumulated over a lifetime.

In a few days, I received word that the new cabinet was to be announced in D.C. at 11:00 A.M. on Thursday, December 11, 1980, with all the appointees present, to be followed by an open press conference. That meant that I had to do what some years before I'd sworn never to do again, take the overnight red-eye flight to D.C. This was not a welcome prospect, since the press conference would be held an hour or so after my arrival, leaving only time for a shave and a clean shirt.

I suppose it was inevitable that my seat on that flight was one row in front of a group whose avowed purpose was to debate philosophical issues through the night. My effort to obtain quiet produced some tense moments, but it finally succeeded.

On arriving in D.C. at dawn, I was met by Ken Cribb, a young man who would become assistant to the counsellor to the president, counselor to my successor as attorney general, and then assistant to the president. We drove to the Mayflower Hotel. After a quick freshening up, I found the other future cabinet members who were gathered, appropriately enough, in the cabinet room of that hotel.

The room was a mass of television cameras, news reporters, and media personnel. After the introductions, the floor was opened to questions. The attorney general's office being what it is, I had more than my share. The questions fell into two principal categories: how would my longtime close relationship with the president affect my performance as attorney general, and what would be our posture concerning civil rights.

The essence of my response to the first question was that given basic integrity and competence, it could hardly be a negative to know someone too well; on the contrary, it was vastly easier to tell a president that under the law he could not do what he wanted to do if you had a longtime relationship with him than if it were a new relationship. Concerning civil rights, I said that this president had been a pioneer in combating discrimination, and that would be a policy of this administration. However, there would be a substantial change in *remedies*, that those that had been a hallmark of the past and had failed—for example, busing and quotas— would be discarded in favor of new and more effective remedies. Some questions concerning antitrust, an area where substantial changes were to be made, telecommunications policy, public lands and natural resources, and so on were also forthcoming. I could see where the media's interests would lie.

Tom Korologos, one of D.C.'s most effective legislative representatives, had been assigned to shepherd me through my confirmation process. I met him following the press conference, and he urged me to make a courtesy call on Strom Thurmond, the new chairman of the Senate Judiciary Committee (before which I would appear for my confirmation hearing). On the way to Capitol Hill, he described the process, and particularly the chairman who would play a key role.

Strom Thurmond is one of the legends of the Senate, a delightful Southerner and a master of the political processes. Then approaching eighty, but married to a beautiful young wife and having four children under twelve, he was energetic, wise, and a consummate politician.

Tom Korologos gave me the script; the senator would be charming, sympathetic, and completely helpful, not only in the confirmation process but thereafter as well. And, said Tom, as I was leaving Thurmond would say, "By the way, I have a very able young constituent who is interested in a position in the Justice Department. If you can help him, I would appreciate it."

Of course, that is exactly the way it happened. And the senator's recommendations, then and later, were invariably on behalf of quality people.

Ken Starr and I returned to California that night. We were to attend a long-scheduled Gibson, Dunn & Crutcher partners meeting at Perino's Restaurant at 7:00 P.M. When we arrived somewhat late, we were greeted by a standing ovation that I found very moving. Later, in response to a toast, when I commented how much I appreciated that welcome, one less-than-solemn attendee cracked, "That was for Ken Starr."

That bit of levity brought warmth, but also a reminder that entering public service must never cause one to lose one's perspective.

❖   ❖   ❖

Before I'd even arrived in D.C., a newspaper columnist had dubbed me a "society lawyer." Without knowing what that is, I found it an interesting designation, particularly since after the navy I had joined a thirty-two-lawyer firm, and over the years had participated in building it into an international firm ranking as the fourth or fifth largest firm in the country—meanwhile engaging during that period in a practice as strenuous as any lawyer is likely to encounter. With certain elements of the press that designation stuck and continued to be repeated, always by those writers who knew least about my history, and apparently were determined not to find out. Epithets were easier than research.

❖   ❖   ❖

The next several weeks involved several trips between D.C. and Los Angeles. Interspersed were meetings of the Presidential Appointments Committee, which I was still chairing (but from which I would soon have to resign because of the press of other business), meetings with the DOJ Transition Committee and its attendant cram courses, efforts to recruit personnel for the top DOJ positions, and sporadic efforts to locate an appropriate place to live in the D.C. area.

The DOJ Transition Committee had been exceedingly well organized by Dick Wiley. The principal areas of concern were ably presented by members with expertise or experience, or both, in those areas. Included were DOJ management and budgeting, civil rights, antitrust, environment and natural resources, tax, law enforcement including the DOJ investigative arms—the FBI and the Drug Enforcement Administration—immigration and congressional relations. Many sessions were held with the Transition Committee during December and early January. This process was essential to prepare for the confirmation hearings and provided an excellent background for assuming the leadership of the department.

Members of the committee included Michael Uhlman, Jonathan Rose, Al Regnery, Hank Habicht, and Frank Carrington, several of whom later took positions in the department.

The process of seeking people for the principal positions of the DOJ was equally arduous. The immediate requirement was to find a deputy attorney general, the number-two position in the department. In mid-December, Bill Casey, later to head the CIA, sent me a memo strongly recommending Edward Schmults, who had been the general counsel of the Treasury Department under George

Shultz in the Nixon-Ford administration, and later deputy counsel to the president. I called Shultz, and received an equally enthusiastic endorsement.

Shortly after I had been designated attorney general, the transition organization had assigned Tim McNamar, later deputy secretary of the treasury, to assist me in the personnel search, and John Herrington, later secretary of energy, to assist in media relations. I therefore had Tim arrange for a dinner with Schmults at the new Four Seasons Hotel. Ed was an extremely impressive person with a superb background in government and the law, among other things, and the managing partner of White and Case, a leading New York law firm. When I offered him the position, he asked for time, which of course I gave him.

The next day I learned that both Jim Baker, the newly designated chief of staff, and Ed Meese, the counsellor to the president, were pressing Ed Schmults hard to take the position of counsel to the president, the president's lawyer in the White House. I was convinced that he would be more valuable to the administration as deputy attorney general. Determined to accomplish this result, I called Bill Casey, who concurred with me, and agreed to support that position. I also called Pen James, the designated director of White House presidential personnel, to cover that base. I then called Jim Baker and Ed Meese to lessen pressure from that quarter, and shortly thereafter Ed Schmults agreed to take the position.

Now we could both proceed with the recruiting effort, and I would have at least some additional time to pursue in particular the preparation for the confirmation proceedings.

Our interviews continued, though at a fast pace, and we were able to designate Rudolph Giuliani as associate attorney general—the number-three position in the department, and the man generally in charge of all criminal investigations of the department—and Robert McConnell as assistant attorney general for legislative affairs. Giuliani had been strongly recommended by Harold ("Ace") Tyler, deputy attorney general in the Ford administration, and became one of the most imaginative and successful persons ever to hold that position.

For three years, McConnell had worked for Congressman John Rhodes of Arizona, the longtime minority leader of the House.

(Years later, after I had left office, Howard Baker, majority leader of the Senate during my years in D.C., told me that McConnell was one of the best, if not *the* best, legislative representatives on the Hill of any agency of government.)

❖   ❖   ❖

It was during this same period that we were confronted with our first crisis—even before the inauguration. The Carter administration officials had negotiated a settlement in a federal district court proceeding that concerned an employment examination called PACE, the Professional and Administrative Career Examination, a civil service competency test used to fill 118 categories of federal jobs, such as customs inspectors, tax examiners, and social security adjusters. This litigation was initiated by civil-rights groups that contended the examination discriminated against minorities. Eleven days before the new administration was to take over—and, I am sure, with malice aforethought—the Carter administration entered into a consent decree phasing out the exam, in effect establishing quotas and practically guaranteeing exam results.

In the only court appearance by the office of the incoming administration before it took office, we requested that our views be heard. Despite that request, the judge, Joyce H. Greene, gave provisional approval to the consent decree. We then undertook negotiations with the civil-rights groups in an effort to eliminate the most egregious provisions of the decree, such as the quota requirement that blacks or Hispanics would have to fill at least 20 percent of the covered jobs before agencies could stop making special remedial efforts to hire minorities. We recognized the formidable task of attempting to repudiate an agreement made by our predecessors and approved by the court. We succeeded modestly, however, and went on to other things.

Two other issues were pressing in on us even before we were in office. Judge Harold Greene was pushing for the position of the new administration in the AT&T antitrust litigation, wanting to know if we were for or against the breakup of the giant telephone company. We were also faced with a decision on whether to ratify the Iran hostage accords initiated by the Carter administration. In the latter case, it is interesting to note that for over a year and a half, President Carter had not been able to do anything about the hostages. It was only after Ronald Reagan was elected in November, with his tough foreign-policy image, that the Iranians started to move on this issue. And they made certain that agreement was reached before Inauguration Day. It was signed on January 19, 1981.

❖ ❖ ❖

Superimposed upon all the official activity was a host of social functions. It was an exciting time. Not only was there a glamorous new president, but also one who had been elected in a landslide and with a strong mandate to change the course of events under way for decades. He generated excitement, and all observers, whether for or against his policies, were fascinated.

And he did all the right things. He visited Capitol Hill, he visited the Supreme Court, he announced that Mike Mansfield, the revered former Democratic majority leader of the Senate, would continue as ambassador to Japan. He also asked the highly regarded director of the FBI, William Webster (who would become a close friend of mine and perennial tennis partner), to stay on.

❖ ❖ ❖

Old Washington, new Washington, and nongovernmental Washington wanted to get into the act. Even Democrats such as Averell and Pam Harriman, the premier Democratic fund-raising couple who undoubtedly despised the new president's policies, hosted beautiful parties for all of us. It was at one of these that Clark Clifford was tape-recorded as referring to the president as an "amiable dunce"—an interesting reference to a man who had been governor of our largest state for eight years and who had engineered one of the few election wins over an incumbent president.

❖   ❖   ❖

During this period, my wife, Jean, was in the process of closing our home of over twenty years in San Marino—a very difficult task under normal circumstances, but particularly so because we both tend to be pack rats and hang on to everything. She commuted regularly between D.C. and Los Angeles, but did not complete the house-closing process until the first of June, until which time I was, essentially, a bachelor.

Further complicating matters was the fact that my secretary of some twenty years, Myra Tankersley, was engaged in the related process of closing my office at Gibson, Dunn & Crutcher in Los Angeles (as well as her home in Pasadena) and was not able to join me for a month after I took office. Myra had been my right hand for years, and although there were longtime, experienced personnel in the attorney general's office, they were not familiar with my modus operandi or my work habits. Myra finally joined DOJ, as confidential assistant to the attorney general, on February 23, 1981 (flying from Los Angeles on Air Force One with the president), and our inner office took shape soon after that.

Jean and I had gone through the usual procedures to locate in D.C. During the inauguration, we had shared a suite at the Madison Hotel (owned and operated by our good friend Marshall Coyne) with Bunny and Jack Wrather, and thereafter took a suite for ten days at the Jefferson Hotel. For a while, Jean looked at houses to buy or apartments to lease, but nothing worked out quite right. Then, as time went on, we concluded, as if by osmosis, that we were doing fine where we were. As a result, we maintained that suite at the Jefferson for over four years. It had two bedrooms, a living room with fireplace, a dining room and, most important, a small kitchen.

Although it was four or five months before Jean was able to join me in Washington, I was greatly aided by our good friend, and the new chief of protocol, Lee Annenberg. During that period, her husband, Walter, the former ambassador to Great Britain, was also unable to be in D.C., and as a result Lee and I accomplished many of our necessary and usually pleasurable social rounds and obligations together.

❖　　❖　　❖

Ken Starr, working with Senator Strom Thurmond, had arrived at January 15, 1981, as the date for my confirmation hearing to begin. The 1980 election had produced a Republican majority in the Senate, and that made Senator Thurmond the Judiciary Committee chairman. One could not have hoped for a more cooperative and helpful chairman.

It became clear that there would be two principal issues in my confirmation hearing: one was my closeness to the president, and the other was my refusal to resign from two clubs that did not admit women.

The first was an issue primarily raised by the media—and oddballs such as Wisconsin Democratic senator William Proxmire. It was a phony issue and difficult for liberals to raise because of the Bobby Kennedy–Jack Kennedy relationship, but they raised it anyway.

The argument seemed to be that because John Mitchell was a close friend of Nixon, that fact had somehow produced Watergate. In the first place, Mitchell was not a close friend of Nixon, and, second, there is no evidence whatsoever that a close relationship produces results harmful to the public interest. To the contrary, the evidence shows that a close relationship has been to the public good. That was true with Bobby Kennedy; it was true with Griffin Bell, a friend and confidant of President Carter; and, if I do say so myself, it was true with me and President Reagan. In none of those regimes did any constitutional crisis arise. Indeed, the relationships were excellent and the public interest well served. I might say, too, that this was not by accident. The relationship produced, rather than impeded, this result. The notion that one can know someone too well is foolish, assuming of course that personal integrity is not in question; if it is, that's another issue. It is much easier to advise someone you know well that he cannot do something than it is for a stranger to do so.

The second and far more intense issue was my refusal to resign from the Bohemian Club. Visitations and requested visitations from women's groups established the intensity. Such visits, rather than being hostile, were more of an effort to make me understand why I should resign. I told them, as I did the committee later, that I did not believe we had reached a point in this country where being a member of the Davis Cup team, the Boy Scouts, or the Little League should be viewed as evidence of a discriminatory intent.

At the *Los Angeles Times* party at the Renwick Gallery, I sat at a table with Roger Mudd, the television personality, and (as usual) a liberal. We discussed this question, and he pointed out that in recent years no appointee had been confirmed who had not resigned from clubs that discriminated, and he urged that I do so.

I pointed out how hypocritical and expedient I thought that result was: the intent to belong to that club had long been established, and resigning to achieve confirmation was the ultimate in hypocrisy—particularly since the pattern was to rejoin the same clubs *after* governmental service was terminated. (The story is that Edmund Muskie, who had resigned to achieve confirmation as secretary of state, later reapplied for membership in the Chevy Chase Club, and was refused—quite properly, in my opinion.) Roger Mudd had no response to this.

That night I also saw Robert Strauss, former chairman of the Democratic National Committee and an old hand in politics in D.C. Strauss strongly advised that I resign, not for reasons of policy or principle but for reasons that were purely pragmatic; if this issue did not exist, he reasoned, then my confirmation would be a cinch, therefore why not resign?

In my view, none of these reasons was sufficient, since I felt that the distinctions upon which the club policy was based were quite valid. Indeed, during a colloquy in response to a query as to why I was so stubborn on this question, I replied: "The simple fact is that it is harder to get into the Bohemian Club than it is to become Attorney General." That facetious statement seemed more readily accepted than any other.

The representatives of four women's groups appeared to testify, not to oppose my confirmation but to urge the Senate committee to require that I resign as a condition of confirmation. In a good-natured confrontation, Chairman Thurmond asked the representatives of these organizations if they admitted men as full-fledged members. One of them—B'nai B'rith Women—had to admit it did not, and that made the point of the day.

It was evident from my courtesy calls on the various members of the Senate Judiciary Committee that certain cardinal rules had to be followed during a confirmation hearing. These were confirmed in our Transition Committee meetings and by Tom Korologos. The first was not to make any commitments on either substance or process. One is particularly vulnerable at this stage because of the relatively unfamiliar areas, a lack of nuts-and-bolts knowledge of what has gone on or is going on, and the desire to establish a good working relationship (among other things, these are the people who are going to vote on your confirmation) and to maintain it, since these are the senators and the committee one will work with on a continuing basis.

Furthermore, agreeing even implicitly (and senators are good at drawing inferences—they can hear what they want to hear) to what appears to be a "motherhood proposition" can be dangerous. Much lies below the surface.

During the courtesy calls, a frequent inquiry was for me to pledge that I would cooperate with Congress in responding to requests to provide executive branch records and documents to the Congress. On the surface, this seemed a reasonable request, but in fact a minefield was involved here, as we shall see. Fortunately, I had been warned on this one. My response, repeated often, was that I would certainly cooperate to the extent it seemed appropriate to do so.

A second "must" was not to pretend to know more than I actually knew. To attempt this is foolhardy. It can be embarrassing at best, and credibility-damaging at worst. Once discovered, such a pretension can be so easily exploited that it can reflect on everything one has said.

All of this called for a high quotient of "I'll be glad to look into that, Senator"; "After I have reviewed the file on that matter I'll get back to you"; "I can answer that in general terms and will deal with the specifics at the appropriate time"; "That sounds controversial, and I'll have to get both sides before answering"; and so forth.

The result of that approach, however, although by far the lesser evil, is that one is accused of not knowing anything, being too cautious, or even trying to cover up. I received a fair amount of that kind of reaction. I did find it interesting, however, that four years later, after I'd left office, I read the transcript of my confirmation hearing, and even with my then-extensive experience I would have changed very little of my hearing testimony.

The hearing took some nine hours in all (fortunately, it was all in one day; Griffin Bell, my predecessor, had undergone a merciless proceeding that required eight separate days of hearings) and covered every subject from philosophy to refugees to antitrust. Although generally a friendly hearing and one that occurred within the context of a new administration just elected by a landslide, it was nevertheless an exhausting experience.

On reflection, there were two aspects that I found most tiring. The first involved the pair of television lights high up on the wall behind the committee—not quite eye level, but close enough. Looking up into these lights for that length of time was extremely wearing. The second was having to concentrate, continuously, on the questions. To answer the wrong question or a misunderstood question would have been perilous indeed. That kind of intense, concentrated effort can cause one to go numb.

Particularly irritating after long hours of this process were the senators' aides scurrying around behind them, busily scribbling long and convoluted questions on cards they would pass to their senator, who would then proceed to read them. After I had testified for several hours, almost by accident I came up with a very useful gambit: After a senator had plodded through a complex, rhetorical, and usually argumentative question, I would say, "Senator, I do not understand the question. Would you please rephrase it for me?" Almost invariably the senator would go on to the next question.

Then-Governor Ronald Reagan and Smith, then-president of the California Chamber of Commerce, at Sacramento Host Breakfast, September 7, 1973, where Reagan was guest speaker. The yearly breakfast always features the governor of California speaking to top business leaders in California. John E. Palmer photograph.

Of course, senators with a propensity to make speeches were particularly welcome—because they used up their time that way, instead of asking questions. They did this because they had their own message, one they wanted to deliver to a constituency. In many cases they were completely uninterested in the answer, but hoped the *question* would make the evening news. In this process they use up so much of their time that the witness has less time to fill with an innocuous answer to an impossible question.

An excellent example of endless verbosity was provided at another hearing by newly elected Congressman Barney Frank, a Massachusetts Democrat, and a member of the House Judiciary Committee. After one of his long, convoluted, noisy, and unintelligible sermons, I made the mistake of saying, "There must be a question in there somewhere." This produced another tirade.

Senators Biden and Kennedy, the latter in particular, are world-class speechifiers; a grunt would suffice in answer to many of their questions.

Following the hearing, it is the custom for certain senators, both those on the confirmation committee itself and those not, to submit written questions for written responses. I received a host of such questions, to which my staff responded. Usually, that's the end of it, although sometimes there are follow-up questions.

The vote of the Senate Judiciary Committee was unanimous for confirmation, and the vote in the Senate ninety-nine to one, with maverick Senator Proxmire voting no apparently because of my closeness to the president-elect.

❖   ❖   ❖

Inauguration Day broke with low temperature and overcast skies, but at noon as Ronald Reagan was taking his oath, the sun came out, right on cue. The festivities started with services in the historic St. John's Memorial Church opposite Lafayette Park. From there we were driven to the inauguration ceremony, which for the first time in history was conducted on the west front of the Capitol overlooking the Mall. I recall that here for the first time we became conscious of rank, as a consequence of how we were seated. (I remember too that outgoing President Jimmy Carter and First Lady Rosalynn Carter were, despite their efforts to conceal it, manifestly uncomfortable if not irritated by the role they were now called upon to play.)

Following the swearing-in, the traditional lunch hosted by Congress took place in the Capitol, our first of who-knows-how-many official meals to follow. More than once during the day I had a feeling of *awe*: I had seen this event so many times in the past from a distance, yet it was still hard to believe that I was part of it this time.

❖　　❖　　❖

The day after Inauguration Day, the president had scheduled a ceremonial swearing-in for all of the new cabinet officers in the state dining room with families present. In effect, that gathering turned into just a reception, when it became clear that the president's choice for secretary of labor, Ray Donovan, would not be confirmed in time. The president was determined that there would be no group swearing-in unless it included *everyone*. (Ray Donovan's confirmation hearing began what turned out to be a six-year battle before he was ultimately vindicated.) Thus, each cabinet officer was sworn in individually as he or she saw fit. I was sworn in at the United States Supreme Court by Chief Justice Burger in his private chambers.

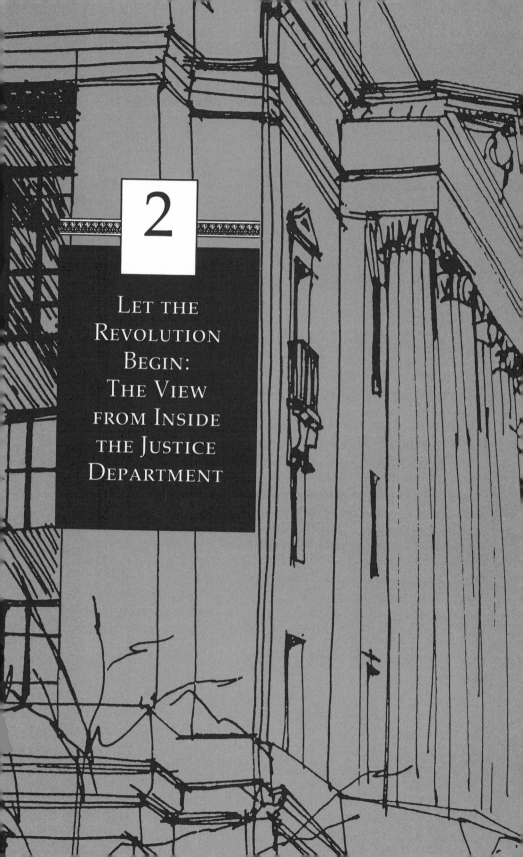

2

LET THE REVOLUTION BEGIN: THE VIEW FROM INSIDE THE JUSTICE DEPARTMENT

O N JANUARY 21, 1981, THE DAY AFTER THE INAU- guration of Ronald Reagan, I walked into the Justice Department for the first time as attorney general. It had been ten years since I had been there; in November 1971, John Mitchell had asked me if I would like to succeed him as attorney general (following an interim period during which his deputy, Richard Kleindienst, would hold the post). I'd declined then—fortunately, as things turned out—but this day in 1981, as I walked through that massive doorway, I was struck by the size and scope of the responsibility that was about to descend upon me.

The fifth-floor AG's office—shorthand is big in the government; AG is in common use—was both empty and quiet. Neither condition would prevail for long.

My first order of business was to secure a desk. My predecessor, Benjamin Civiletti, had used a small, circular French desk, but, being a pack rat, I wanted a large wooden desk with lots of drawers. My request for such a desk produced my first experience with the federal bureaucracy—four large men showed up to escort me around the building until we found one (which wasn't already in use) that I liked.

We were a skeleton crew in those earliest days of the Reagan Justice Department. Ed Schmults, the new deputy attorney general, was there, as were Ken Starr and one or two members of the transition team, such as Doug Marvin, who were helping out temporarily. Doug, an able member of the DOJ transition team and a partner at Williams and Connolly in Washington, had been a close adviser to Attorney General Edward Levi during the Ford administration. Charles Renfrew, the outgoing deputy attorney general, had agreed to stay on for a few weeks, for which we were grateful, and as things turned out I definitely had work for him to do.

The news at that time focused on the horrible situation in Atlanta involving the kidnapping and murder of some seventeen young black men. The cry for help was loud and anguished. It would have been logical within the DOJ to turn to the FBI, but their jurisdiction was limited. As one of my first acts as attorney general, I asked Ken Starr and Charles Renfrew to go to Atlanta and see if something could be worked out.

They did so, and opened the door for the FBI, which did a magnificent job of helping to identify and apprehend Wayne Williams, the man convicted in two of the killings, and the chief suspect in many of the others. For me, it was an inspiring demonstration of the power of the Justice Department to do good.

❖   ❖   ❖

From my first day on the job, it was obvious that there was a crucial need to fill the top positions at the department, and to do it quickly. Ed Schmults and I made this our first priority. However, once I learned the vast Justice Department organizational chart— the department consists of thirty-one separate divisions, boards, and bureaus, all headed by presidential appointees—I knew it was not going to be an easy task.

In a sense, the Justice Department touches the lives of a broader cross-section of the American people than any other department— at $191 per capita to run the entire national justice system. Compared to the vastly higher costs involved in defense, education, and social programs, it's a real bargain.

Obviously, then, the people we selected to head the various divisions, boards, and bureaus had to be special people—talented and experienced individuals with initiative, imagination, judgment, and the ability to lead. In some cases they would have to be specialists (especially in such areas as civil litigation, antitrust, tax, and criminal practice) in order eventually to earn the respect of the career professionals they would be directing. Finding such people was my next task.

Spot by spot, and only after we had examined innumerable résumés, we began to fill the top posts. The six "highest-profile" slots were the assistant attorneys general in charge of civil rights, antitrust, land and natural resources, the criminal and tax divisions, as well as the post of solicitor general.

Our choice to head the Antitrust Division was William Baxter, a Stanford Law School professor who definitely had the requisite talents and philosophy. His appointment was somewhat controversial because of some public comments he had made about the AT&T case, but he explained them to our satisfaction during the interview process. We were being especially careful because the changes we contemplated making in the economic area would be more dramatic, revolutionary, and far-reaching than any others in the entire history of the Antitrust Division.

For land and natural resources our pick was Carol Dinkins, a Texas lawyer from the prominent firm of Vinson & Elkins, who came highly recommended by Governor William Clements. She was well known to him for having done an outstanding job in heading up a Texas environmental commission—she had a strong background in environmental law—and he was very enthusiastic about her.

As for the solicitor general's post, we had an embarrassment of riches—three exceptional candidates: Dallin Oakes, dean of the Law School at Brigham Young, Antonin Scalia, later a judge of the U.S. Court of Appeals for the District of Columbia Circuit and associate justice of the United States Supreme Court, and Rex Lee, formerly head of the Civil Division under Ed Levi. The job eventually went to Rex Lee, but I almost could have flipped a coin to make the choice; it was that close.

To head the Office of Legal Counsel—the most prestigious group of lawyers in government (except possibly for those in the Solicitor General's Office)—I selected Ted Olson, a former partner and a fine lawyer. This was a key job, providing legal advice to the president and the attorney general and other agencies, and Ted's and my previous relationship ensured that we would work well together here. Ted Olson's sense of ethics, sound judgment, and insistence upon excellence, together with an unusual combination of aggressiveness and caution caused him to be labeled the "Iron Duke." If anything got past Ted, it had to be okay, an irony considering the disgraceful and outrageous action taken against him (and detailed later).

William H. Webster, the able head of the FBI appointed during the previous administration, had been advised before the inauguration that the president wanted him to stay on. Otherwise, this would have been a very difficult position to fill.

In due course, Paul McGrath, head of the litigation department of Dewey, Ballantine, Bushby, Palmer & Wood, was nominated and confirmed as assistant attorney general for the Civil Division, and Glenn Archer was named to head the Tax Division. To head the Criminal Division we found another ideal candidate, Lowell Jensen, the district attorney for Alameda County, California. He was a Democrat, but was highly thought of throughout California. He later was designated as associate attorney general to succeed Rudy Giuliani when he left to become the U.S. Attorney for the Southern District of New York.

The head of the Immigration and Naturalization Service was a particularly difficult position to fill, and we did not do so for several months. It was important, because the agency had been without leadership extending back into the previous administration—and it was without policy direction. In effect, it was chugging along on momentum without either leadership or an effective blueprint. We finally recruited Alan Nelson from the Pacific Telephone and Telegraph Company, as it was then known. His leadership, plus the policy provided by the Immigration Reform Act of 1985, reinvigorated that agency.

The last assistant attorney general position to be filled was the hardest and the most controversial—civil rights. We wanted someone who was not only dedicated to protecting the rights of all citizens, but also someone the public perceived to be so dedicated.

And, of course, his views on such matters as busing and quotas as remedies for civil-rights violations had to be compatible with administration philosophy.

Erwin Griswold, former solicitor general, and longtime dean of the Harvard Law School, was the first to call to my attention the man who eventually got the job—William Bradford ("Brad") Reynolds. Dean Griswold, who had been Reynolds's boss in the Solicitor General's Office from 1970 to 1973, used nothing but superlatives to describe him.

Interestingly, Reynolds, who would become very controversial, originally wanted to head the Civil Division. He nonetheless agreed to take on civil rights. Ironically, Ed Meese, whom Brad would later defend so staunchly, opposed Brad. Meese, then serving at the White House as counsellor to the president, thought we should have picked someone with more experience in civil rights, and someone with a stronger political background. Ed Schmults and I interviewed Brad at length, quizzing him about his views on civil rights to learn the extent of his commitment to protecting the rights of *all* citizens, and his views on administration policy. He was strong on both counts, and we overcame the objections of the White House.

Generally speaking, particularly at the beginning of an administration, it is heartening to know that so many fine and able people are willing to serve in government. Because one must compete in various areas with other departments and agencies, and despite the fact that the Justice Department does well in such competitions, we did on occasion lose someone we wanted.

(For the final line-up of the Reagan Justice Department, see charts 1 and 2.)

❖   ❖   ❖

The policy changes we were now about to undertake were dramatic—in several areas they would reverse the established practices of many years, indeed decades. All of these were positions that the president, during his years of speaking and campaigning, had long consistently advocated. Having won the election by a

Chart 1
Principal Officers of the Department of Justice, 1981–1985

Attorney General
William French Smith

Counselor to the Attorney General
Kenneth W. Starr
Tex Lezar
Ronald L. Blunt

Confidential Assistant to the Attorney General
Myra L. Tankersley

Deputy Attorney General
Edward C. Schmults
Carol E. Dinkins

Solicitor General
Rex E. Lee

AAG Legal Policy
Jonathan C. Rose
Roger B. Clegg (acting)
Tex Lezar
James Milton Spears (acting)

AAG Antitrust
William F. Baxter
J. Paul McGrath

AAG Civil Rights
William Bradford Reynolds

AAG Justice Assistance
Lois Haight Herrington

AAG Lands
Carol E. Dinkins
F. Henry Habicht II

Special Assistants to the Attorney General
F. Henry Habicht II
Thomas P. DeCair
Carolyn B. Kuhl
David D. Hiller
John G. Roberts
Emma C. Jordan
James K. Stewart
Roger B. Clegg
Catherine L.O. Anderson
Terry Eastland
Ronald L. Blunt
Kenneth O. Simon
Robert E. Steinberg
Judith L. Hammerschmidt
Hugh Hewitt

Associate Attorney General
Rudolph W. Giuliani
D. Lowell Jensen

AAG Legislative Counsel
Theodore B. Olson
Ralph W. Tarr (acting)

AAG Legal Affairs
Robert A. McConnell
Phillip D. Brady (acting)

Chart 2
Department of Justice

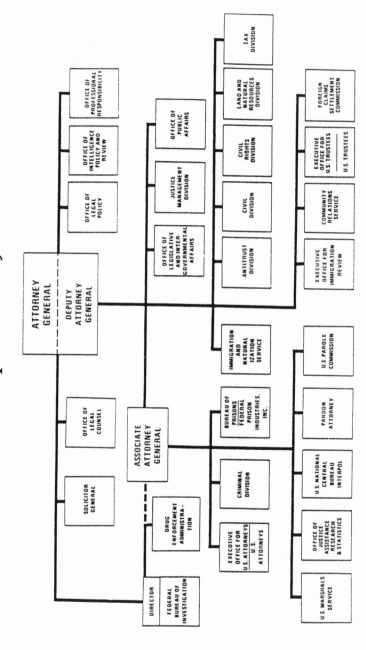

landslide, these policies had the imprimatur of public mandate. These changes were to permeate the department, and in several areas were high-profile, and affected large and well-defined constituencies. In others, changes were more esoteric, or at least less controversial (if, indeed, in Washington any change is not controversial to *someone*) but no less significant.

The Department of Justice is a remarkable institution blessed with an abundance of remarkable people. Both the career officials and the political appointees are highly respected, outside government as well as inside. The department is remarkable for another reason. The variety and complexity, not to mention the volume, of the problems that either originate or pass through the DOJ is staggering. Herbert Brownell, a Republican predecessor, is said to have once described life in the DOJ as "one goddam thing after another."

The department is, literally, at the crossroads of government. Whenever any agency has a problem, sooner or later it seems to arrive at Justice. And, as distinguished from so many other areas, public and private, an inept decision is often very quickly exposed. The fact that so many things have to be crowded into so little time makes the position of attorney general both high-risk and high-profile. It is remarkable but true that you can grapple with, and make, an extremely important decision, and then, because of the urgency and volume of equally important opinions, thirty minutes later you can't remember what you did a few moments ago.

❖   ❖   ❖

On Thursday, March 5, 1981, less than six weeks after Ronald Reagan took the oath of office as president of the United States, I held my first formal press conference. It was to be followed by many others over the next five years. Looking back, what strikes me about this particular exchange is that it set the tone for the others that were to follow. I tried hard to give the press the answers I wanted to give, and the press tried at least as hard to elicit the answers they wanted to get.

In the end, while neither of us was entirely satisfied, we were not exactly disappointed either. In the process a good deal of information was transmitted. Perhaps, over the long haul, that's all anyone can hope for in Washington.

It is important to understand, however, that the media's focus is always going to be on the immediate, the tangible, and the dramatic. Journalists are interested in results, not so much the legal process or philosophy that produces them. This might not be a problem in other fields, but it definitely is not the way the Department of Justice should be covered.

I can see, in retrospect, that no matter how hard I pressed to interest the media in what we felt was the big story—say, the reorganization of the Justice Department, which would have far-reaching effects—their angle would always be sharper, closer, more acute, and pegged more directly to events of the day, not issues with long-range consequences. That made for some lively exchanges.

Before I permitted questions at that first press conference, I made a few points that I wanted to be certain got made. I spoke of the great pleasure I took in announcing that Ed Schmults and Rudy Giuliani (the new associate attorney general in charge, essentially, of law-enforcement matters; later the U.S. Attorney in New York City and a candidate for its mayor) had just come aboard, and that we had carved out a brand new Office of Legal Policy (OLP), which provided an important element in our streamlined management structure. (Under Professors Dan Meador and Maurice Rosenberg, OLP's predecessor, the Office for Improvements in the Administration of Justice, had its mandate expanded.) I also announced the formation of the Attorney General's Task Force on Violent Crime, to be co-chaired by former Attorney General Griffin Bell and Illinois governor James Thompson. After talking about the scope of the task force, I opened the floor to questions.

What I find so interesting, looking back, is that by and large many of the issues raised in that very first press conference would remain the key issues of the Reagan Justice Department.

For example, the second question had to do with affirmative action. That was followed by questions on violent crime; how we expected to fight crime *and* cut spending; Congress vs. the courts in regard to busing, abortion, and school prayer; the war on drugs, in particular the relative roles of the FBI and the DEA (Drug Enforcement Administration); the criminal law issue of preventive detention in federal cases; and civil rights and school desegregation.

Toward the end, two issues that I considered far less important came up, and took far more time than they should have. One I disposed of quickly, and I think with at least a touch of humor, but the other I grappled with for far too long. And even that was not to be the end of it.

The first issue had to do with telephone logs, the second with Frank Sinatra.

QUESTION: Are you going to publish your telephone log?

AG SMITH: No.

QUESTION: Why not?

QUESTION: Definitely not?

AG SMITH: Well, one reason is that I think that that is really a part of the Watergate overreaction. I do not consider that to be an appropriate method of disseminating information. I know of no other department of government that follows any such procedure, and, as a matter of fact, I even understand that that was true during the previous administration, except for the Department of Justice.

It was a practice that somehow got started, I think, during Attorney General Bell's term. And I just don't think it's an appropriate method of disseminating information. . . .

QUESTION: Sir, what is inappropriate about that? And are you trying to avoid making public the number of your contacts with President Reagan?

AG SMITH: Not at all; not at all.

QUESTION: Then what's inappropriate about it?

AG SMITH: Well, I think that the information that comes from this type of document, which really says something and yet doesn't say anything, it may indicate a telephone call to somebody that has no indication as to the content, whether it's a golf game, whether it's a matter of substance. I just think it is a very poor practice with respect to the dissemination of information.

If that kind of information is necessary to be disseminated, it should be disseminated in a proper way and not piecemeal and in possibly deceptive ways. And a telephone log tells you very little. It may provide a lot to speculate about, but that's not the basis. . . .

However, I want to emphasize that we do intend to—well, I say improve—establish procedures which will disseminate the kind of information we should be disseminating. I think there are a lot of things that you should know about, and there are a lot of things we would want you to know about.

QUESTION: Such as?

AG SMITH: Well, for example, we had meetings with representatives of Hispanic groups not too long ago. We've met with the black caucus. We are meeting regularly with . . .

QUESTION: You mean you're talking about the ones you want us to know about but not the ones you don't want us to know about?

AG SMITH: Well, we have to leave a little something to your initiative, you know.

❖   ❖   ❖

My response got, if not a laugh, certainly a chuckle, and that was the end of that. (For the record, I never made my telephone logs available. Instead, we responded to the media's requests for specific information of that sort on a case-by-case basis.)

The press conference exchange relating to Frank Sinatra was a little more heated, and it did not end with a chuckle.

QUESTION: General, last week one of your spokesmen said you were not presently receiving sensitive case reports on Frank Sinatra. Do you feel without those case reports you are in a position to advise the president on any sensitive matters that may arise in the New York federal investigation that is said to involve Mr. Sinatra?

AG SMITH: Well, as a matter of fact, you are assuming a few facts not in evidence, as we would say.

I am not in any position to talk about the status of any investigations, either—whether they exist, don't exist, or what their progress is. All I can tell you is that I am not—and would not ordinarily—be personally involved in anything involving the subject matter of your question.

We left that topic for a few questions, but another reporter returned to it only minutes later.

QUESTION: Have you recused yourself from any matters pertaining to Mr. Sinatra in the department?

AG SMITH: No, I have not. As a matter of fact, all of the procedures that are involved in criminal investigations would not normally involve me in the process at all. Needless to say, because of the attitudes of some of you gentlemen, if anything should develop which involved this particular individual or any other individual similarly situated, I would, I'm sure, not participate in any way.

QUESTION: You said that some facts were not in evidence. The question had as its predicate that there was an investigation in Westchester County, New York, involving Mr. Sinatra.

AG SMITH: That's right.

QUESTION: Do you mean to imply that you have information that he is not involved in that investigation?

AG SMITH: No, no. I don't mean to imply anything. As a matter of fact, I have no comment with respect to what is going on in that investigation other than to say that I have not had, and don't expect to have, any personal involvement.

QUESTION: You haven't recused yourself, but you don't expect to have . . .

AG SMITH: Well, I haven't had any occasion to and don't anticipate it.

QUESTION: Isn't he a personal friend of yours? How could you impartially preside over it, make decisions about it?

AG SMITH: Well, this is what I have thought I just said, namely, that to the extent that anything were to involve him or anybody else similarly situated, I would just have no participation in it, of any kind.

QUESTION: Well, what is the role of the attorney general at some point not involving a specific individual named here, but the attorney general often, as we saw in the Billy Carter case quite frequently, may find that there is somebody who is a relative, a friend, something to a president, who is a danger to him because he is involved in the various activities. But you are totally disassociating yourself from this. Who is going to tell the president?

AG SMITH: Well, as a matter of fact, that really . . . I don't know if that is a problem because if there were a situation that involved my brother or somebody that was in a category where I would normally disqualify myself, then the functions that I would normally perform would devolve on the deputy attorney general. And he would just carry the function on.

❖   ❖   ❖

Believe it or not, there were a few more follow-up questions on the Sinatra matter. I bother to go into it at such length here only because the media's preoccupation with the subject was symptomatic of the way it so often performed during the four-plus years I was in Washington. The story with the glitter always commanded more attention than the story with the substance.

To illustrate, let me again use the Sinatra example. What makes the whole situation so odd is that although I was acquainted with Frank Sinatra, we were not close friends. Yet my "friendship" with him, as indicated by the persistence of the press at my March 5 press conference, became one of the biggest stories during the first month or two of my tenure as attorney general.

Here is how it all got started: One Friday night in December 1980, halfway between the election and the inauguration, Jean and I attended Sinatra's birthday party at his home in Palm Springs. We received the invitation, and agreed to attend, long before Ronald Reagan asked me to be his attorney general, and I saw absolutely no reason not to attend.

Although we had some close mutual friends, and I had played tennis with Barbara Sinatra a few times, Jean and I did not know the Sinatras particularly well. We made the trip from Los Angeles to Palm Springs in a friend's plane, along with others, and returned the same night. The party was a fascinating blend of people from the worlds of entertainment, business, and society. It was an enjoyable, if uneventful, party.

About a week later, Myra Tankersley, my secretary and confidential assistant of many years, received a phone call from Maxine Cheshire, a *Washington Post* "Style" section columnist. Ms. Cheshire asked if it were true that I had attended a party for Frank Sinatra.

The ever-discreet Myra was noncommittal. Nonetheless, a column soon ran that asked what the attorney general–designate, the man in charge of federal law enforcement, was doing at a party for a man linked to the underworld. Although it may be true that over the years there had been rumors about Sinatra associating with organized crime figures, it is equally true that he has never been charged or, so far as I know, ever been close to being charged with any crime or any participation in unlawful activities. I did not respond to the Cheshire column.

Her theme, however, was picked up, and expanded upon, by William Safire, the *New York Times* columnist (who'd had some run-ins with earlier attorneys general). *His* column was a bigger and more hyperbolic version of the Cheshire column. To quote a few salient points:

> On . . . the day after he was designated by President-elect Reagan to be the next attorney general of the United States, William French Smith went to the 65th birthday party of a man that *Newsweek*

magazine reports is the subject of a federal grand jury investigation in New York.

The future head of our Justice Department joined 200 other guests to honor Frank Sinatra, whose lifelong gangland friendships have become part of his own legend. . . .

It was bad enough that Ronald Reagan turned to Sinatra for fund-raising help during the campaign; bad enough that he attended a Sinatra anniversary party last summer; bad enough that he selected Sinatra to organize entertainment for the inaugural gala on Jan. 19.

But the involvement of the designee for attorney general in the rehabilitation of the reputation of a man obviously proud to be close to notorious hoodlums is the first deliberate affront to propriety of the Reagan administration. . . .

Let birthday-party-goer Smith review the FBI's Sinatra file. Then let him tell the Senate to what extent he thinks it proper for a friend of mobsters to profit from being a chum of the chief executive and of the man who runs the Department of Justice.

All this was taking place before the new administration had been sworn in. Although I see in retrospect that I would have been better off simply to let the matter drop, I allowed it to get under my skin. I found the suggestion that my new position, which I had not as yet assumed, meant I would call back and refuse an invitation we had already accepted, from a man who was neither charged with nor convicted of a crime, simply odious. In a sense, it would have been tantamount to saying that I didn't believe in the presumption of innocence.

And that, perhaps unfortunately, was my mind-set on the evening I attended a pre-inauguration party given by the *Los Angeles Times* at the Corcoran Gallery in Washington, D.C.

During the cocktail hour, I happened to walk up to an old Los Angeles friend, Franklin Murphy, the chief executive officer of The Times Mirror Company, who was standing and talking with Bill Webster, the head of the FBI, and a third man whom I did not recognize. That man turned out to be William Safire, former speechwriter for President Nixon, and current scourge of my new office.

Franklin and Bill introduced us, and Safire said hello quite civilly. But I took the opportunity to let him know, in terms that seemed to shock even a columnist, what I thought of his column regarding me. Safire, again with civility, said perhaps we could have lunch one day and discuss it.

"Not until you've retracted that irresponsible column," I said testily, which was of course precisely the wrong thing to say and do.

Before the evening was out, I had an object lesson in how I *should* have conducted myself. Ronald Reagan, the president-elect, was also at the party, and Safire managed to corner him and ask him about his friend Frank Sinatra.

"Those things have been said about Frank for years," responded Mr. Reagan equably. Then he dismissed the subject by saying, simply, "Let's hope they're not true."

It was exactly what I should have said.

Unfortunately, it came as no great surprise to me, considering the tack I'd taken, that Safire's *next* column on the subject was even more blistering than the first. (Indeed, it was so unrelentingly petulant that it turned off a great number of readers.)

This time I kept my mouth shut about my reaction. After a while, I learned that in addition to having Franklin Murphy as a mutual friend, Safire and I were each acquainted with a most accomplished gentleman, Walter Annenberg, and Armand Deutsch, another friend. When I got notes from both Walter and Armand suggesting I have a make-nice lunch with Bill Safire, it finally struck me as a good idea.

I played host in the attorney general's dining room at the Justice Department, and this time we got on well.

Months later, he happened to mention me, peripherally, in another column, but this time all he said, in reference to our earlier "feud," was "We had lunch—and I sold out."

I would hear one other reference to this matter almost three years later. I was giving a speech at Harvard (of which college, incidentally, Uriah Oakes, my great-great-great-grandfather, had been the fourth president). A young woman who appeared to be a very young undergraduate said, "Given your responsibilities as the attorney general, how can you socialize with someone like Frank Sinatra?"

This time, instead of blowing up, I gave a reasoned answer. Perhaps it is possible to learn something in Washington after all.

❖   ❖   ❖

I give prominence to the Sinatra incident for one reason. It strikes me as a perfect illustration of how easy it is in Washington—for those on either side of the governmental wall—to lose sight of the real issues. I won't pretend that this was a lesson I learned early and well. I made, if not the same, then similar mistakes again and again.

Those failures to keep this sort of thing in perspective each time it occurred, however, do not excuse the short-sightedness of the men and women whose job it was to chronicle the *doings*, the accomplishments or lack thereof, of the Reagan administration, the first ideologically exciting administration to hit Washington in many years. One has to search back for decades to find another new president so firmly pledged to change "the way the [American] world works."

Jerry Ford? He did not have a chance. Richard Nixon? Close, but not really. Lyndon Baines Johnson? Possibly. JFK? No, not really. Ike? No.

Let's face it. The changes promised by Ronald Reagan can, in fairness, be compared only to those promised by FDR. (And, it's intriguing that FDR was the first political hero of "RR.") I don't mean to suggest that Ronald Reagan, in his two terms in office, was able to introduce as many long-lasting changes in the structure of American government as did Roosevelt in his three-plus terms. Indeed, I think it is quite enough to say that the Reagan presidency was a watershed administration. Its legacy will reside in its having changed the thinking and attitudes—the very ambience—of government and the people it serves, rather than having *immediately* altered direction or policy (although certainly there were dramatic reversals in some areas of decades-long practice).

The media, however, took a long time before they got beyond the personalities of the new administration. By that point, for better or for worse, and (pun intended) for richer or for poorer, the wedding was over and the marriage, such as it was to be, had already begun.

The most disconcerting problem in regard to the media—indeed, in the federal establishment itself—and especially for someone used to dealing with the merits of an issue, is that in Washington one rarely is able to reach the merits of a problem. Layers and layers must be penetrated to get to the heart of the matter.

The first layer is that of perception—not how things *are*, but how they are *perceived* to be. Many issues are disposed of on the basis of perception. If one pierces this layer he confronts layer number two, that of politics. Political obstacles and feasibility settle many an issue. The third layer is that of personalities, considerations of "turf," and internecine warfare. Sometimes such matters have an intensity that will sidetrack responsible debate. If one finally manages to get past that layer, then he may at last reach the actual merits of an issue.

I don't believe much of this is going to change. Frankly, my advice to anyone contemplating government service or interested in learning about it is that the key to survival in Washington is to recognize the milieu and adapt to it because it is simply a fact of life. At the same time, one has to recognize the obvious—that to do so is not an easy task.

❖   ❖   ❖

In some ways, it was just as well the media took a while to get us all in focus, because, in truth, we were having the same problem ourselves. As I would soon discover, starting a revolution is one thing, but getting results is quite another.

Did we come in each morning and say, "What steps shall we take today to advance the conservative movement?" Of course not. We were far too deeply involved in day-to-day issues.

That is not to say, however, that we did not have the goals of the Reagan administration firmly in mind. We did not have to have them spelled out for us each and every day. We knew the man we had helped to elect and were pledged to serve. And we knew where he, and therefore we, stood on the issues in general, and in particular on such issues as antitrust, civil rights, and the environment. We also knew what we intended to do.

My favorite example of day-to-day, business-as-usual activity in Washington has to do, by coincidence, with a small Antitrust Division office in an equally small town in Ohio, miles and miles from Washington, D.C.

A preliminary review of our field office situation indicated that we no longer needed this particular office. It was simply not efficient to keep it open, and so I began to implement the process necessary to close it.

There was no question that I had unfettered authority to shut down this office and transfer its eight employees elsewhere. Yet, in my four-plus years in Washington as the attorney general of the United States, I could not accomplish this seemingly simple task.

The reason, of course, was that the elected officials in Ohio— local, state, and federal—rushed to the defense of "their" antitrust office. They soon made it a bargaining chip in the inevitable trade-off sessions on Capitol Hill that are so much a part and parcel of life in Washington. To me, my continuing inability to close that little DOJ office became a symbol of the way the world works, Washington-style.

The same phenomenon could be observed in much larger and more significant matters. For example, during my first year as attorney general, the administration took a very hard and serious look at the possibility of revising the social security program. If any question at that time was deserving of serious debate it was this one, yet that debate never took place. Why not? Because politicians—quickly followed by the media—smelled an issue that would play to the voters. Charging that we were about to dismantle the social security system, they jumped on the bandwagon with both feet, and that was the end of that.

The same overreaction occurred in the Bob Jones University case (which will be dealt with in detail in Chapter Six). The high emotional atmosphere generated by civil-rights groups, politicians, and the news media—which at times bordered on hysteria—

meant that the real issue in the case was never discussed on its merits.

As I will explain later, the basic issue had nothing to do with civil rights. It involved whether Congress could change laws by failing to respond affirmatively to actions by the courts or bureaucrats. Hard as that may be to believe, the essence of the Bob Jones University case was that Congress could change laws by "acquiescence"—not by voting on bills.

Perhaps even harder to believe is that no less a liberal establishment figure than Laurence Tribe, of the Harvard Law School, came around to agree with us to a surprising degree on that point.

Yet another example of Washington's myopia was the dispute (also treated fully in a later chapter) between the Environmental Protection Agency and the Congress in 1983. The central question in that case was not, as the man or woman on the street would undoubtedly tell you today, danger to the environment, or mismanagement at the EPA; it was the doctrine of executive privilege— the capacity in that case of the law-enforcement officials to formulate strategy and to consider filing charges without public and congressional participation in those delicate and sensitive decisions.

The issue was power in our system of separated powers. Once again, the layers of obfuscation were never peeled away, and the true issue, which remained submerged, never became the subject of rational debate.

And that, believe me, is the way things are in Washington, D.C.

3

ANTITRUST: BIGNESS IS NOT NECESSARILY BADNESS

O N January 15, 1981, the Senate Judiciary Committee held its first hearing on my nomination to be the seventy-fourth attorney general of the United States. When Senator Howard Metzenbaum, the liberal Democrat from Ohio, got his turn to question me, he devoted all his time to my views on antitrust policy. I sincerely welcomed his questions, as I considered antitrust to be one of the most important responsibilities of the Department of Justice.

The following is part of our give-and-take.

Senator Metzenbaum: What are the principal purposes that antitrust laws serve?

Mr. Smith: Perhaps I can put it this way: I would be a vigorous enforcer of the antitrust laws for the very simple and basic reason that I think competition is as fundamental to the preservation of the free enterprise system as I think the right of free speech is to the political system. Therefore, I have no problem whatever with respect to stating we would vigorously enforce the antitrust laws.

I do know that there are procedures to accomplish the end result which are subject to some controversy as to whether they are good procedures or not, or procedures which should be utilized. I also know that there is a certain amount of feeling that the situation overall has changed because of international competition, and the system being different now because of the tremendous change in the circumstances, vis-à-vis our international competitors.

SENATOR METZENBAUM: Are you suggesting that there should be special exemptions provided in the antitrust laws in connection with international trade?

MR. SMITH: No. As a matter of fact, I am not really suggesting anything of a specific nature because I am just not in a position to do so at this time. Certainly the new administration will formulate an antitrust policy, and in the process of doing that will review these various areas.

I can certainly assure you that as far as the basic proposition is concerned the need for free competition and the the importance of that concept to the free enterprise system is something we are very strongly for.

Moments later, Senator Metzenbaum touched upon a key issue when he brought up my long-standing friendship with Ronald Reagan.

SENATOR METZENBAUM: Historically the Justice Department and in particular the Antitrust Division have been the advocates of strong procompetitive policies even when such policies have conflicted with those of the president or other parts of the administration.

Knowing of your close relationship with the president-elect, would you plan to continue this traditional role of independence for the department in connection with antitrust proceedings?

MR. SMITH: Of course, I am hopeful there will be an overall administration policy with respect to antitrust so there would not be any competition of viewpoints. To the extent that was necessary, I am certain I could uphold the necessary standards of the Department of Justice. In other words, I guess I could hold my own against whatever the forces of onslaught might be.

SENATOR METZENBAUM: Let me give you an example. David Stockman, who has been selected as the president-elect's nominee for the Office of Management and Budget, recently expressed the following attitude toward antitrust enforcement:

You don't have to structure competition. That's where I disagree with the whole antitrust position which has been very strong in the Hart Committee, the FTC Bureau of Competition. That's wrong. My view is that a monopoly never develops unless it is sanctioned by government authority. There is no such thing as a privately-developed and composed monopoly. You can go into a long debate about history. In modern times, in a global economy with multinational corporations and a swift ability to deploy capital and production all around the globe, you don't have monopoly. So you don't have to define the rules of the game in terms of competition.

That is contrary to what all the other Republican advocates of antitrust laws have stated over a period of many years.

Are you, as the new attorney general, prepared to accept this concept which is so totally different from that which many others have expressed over a period of time? He is saying you have monopoly only if government creates the monopoly.

MR. SMITH: I am familiar with that approach. I will have to talk to Mr. Stockman about it. The degree to which it may represent administration policy I don't know. I would be surprised if it did, only for the reason that as far as I know there has been no antitrust policy established by the administration as yet.

SENATOR METZENBAUM: It may be necessary to take the young man over your knee.

MR. SMITH: Just so long as you don't take that as a commitment.

❖   ❖   ❖

When he was almost done questioning me, Senator Metzenbaum replayed that same theme. "You will be the policymaker," he said to me. "Antitrust is not a foreign subject. It is as if somewhere down the line there will be somebody who will come down with a suggestion from on high as to what the policies ought to be. Since it is the attorney general who indeed makes those policies, is it not reasonable of us to inquire of you concerning that, and not assume that Mr. Stockman or Mr. Meese or the president-elect will set the policy but rather that the attorney general will?"

I assured him that he was correct. "The attorney general will play a major role." And that, I am pleased to report, is just what happened.

❖   ❖   ❖

On the first anniversary of my swearing in as attorney general, my staff surprised me with a party. There were several gifts, some serious, some lighthearted. Among the latter category one stood out. It was a handsomely framed enlargement of a photograph that had originally run in *Newsweek* magazine. Taken at one of the formal dinner parties during inaugural week, it appeared to show me peering intently ("ogling" might be a better word) at an unusually well-endowed young woman wearing an exceptionally low-cut gown. I was actually gazing beyond this young lady, and could have said so but, knowing that such protestations are rarely given credibility, I simply said nothing. In any event, the photo bore the bold (and appropriate) caption: "BIGNESS IS NOT NECESSARILY BADNESS."

The staff was chiding me for my frequent use of that phrase over the previous twelve months as we developed and implemented our new antitrust policy. I appreciated the gift, and I didn't mind the ribbing, for I was particularly proud of our stand on antitrust issues. After all, it was on the basis of bigness not necessarily being badness that we had dismissed the hugely expensive and futile IBM case, thereby setting the tone for the new Reagan antitrust doctrine.

When we—the Reagan administration—took office in early 1981, we did so armed with a coherent economic vision. Our goals for the economy included increasing U.S. employment; maintaining U.S. technological leadership *and* increasing our competitiveness overseas; and minimizing the costs of government intervention in the marketplace. Whether we could reach those goals depended in no small part on the theory and practices of the department's Antitrust Division and, clearly, some basic changes were in order.

Those economic goals could only be achieved by the maintenance of free markets—markets conducive to rigorous competition and free from collusive arrangements, such as market-sharing agreements that would undermine the vigor of competition. Under prior administrations, the division had fallen into an error that was, at bottom, the responsibility of the Supreme Court during the tenure of Chief Justice Warren. The division, however, had done much to perpetuate that error, and to find new applications for it.

The error is to equate the state of competition in a market with the comfort level of the competitors. Rigorous competition drives prices down and tends to hold profits at levels minimally sufficient to attract necessary capital and resources, even for the most efficient firms. Vigorous competition drives inefficient firms out of the market, sometimes through business failure, alternatively by withdrawal to other markets where those firms can behave efficiently. Rigorous competition, in short, tends to reduce the number of firms in the market and to make life very *uncomfortable* for all but the most efficient firms. Efficient firms tend to grow and increase their market share; inefficient ones lose market share as they approach their exile from the market. The Warren Court interpreted the antitrust statutes as a delegation of judicial authority to shelter small firms, to suppress competition, and, thus, to preserve comfortable lifestyles for less efficient firms.

The result was that the goals of antitrust law—which were intended to foster competition to achieve social, political, and economic gains—had actually come to inhibit competition in the world economy. Economic good sense, rather than outmoded practices, should have been the guide. Hostility to size and to concentration was not enough.

The Antitrust Division had begun to turn away from these false concepts of antitrust before we arrived in 1981, but it had done so surreptitiously, out of reluctance to criticize judicial precedents and unwillingness to cross swords with the populists in Congress who found a protectionist version of antitrust to the liking of their constituents. Our course was unique in that we rejected "protectionist antitrust" loudly and frequently, and welcomed rigorous, competitive markets with equal enthusiasm. That articulation was essential if change were to be achieved, for, although the division litigating can improve market performance by punishing market-sharing arrangements in the courts, it cannot command rigorous competition. That spirit must come from the business community, and in 1981 the business community had to be assured that rigor was welcomed, and that the protectionist era had come to a close.

We made those changes. In fact, over the four years of the first term we produced a revolution in the government's attitude toward enforcement of the antitrust laws. A case could be made that the most dramatic change in economic policy throughout the administration took place in the Antitrust Division of the Justice Department. The implementation of that policy had dramatic, and salutary, effects on our economic system, and was much needed.

The promulgation, in June 1982, of the merger guidelines was probably the administration's most important and valuable antitrust initiative. For reasons having nothing to do with antitrust, merger activity was at a high level in the eighties. It became the focus of the antitrust controversy. There was no persuasive economic evidence that the merger practices of the past had created *anti*competitive effects. Increased market share was at least as likely to be the result of skill, hard work, and efficiency.

In addition, unless there were significant barriers to new competitors seeking to enter the market, concentration in the market resulting from factors other than efficiency was not likely to endure.

In short, in order for the Justice Department to be permitted to block a merger, we had to establish, with sophisticated economic analysis, that the proposed merger was indeed likely to be anticompetitive. The 1968 merger guidelines focused on economic concentration within an industry that did not constitute an acceptable basis for policy.

Accordingly, we undertook a systematic review of antitrust theory that was based on sound economic principles. The result was the Antitrust Division's new set of merger guidelines, issued in June 1982 and revised two years later.

The new guidelines recognized that most mergers do not threaten competition, and that many are in fact procompetitive and beneficial to consumers. The guidelines reflected a move away from a test based on concentration and established a sophisticated, economically oriented approach to market definition. They emphasized production suitability and ease of entry. At the same time, the guidelines set forth clear standards enabling businesses to avoid antitrust problems when planning mergers. They virtually eliminated vertical and conglomerate mergers as a cause of competitive concern.

Over the course of the first term, our Antitrust Division took a number of other important initiatives. First, the department moved quickly to jettison the huge, costly, and unwarranted case against IBM. That dismissal both paved the way for IBM to compete freely and efficiently in international markets, and sent a clear signal that the division had rejected the ill-advised, populist notion that efficient business practices would be condemned simply because of a company's size.

Second, the department also approved a settlement in the AT&T case, under which AT&T agreed to divest itself of the Bell Operating Companies in exchange for the freedom to compete in both unregulated markets and international markets. The final divestiture was accomplished on January 1, 1984, and the nation's communications system was thereby positioned for the challenges of new technologies and novel consumer demands.

Third, the department recognized that some joint efforts among competitors may enhance productive activity, as in industries whose advanced technologies require extensive research and development. Thus we led the successful fight to pass the National Cooperative Research Act of 1984. This act limits to single damages any antitrust recoveries against research and development joint ventures, and requires that these ventures be analyzed under the antitrust rule-of-reason rather than a rule of *per se* illegality. The passage of this legislation has encouraged innovation by removing much of the uncertainty surrounding research and development joint ventures.

Fourth, the Antitrust Division helped champion legislation that, when it passed in October 1984, gave units of local governments immunity from damage suits brought under the antitrust laws. The Local Government Antitrust Act of 1984 prohibits private treble antitrust damage actions against municipalities, while allowing courts to enjoin anticompetitive municipal conduct. Many small cities felt that their fiscal integrity would have been in doubt had such a law not been passed.

Finally, the Antitrust Division focused its resources on bid-rigging conspiracies in the fields of public highway, airport, utility, and electrical construction. The cost of public construction projects is expected to diminish significantly as a result of these efforts, yielding savings to both federal and state governments.

Our efforts against bid-riggers depended on successful criminal prosecutions. These prosecutions, visible as they are, have helped create a climate in which contractors for the first time realized that their actions would be submitted to the strictest scrutiny. To achieve deterrence, it was necessary to maintain a steady pressure of enforcement activity—and we did that.

In four years, the Antitrust Division initiated 297 criminal prosecutions involving 283 corporate defendants and 273 individual defendants in connection with conspiracies to rig bids on public highway and airport construction projects in twenty-one states. Of these cases, 237 yielded guilty pleas; fines totaled $58 million; and the aggregate jail time added up to more than fifty-three years.

The offensive against bid-riggers, which produced savings to taxpayers in millions of dollars, far beyond any previous effort, was only one part of the criminal law enforcement picture. The numbers clearly reflect the stark contrast: From 1977 to 1980, the Antitrust Division brought an average of thirty-eight criminal cases per year. For the years 1981 to 1984, the average number skyrocketed to ninety-one cases per year.

In contrast to the politically charged developments mentioned above, some of the most important activities of the division were too arcane to receive public attention

One of the more important steps taken during the first administration was rather technical and barely visible outside the specialist community affected. In the 1970s, the Antitrust Division had announced nine specific restrictions on the way valid patents could be employed or licensed to others. There is little or no legal justification for those restrictions, and absolutely no economic justification. Nevertheless, the threat of suit by the division was sufficient to deter much desirable economic behavior by innovative companies and to reduce significantly the value of patents in the hands of such companies. These restrictions became known in the profession as the "nine no-no's."

Shortly after taking office we explicitly repudiated the nine no-no's. Our repudiation was helpful; some bold companies began taking advantage of the opportunities newly afforded. A high level of uncertainty remained, however, about how the courts would respond in the event of private antitrust litigation. Even now, nine years later, the damage done by the nine no-no's has not been completely eradicated. Nonetheless, an increasing number of companies are employing the once-prohibited licensing techniques. The repudiation of the nine no-no's has been one of several forces in recent years that has brought about renewed attention to and respect for the importance, not just of patents but of all forms of intellectual property and the importance of its alienability through licensing and other modes of transfer.

The nation's business depends on a forward-looking Antitrust Division. That vision was brought into our daily life during the first term, and the country's economy has been far better for it. The practical results of this, the most significant change in antitrust policy in recent history, have spread throughout our economy, and have played no small role in sustaining the longest period of prosperity in decades.

❖   ❖   ❖

My choice to run the Antitrust Division, with its almost four hundred attorneys, was William F. Baxter, a law professor from Stanford. Bill Baxter struck me as offering an ideal combination of brains and backbone, which was just what the job called for. Bill soon proved that he could take the heat we knew our "bigness-is-not-necessarily-badness" shift in approach would generate.

Many U.S. publications, newspapers and magazines alike, took us to task for our proposed shift in emphasis, but the highly respected British publication, *The Economist*, struck what seemed to me just the right note. It reported:

> America's trustbusters are in retreat, but not disarray. The new boss of the Justice Department's Antitrust Division, Mr. William Baxter, a Stanford University law professor, intends to curb the use of antitrust laws to interfere with mergers, markets dominated by a few big firms, and joint trading ventures. Cheering big businessmen should realise, however, that his division will root out with renewed vigour price-fixing, market-sharing, and many other such collusive practices.
>
> The Reagan administration wanted to signal a sea-change in antitrust policy. That is why the attorney general, Mr. William French Smith, chose Mr. Baxter, a fellow Californian, a free marketeer. . . .
>
> American antitrust policy has already been moving in the direction Mr. Baxter advocates. There is considerable agreement among liberals and conservatives that the antitrust framework laid down by Senator Sherman in the 1890s is increasingly irrelevant (even harmful) to America in its current economic predicament. . . .
>
> Not all companies will be able to breathe easier. "Republicans have traditionally been just as tough at trustbusting as Democrats," says Mr. Ira Millstein, an antitrust lawyer and Mr. Baxter's close friend. "Baxter believes in competition; he will be tougher than many businessmen think."

And he was. Nonetheless, the contrast to the record of the previous administration was a sharp one.

In his first fifteen months at the helm, Baxter and his troops filed only five lawsuits to block mergers. The Carter administration filed twice that many in their last year in office alone.

One of our most vocal (and most politically partisan) opponents was then-Congressman Peter Rodino (D–N.J.), the chairman of the House Judiciary Committee. He saw a red flag whenever he looked at the Antitrust Division, accusing us of showing "aggressive indifference" to corporate mergers. According to Rodino, "In 1981, the number of mergers and acquisitions increased 27 percent over 1980. There is no doubt that administration rhetoric has fed this bloat."

Congressman Rodino showed not just his opposition but also his pique by "roadblocking" us. We wanted to go public with the changes we wanted to make in the antitrust laws, but he refused to hold hearings. In part, he was motivated by substantive disagreement, but another motive was his fear that if the changes worked for the better, the Reagan administration would get the credit. He made it clear he did not want that.

On certain issues we also had disagreement within our own ranks. Regarding the AT&T case, which we had inherited from the Carter administration, both Secretary of Defense Cap Weinberger and Secretary of Commerce Mac Baldrige wanted us to drop it. According to Bill Baxter, however, "Dropping the case would have meant perpetuating a major problem and a complex regulatory system. The consent decree I achieved permitted deregulation. It's no criticism of either Mac or Cap to say they simply didn't understand the issues—it wasn't their job to do so—but they were responding to AT&T lobbying."

The specifics of the AT&T case, while daunting to some, are really rather simple. Bill Baxter explains it this way:

> AT&T had control of the "local loops," the two strands of copper wire that run from every phone to the most local telephone office. The local loop is the only part of the entire phone system that has natural monopoly characteristics and really requires regulation. By denying all other companies the opportunity to have their equipment connected to the local loops, AT&T had acquired unnecessary monopolies over all switching equipment manufacture, all long-distance service, etc.

> And to cope with all those monopolies, regulatory bodies had expanded to correspond with AT&T's scope. The offense under Sec. 2 was needless denial of interconnecting with local loops.

What also made things more difficult for Bill Baxter in the AT&T fight was that both Ed Schmults and I had to refrain from participating because of prior legal services for the telephone industry.

Not only did he have to carry the fight by himself, so to speak, but he had to do so as a non-cabinet-level officer—which made it even more difficult to fight off Cap Weinberger and Mac Baldrige. But he did it. Bill Baxter was resourceful, tenacious, brilliant, and confident. He was not timid or bashful about his convictions.

❖   ❖   ❖

I, too, had some problems with other members of the administration, in particular and not surprisingly Mac Baldrige, the secretary of commerce. He went public with his opinion opposing the division's resistance to the proposed merger of the LTV Corporation and Republic Steel, saying that the Justice Department's stance was "out of touch with the real world," and a "world-class mistake."

He had gone public without any notice to or discussion with me, which was irksome. For once I responded in kind—by going public myself (although I called him in advance and advised him of what I was about to do).

❖   ❖   ❖

One of the finest tributes that Bill Baxter received for his no-nonsense performance as head of the Antitrust Division came from Melanie Stewart Cutler, a staff attorney who had served three consecutive antitrust chiefs. In a letter to the editor, she took issue with a *Wall Street Journal* article that claimed there had been a drop in morale and commitment to enforcement in the Antitrust Division. She wrote, in part:

> Contrary to the article, the department's merger standards have not been loosened. Rather, the new guidelines embody an articulation—unprecedented in the detail they offer—of the methods of analysis employed by the division in evaluating proposed mergers. While the guidelines do outline some innovations, they

are not so much a revolutionary as an evolutionary reflection of what the division has been doing for some time. . . .

With respect to price-fixing enforcement, I can only echo section chief Tony Nanni's sentiments: Bill Baxter has not been timid about enforcement. Moreover, the very graph employed to illustrate the plunge in enforcement activity gives the lie to these allegations. From 1981–1982, a period during which Mr. Baxter was in office, the graph shows an upswing which has continued into 1983. Indeed, the most recent "disastrous plunge" appears to have been from 1980–1981, prior to Mr. Baxter's assuming office. The key point, however, is that one should not credit any of these figures with much significance. In fact, the period 1980–1981 was a time of vigorous enforcement and unparalleled commitment to responsible and aggressive prosecution. In short, these simplistic graphs and numbers games say virtually nothing about what is really going on in the Antitrust Division.

If Mr. Baxter's personal style has offended some, that is regrettable. However, I venture to say there is not an assistant attorney general in memory who has escaped such criticism. Mr. Baxter's invaluable contribution to the division has been to insist on rigorous and thoughtful analysis as a precondition to the initiation of any enforcement activity. Can anyone seriously debate the merits of such an approach?

❖   ❖   ❖

To which I can only say, amen.

4

Judicial Activism and the Search for Sandra Day O'Connor

L ESS THAN TWO WEEKS AFTER HIS ELECTION, RONALD Reagan received an eleven-page memo from Richard Nixon. In this candid and far-reaching document, the former president offered the president-elect suggestions as to whom he should name to the high posts of the new administration.

Here, in its entirety, is what President Nixon recommended regarding the office of attorney general:

This is one of your most important positions. Above all, he must be a man whose personal loyalty to you is unquestioned. In addition, of course, he must be an outstanding lawyer and a good administrator. William French Smith fits the bill above anyone else I can think of. As you probably know, I strongly considered him for appointment to the Supreme Court. He is a legal heavyweight with impeccable credentials and has been one of your devoted supporters for years. Another point that should be made is that your attorney general will be making recommendations to you for all judicial appointments and particularly to the Supreme Court. The importance of this is obvious when you consider the fact that you will probably appoint at least four and maybe five justices in your first term. I very deliberately appointed conservative justices to the Court who shared my philosophy that it was the responsibility of the Court to interpret the law rather than to make it. Because he had a liberal attorney general, Ford appointed Stevens, who has lined up with the liberals on the Court in virtually every significant case. With someone like Bill Smith advising you, I am confident you would not make that mistake. You will leave a great legacy both in your new approach to economic policy and in your foreign policy. But the most lasting legacy will be your impact on the Supreme Court. That is why it is so important that you appoint as attorney general someone who shares your conservative views about the role of the courts in our system of government.

At the risk of appearing immodest, I include President Nixon's comments about me. Far more important, of course, are his remarks about the importance of choosing wisely and well when it comes to the federal judiciary. With the possible exception of his prediction that President Reagan would get to name four or five justices to the Supreme Court in his first term, Richard Nixon once again proved himself to be a good prognosticator. No one could argue with his observation that the opportunity to name federal judges is a rare and powerful chance to leave one's mark on history.

We took that opportunity very seriously. The main reason we did was our firm belief that judicial activism—the policy of judges' substituting their own attitudes and feelings for the laws as passed by the legislatures—had become far too widespread.

We believed that the groundswell of conservatism that swept Ronald Reagan into office in 1980 made it an opportune time to urge upon the courts a return to fundamental legal principles, thereby diminishing judicial activism. Courts are not unaffected by major public changes in political attitudes, a lesson history continues to offer us from time to time. As Justice Cardozo once put it, "The great tides and currents which engulf the rest of men do not turn aside in their course and pass the judges by." More prosaically, as Finley Peter Dunne had his Mr. Dooley say, "The Supreme Court follows the illiction returns."

Whether we are talking about today or about the turn of the century, when Mr. Dooley made his observation, although federal judges remain free from direct popular control, basic changes in public sentiment can still affect judicial philosophy. Various doubts about past conclusions have always been expressed in Supreme Court opinions, concurrences, and dissents. Thus we saw the first few years of the Reagan administration as a golden opportunity for urging modification upon all of our courts.

We started right away. Early on, Solicitor General Rex Lee asked the assistant attorneys general to identify those key areas in which the courts might be convinced to desist from actual policymaking. In some areas, we hoped to be able to correct what we considered errors of the past, and in others we thought we might at least make an attempt to halt trends and substitute new approaches.

It was clear that, since the thirties, the Supreme Court not only engaged in but also fostered judicial policymaking under the guise of substantive due process. During those years the Court weighted the policy balance in favor of individual interests against the decisions of state and federal legislatures. Using the due process clauses, judges—who, it should be stressed, were *not* elected—substituted their own policy preferences for the determination of the public's elected representatives.

We were determined, in 1981, to focus on the doctrines that led to such activism. We hoped to reverse the unhealthy flow of power from state and federal legislatures to federal courts—and the concomitant flow of power from state and local governments to the federal level.

We were most interested in three particular areas of judicial policymaking: first, the erosion of restraint in considerations of justiciability (what will or will not be decided by the courts); second, certain of the standards by which state and federal statutes had been declared unconstitutional (especially some of the analyses of so-called fundamental rights and suspect classifications); and, third, the extravagant use of mandatory injunctions and remedial decrees.

Article III of the Constitution limits the jurisdiction of the federal courts to the consideration of cases or controversies properly brought before them. Nevertheless, in the years immediately preceding the election of Ronald Reagan, a weakening of the courts' resolve to abide by the case or controversy requirement has allowed them greater power of review over governmental action. Often in the past, the federal government itself has moved courts to show less deference to the boundaries of justiciability—in particular in environmental litigation.

Thus I pledged on taking office that the Reagan administration's Justice Department would show what I considered to be a more responsible concern for such actions. We would assert that cases should not be adjudicated where the party bringing the case had only a remote connection with the issues; where the underlying dispute was not "ripe" for judicial review (for example, a true conflict did not yet exist, where the dispute was over with—had been resolved in some fashion—and where the matter was properly resolved by the political branches, Congress or the executive, not the courts).

Granted, this terminology smacks of a legal seminar or a law-school classroom. But these are the standard elements by which one judges whether or not an issue gets to court. We knew at the time that if we could vindicate these principles, it would be a big step toward getting the courts to pay proper attention to the actions of the elected branches.

Just as the courts have sometimes overstepped the proper bounds of justiciability, their analyses of the principles of equal protection have also often trespassed upon the rightful role of the legislatures. Through their determination of what they term "fundamental rights" and "suspect classifications," in the past courts had sometimes succeeded in weighting the balance against proper legislative action.

In the past forty or so years, the number of rights labeled "fundamental" by the courts has multiplied. They now include not only First Amendment rights and the right to vote in most elections, rights clearly mentioned in the Constitution, but also rights that are only *implied* by the Constitution. The latter group, which has become a basis for expanding federal court activity, includes the right to marry, the right to procreate, the right of interstate travel, and the right of sexual privacy (that may have helped spawn a right, with certain limitations, to have an abortion).

It was not that we necessarily disagreed from a policy standpoint with the results of these cases, but that the application of their principles has led to some unwise—and constitutionally dubious—intrusions upon the legislative domain. We also felt that the very arbitrariness with which some rights have been discerned and preferred revealed a process of subjective judicial policymaking as opposed to reasoned interpretation.

This multiplication of implied constitutional rights, and the unbounded strict scrutiny they produced, had gone more than far enough. We pledged to resist further expansion of these techniques to undermine or displace legislative judgments. We also intended to return to the legislatures those issues whose very nature requires the fact-finding and deliberative resources of a legislative body to resolve. We also determined to contest any expansion of the list of suspect classifications that, once established by a court, almost inevitably result in the overturning of legislative judgments.

The extent to which the federal courts had inappropriately entered legislative terrain could be seen—and felt—most clearly in their use of mandatory injunctions and attempts to fashion equitable remedies for perceived violations. Throughout history, the equitable powers of courts have normally reached only those situations a court can effectively remedy. Implicit within that historical limitation is the recognition that some kinds of remedial efforts require resources and expertise beyond those of a federal court.

Nevertheless, federal courts have attempted to restructure entire school systems in desegregation cases, and to maintain continuing review over basic administrative decisions, such as prison systems and public housing projects. They have restructured the employment criteria to be used by U.S. business and government, even to the extent of mandating numerical results based on race or gender. (One federal judge even attempted to administer a local sewer system.)

It seemed to us that in the area of equitable remedies the federal courts had gone far beyond both their abilities and, more fundamentally, their appropriate role. In so doing they forced major reallocations of governmental resources, often with no concern for budgetary limits and the dislocations that inevitably result from a limited judicial perspective.

We planned to seek to ensure better responses to the problems by the more appropriate branches and levels of government. We had already begun that process in the case of busing and quotas— both of which have largely failed as judicial remedies.

It is one thing to list, as I have just done, the things that we intended to *do*. It is also necessary, in fairness and fullness, to admit that there were a few things we took office knowing we *could* not and *would* not do. Some conservatives believed that President Reagan's election meant the automatic repeal of all the laws with which we did not agree. Not true.

The Constitution directs the president to ensure the faithful execution of the laws—*all* the laws, including those with which the administration does not agree. Such statutes are the law of the land, and as such must be fully enforced by the executive branch when their validity and meaning are clear.

Despite the predictions to the contrary by some of our detractors, we took office pledged to keep the Reagan Justice Department in sync with the Constitution. Were we to do less, we would have been guilty of the same sins I had decried on the part of the judiciary.

Under the Constitution, the executive branch cannot unilaterally alter the clear enactments of Congress anymore than the courts can. When it disagrees with a law, the executive branch can urge and support *legislative* change. In the case of laws that are clearly unconstitutional, the executive branch can refuse to enforce them or urge the courts not to validate them. That is our responsibility under the Constitution, regardless of our views on substantive policy.

In the case of ambiguous laws, the executive branch can in good faith urge and pursue those interpretations that seem the most consistent with the intentions of Congress, the policies of the administration, and the other laws of the land.

The executive branch can do all these things, but, constitutionally, it cannot do more.

❖   ❖   ❖

Every attorney general has both bad days and good ones, and I had at least my share of the bad. But every once in a while there was a day so gratifying that it served to eclipse the memory of the days that did not go the way I had thought, or hoped, they would. One such occasion took place on September 11, 1981. That was the day on which the United States Senate confirmed Sandra Day O'Connor as the first woman justice on the United States Supreme Court.

We made more than just legal history that day, for the confirmation of Justice O'Connor capped a four-month, undercover "talent search" for the person to replace retiring Supreme Court justice Potter Stewart. Rarely had an important secret been kept in Washington for so long.

It all began on March 4, 1981, with a phone call from the vice president. George Bush was calling to advise me that his close friend, Supreme Court justice Potter Stewart, had asked him to arrange a meeting with me. I called the justice immediately, and scheduled a meeting at his home for March 26.

Actually, this story began even earlier, and I should back up a bit and include that part of it.

I keep my desk, whether at the office or at home, relatively neat. But I do have the habit of leaving certain pieces of paper on top of the desk for long periods of time, either as reminders of something important or as "master lists" related to key projects.

One such list, scribbled on the back of a pink telephone message slip, floated about my desk at the Justice Department from the very beginning. Now and then I'd pick it up and jot down a name. Sometimes I'd add an identifying phrase or title, but not always. On that list were the names of four women. Somewhere along the line I had picked up that list and jotted down a new name— "O'Connor."

Perhaps the reason I did not treat this list-making in a more formal manner was that I thought it would be a long time, if ever, before it became relevant. However, Vice President Bush's March 4 call made the list instantly relevant.

On March 26 I met with Justice Stewart at his home in the Palisades section of northwest Washington. We had a most pleasant meeting, in his solarium, during which he informed me that he planned to step down from the Court at the end of its present term. However, he did not want his decision known until he could announce his retirement, which he would do when the current Court term ended in June.

We talked for a while about possible successors, and then, after promising to keep his decision a secret, I left. As I rode back to the Justice Department I thought of that list tucked away somewhere on my desk, for it contained the names of the top women candidates for nomination to the United States Supreme Court.

Repeatedly during the campaign, Ronald Reagan had said he would give serious consideration to naming a woman to the Supreme Court. As the car neared the Justice Department, I realized I was now about to begin, in secret, the process by which that historic event might take place. For I knew that when he made that promise, Ronald Reagan was dead serious—and the reason I knew was that not long after the election, he reminded me of it!

The very next day I directed Ken Starr, who was counselor to the attorney general, to begin to research possible candidates for the Supreme Court, just so that we would be "prepared" in case a vacancy developed. I did not, however, tell Ken anything about my visit with Justice Stewart.

As Ken was about to leave my office, I handed him the back-of-the-phone-message-slip list that contained the names of the five women candidates.

He gave it a quick glance and said, "Who's 'O'Connor'? All you've got here is a last name."

"That's Sandra Day O'Connor," I said. "She's an appeals court judge in Arizona."

Ken Starr promptly began the research necessary for compiling a list of possible candidates. The writings and judicial opinions of all of the candidates were gathered together and then analyzed by Ken and a team we put together, consisting of: F. Henry ("Hank") Habicht, special assistant to the attorney general (now deputy administrator of EPA); Emma C. Jordan, who was then serving as a White House Fellow and a special assistant to the attorney general; Solicitor General Rex E. Lee; Jonathan C. Rose, assistant attorney general, Office of Legal Policy; and Bruce E. Fein, associate deputy attorney general. A list of twenty-one men and women was compiled, with appropriate background information. The list was then given to me for review.

On March 30, 1981—the Monday following my Thursday meeting with Justice Stewart—President Reagan was shot and hospitalized, the near-fatal victim of a crazed assassin. Therefore it was not possible to tell him of the impending Supreme Court vacancy until April 21, by which point he had returned from the hospital. That evening, I met privately with the president in his third-floor White House study. I advised him of Justice Stewart's intention to resign and of our search for a successor, which by then was well under way.

On May 15, Ken and Hank gave me a preliminary report regarding various candidates, and followed these up, on May 28, with thorough briefing memoranda. I reviewed these materials and asked the staff to research the records and backgrounds of certain other candidates.

Up to this point, the process had moved along nicely, and with no media attention. All that changed on June 18 when Justice Stewart formally announced his retirement, and the process was intensified. Additional names were added to the list, and more information was gathered regarding the writings and records of individuals already identified.

On June 23, I met with the president to discuss with him the various candidates. We agreed that one of the candidates whose background clearly merited additional and in-depth review was Judge O'Connor. As a result, I sent Hank Habicht the next day to Arizona, where he spent two days obtaining (on a confidential basis) even more background and information concerning Judge O'Connor.

Although Judge O'Connor was a leading candidate at this point, other candidates were also being considered, and we were doing similar checks of the backgrounds of some of them.

Although my staff was not aware of the coming vacancy, throughout the search process I had emphasized the need for confidentiality. The staff's goal in reviewing local Arizona sources was to obtain, discreetly, as much information as possible and to gain an assessment of Judge O'Connor's reputation and interests in the community.

Despite the constraints imposed on him—because of the need for confidentiality—Hank Habicht did a fine job. He reviewed legislative journals and newspaper clipping files, and spoke, in confidence, to certain people in Arizona who we had already determined were in a position to provide helpful information.

The available journals led to principal bills sponsored by then-State Senator O'Connor, or bills upon which she had requested that brief comments be published. The documentary search indicated that Judge O'Connor, one of the few lawyers serving in the Arizona legislature during her terms, was publicly identified with three principal issues.

The first was the administration of criminal and civil justice (including death-penalty legislation, increased penalties for drug offenders, improved prisons and mental institutions, and merit selection of judges). Second was state revenue law reform, along the lines of California's Proposition 13. Number three was women's rights, including amending provisions of Arizona statutes that appeared unduly discriminatory toward women.

There was no indication of her having taken any public position on abortion.

All my sources confirmed that Judge O'Connor had earned bipartisan respect and affection in Arizona, both as a professional and as a family woman. Our search turned up nothing controversial, and certainly nothing that could have disqualified her.

The next step in the process was for me to call the judge personally, which I did on Thursday, June 25. As I picked up the telephone, I hesitated slightly—not from any second thoughts, but from the realization that what I was about to do could well change history, and Judge O'Connor's life.

On the phone, I told her that I would like to consider her for a "federal position," and I asked if she would agree to be interviewed, in Phoenix, by two of my top aides. She agreed, and two days later Ken Starr and Jonathan Rose were sitting in the O'Connors' living room.

I liked what I heard about that daylong meeting, and so I called the judge again. This time I invited her to Washington for further talks. Again she agreed, even though neither one of us mentioned the identity of the court we both knew we were talking about, which is the way that dance goes. As it turned out, she was coming back to Washington anyway for a meeting of the Judicial Fellows Commission.

That same night she flew to Washington and had dinner with my wife and me at the Jefferson Hotel. My passion for secrecy extended to the point that even though Jean knew Judge O'Connor was being considered for a high federal appointment, she did not know which one. Nevertheless, I was particularly interested in Jean's opinion of Mrs. O'Connor as a person, because she has excellent instincts about people.

We had a most pleasant evening. Jean and I agreed that the judge was a highly intelligent, straightforward, and altogether charming person. Perhaps it was the power of suggestion, or the example set for decades by her fellow-Arizonan Barry Goldwater, but it seemed to us that Sandra Day O'Connor, both in her looks and in her personality, had that same direct friendliness one associates with the wide-open territory where she lived.

Based on all that I had learned, I concluded that I would recommend to President Reagan that he name Judge O'Connor as the newest associate justice of the United States Supreme Court. (I must emphasize that we were looking for the finest possible candidate for the Supreme Court. It is true that we were interested in a woman, but she had to have qualifications equal to those of any man on the list—and Sandra Day O'Connor did.)

Next, I arranged for the judge to have breakfast the morning after our dinner, with me and two other men whose opinion would be important to her "candidacy," Deputy Secretary of State William P. Clark (a former justice of the California Supreme Court) and Deputy Attorney General Edward C. Schmults, my close aide.

As the site of the breakfast I chose L'Enfant Plaza Hotel, a good hotel that had the added distinction of *not* being, like the Madison and Jefferson, within sprinting distance of the *Washington Post*. Later that afternoon, and also at L'Enfant Plaza, I introduced her to the White House staff "Troika"—Ed Meese, Jim Baker, and Michael Deaver.

All who met her that day were highly impressed, so I went ahead with the next step. I called President Reagan and told him I would like him to meet Judge O'Connor the next day.

Now I really had my work cut out for me if I wanted to keep

the impending appointment secret. Meeting the president meant going to the White House—one couldn't expect the chief executive to slip over, unnoticed, to a Washington hotel, even a chief executive as accommodating as Ronald Reagan. What's more, by this point there'd been considerable speculation in the media, especially by the press, that Judge O'Connor was a "finalist," and it seemed to me that if I escorted her to the White House, any number of reporters would run with the story. So we arranged that my confidential assistant, Myra Tankersley, would be the judge's escort.

Come the next morning, we still did not have a specific time set for the meeting, and Judge O'Connor had a number of meetings she wanted to attend. We arranged that she would leave with Myra the telephone numbers where she could be reached, and as soon as we had a definite time for her meeting with the president, we would call her and she would have fifteen minutes to meet Myra and the driver and get to the White House.

Shortly after 9:30, I got word that the president would meet with Judge O'Connor at 10:15. Scrambling, I told Myra to call the judge immediately. She did, and then prepared to leave. Watching Myra, I marveled at her calm.

"Where are you going to meet?" I asked her.

"In front of the People's Drug Store on DuPont Circle," replied Myra, as if she were talking about a lunch date with a friend.

"Wait a minute," I said, suddenly remembering that Myra had never met the Arizona judge. "Do you know what she looks like?"

"No," said Myra with a smile, "but she told me she's wearing a lavender suit."

Despite my fears, everything went smoothly, and Judge O'Connor got to the White House on time for what had to be one of the biggest moments of her life.

The meeting itself went swimmingly. In addition to the president and Judge O'Connor, Baker, Deaver, Meese, and I were also present. Immediately following the meeting, President Reagan made his decision to nominate Sandra Day O'Connor to be the first woman in history to sit on the United States Supreme Court.

Justice Stewart's intentions had not leaked for some four months. Following the meeting with the president, all agreed that Judge O'Connor's nomination would be kept secret until the president could officially notify her, and until other processes could be completed. However, what would later become common knowledge concerning White House leaks was well demonstrated here. True to form, on the very next day, Thursday, July 2, 1981, the *Washington Post* broke the story that Judge O'Connor was the leading candidate for the vacancy created by Justice Stewart's retirement!

Deliberations continued over the next few days. On Monday, July 6, the president telephoned Judge O'Connor in Phoenix and informed her that he would like to nominate her to fill the vacancy on the United States Supreme Court. She accepted.

On Tuesday, July 7, 1981, I accompanied the president to the White House press room where he announced his intention to nominate Judge Sandra Day O'Connor. The president accurately praised her as a person "for all seasons."

Judge O'Connor was in Phoenix at the time of the announcement. Peter Roussel, a press aide on the president's staff, had been assigned to assist her. She held a morning press conference where she thanked the president for his support. On July 15, at a formal ceremony in the Rose Garden, the president presented Judge O'Connor.

❖   ❖   ❖

During the months the process had taken, I had learned one thing for certain: There were four people in Washington who could keep a secret—President Reagan, Vice President Bush, Justice Stewart, . . . and me. What's more, the four of us had kept that secret for *four months*. In Washington, that's an eternity!

❖   ❖   ❖

The confirmation hearings opened on Wednesday, September 9, and continued to Friday, September 11. It was my privilege to introduce Judge O'Connor to the Senate Judiciary Committee on September 9 in the Senate Appropriations Hearing Room of the Dirksen Building.

Her nomination was approved unanimously by the Senate Judiciary Committee on September 16, and was confirmed by the full Senate on September 21 by a vote of ninety-nine to zero.

On September 25, 1981, she took the oath of office when, with great pride, I presented her credentials to the sitting Supreme Court at her investiture. This impressive ceremony was preceded by a gathering of the president and Justice O'Connor in the office of the chief justice, and then the presentation to the other members of the Court in the famous conference room. The president was also present in the conference room for the investiture.

It was a particularly important day when the first woman took her seat on the highest court in the land. I was proud to have earned a footnote in that important chapter in our history.

❖   ❖   ❖

Rarely does the search for a judge, Supreme Court or lower court, go as smoothly as it did in the case of Justice O'Connor. A couple of our other candidates who also looked good initially turned out, on closer inspection, to have oversized skeletons in their closets.

One woman we'd been interested in for a judgeship turned out not to have paid her income taxes—in fact, she hadn't even filed for a number of years. The FBI check had revealed her to be a superb candidate, with this single astonishing exception. At the time, we had mounted an aggressive campaign to name more women and minorities to the bench, but our critics didn't believe us, and were being very vocal with their skepticism. Although it would have been helpful to say that we had been considering this woman, we could not very well do so because we couldn't reveal *why* she had not been chosen!

We also had another highly qualified person brought to our attention, a man this time, only to learn that despite his having a wife and children, he had had a homosexual relationship in the

*The president, Judge Sandra Day O'Connor, and the attorney general
meet in the Oval Office before the ceremony in the Rose Garden at which
Judge O'Connor will be presented. July 15, 1981. White House
photograph.*

past. Unfortunately, it was not much of a secret; staff members of
several senators who would be involved in the confirmation process knew of it. We left it up to the candidate as to whether he
wanted us to proceed with his nomination process, and he decided
against it.

It was proposed to us that we discontinue the practice of submitting nominees' names to the American Bar Association's Committee on Judicial Qualifications. Many senators opposed this practice. We thought the process was beneficial, on balance, although
not without its shortcomings.

Over the years, the ABA's Committee on Judicial Qualifications
has been made up of very responsible members of the bar, and
has been helpful in improving the quality of the federal bench.

Very few problems have resulted from our use of this process. It had been suggested, however, that in recent years the committee had become too liberal. I had no direct experience with this affecting the reports on the candidates while I was attorney general, and would have been most distressed had it proved to be true. (I must say that the conduct of some of the committee members—and their obvious political bias—in connection with the nomination of Judge Robert Bork was very disappointing, however, and certainly cause for alarm.)

Early in the administration, Ed Schmults and I met with key members of the Senate leadership to discuss the question of judicial selection, and the understanding we reached was memorialized in a letter. In essence, we agreed that each senator would submit three to five acceptable names for each district court vacancy, and the president would choose a name from that list. This became the basis for the selection of federal district court judges for the duration of the term.

In selecting court of appeals judges, the administration had a freer hand because, with each circuit encompassing several states, no senator would have a specific claim to a vacancy. There were, however, substitute issues, such as whether a given vacancy should be filled from a particular state, or whether a given seat "belonged" to a given state. As had always been the case, the senators—being politicians—had an interest in every significant appointment.

In administrations prior to that of President Carter, there was always a tendency to appoint at least *some* members of the opposite party. In fact, we took some heat from certain California Republicans for having appointed so many Democrats during Ronald Reagan's tenure as governor—20 to 25 percent of the total during his eight years in office. But during the Carter years, to my knowledge *no* Republicans were appointed. And the folks who were appointed during those years were, consistently, of the most liberal stripe.

It has always been charged that during the Reagan administration we applied a political litmus test to judicial appointees. That was not the case during my tenure. Although we were interested in quality and judicial philosophy, we never inquired as to positions on specific issues. We read much in the press about Ronald

Reagan imposing these litmus tests, and "packing" the Court with conservatives. I can't recall any articles in the press accusing the Carterites of packing the Court with liberals, however.

As a last word on this subject, let me quote part of an op-ed-page column I wrote for the *Los Angeles Times* in reference to the nomination of Judge David Souter:

> It is my fervent hope, and I suspect the hope of most Americans, that [Judge Souter's confirmation] hearings will signal an end to the Roman carnival atmosphere that has come to envelop such events.
>
> . . . Political campaigns that inflame passions at the expense of reason and commitment to the public good, and in which lying and distortion play a key role, are always bad. But there are special and important reasons why a campaign of this sort involving a Supreme Court nominee is dangerous.
>
> . . . One argument is that in order to deserve confirmation, Souter must be willing to state in advance how he will decide cases involving abortion. Somewhat more subtly, others are insisting not that he make commitments on particular issues, but to particular constitutional doctrines, such as the right to privacy.
>
> There *is* widespread agreement that Souter should not make any promises about particular cases. But, as Justice John Paul Stevens explained in a recent speech, the attempt to get commitments about doctrines is also wrong. It is at best futile and at worst very dangerous . . . dangerous because we want our judges to be open-minded, to decide cases on the basis of law, not on the basis of promises made in order to get confirmed.
>
> As [Justice] Stevens said, "That's not part of the independent judiciary that's such an important part of our tradition and our history."

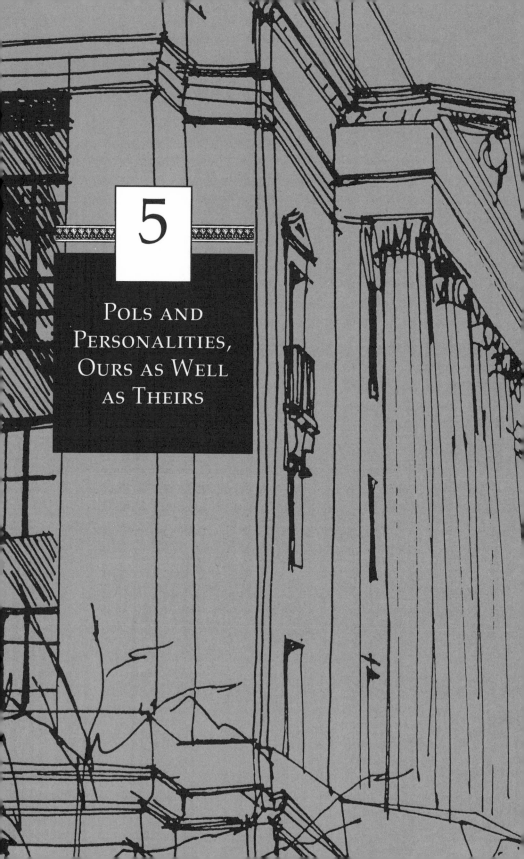

5

Pols and Personalities, Ours as Well as Theirs

T HE LATE SECRETARY OF COMMERCE MALCOLM BAL- drige had a substantial and entirely proper concern for the principle of free trade and the ability of U.S. business to compete in the increasingly competitive world markets. Mac was a good friend and a highly respected businessman and cabinet officer, but he also had a certain disdain for lawyers. Thus, when his interest in promoting business and the Department of Justice's interest in upholding the antitrust laws came into conflict, it should surprise no one that sparks flew.

Contrary to what some of our partisan critics have charged, the Justice Department under Ronald Reagan was committed to en- forcing the antitrust laws as they existed on the books. In the process of doing so, in early 1984, we raised strong objections to the proposed $747 million acquisition of Republic Steel by the LTV corporation.

We feared that the resultant company would unfairly dominate the market for three steel products, and thus we would only approve it, we said, if certain conditions were met.

If our objection was strong, Secretary Baldrige's objection to our objection was even stronger! In fact, he took the unusual step of attacking our decision (and my antitrust chief Paul McGrath) pub- licly—and he did it without even telling us he was going to do so.

Mac felt strongly that this type of merger in one of our basic industries was necessary to meet foreign competition. Consequently, as I noted earlier, he labeled the Department of Justice stance as being out of touch with conditions in "the real world," and called our decision "a world-class mistake for the U.S." As his denunciation included the name of a Justice Department subordinate official, protocol—and fairness—required me to defend him. My defense of the official, and our policy, was immediate and forceful. Our press release pointed out that our

> law "enforcement decisions" in antitrust or any other area—would be made in the future, as they have been in the past, on the basis of the facts and the law, without regard to how popular they may be inside or outside the government.

❖　　❖　　❖

I didn't like having to put out that press release, because it made an internal squabble public, but that was the lesser of two evils. And I did what Mac had not done—I called him and told him what was coming, and chided him for not having given me the same courtesy.

Of course the media loved it. The *Baltimore Sun* weighed in almost immediately with an editorial entitled "Feuding Cabinet":

> Move over Donald Regan and Martin Feldstein. This month's wrestling match between cabinet officials features Commerce Secretary Malcolm Baldrige and Attorney General William French Smith. They are the latest Reagan administration officials to go public—after a decision has been made—with a dispute over which course the administration should have taken.

As things were worked out, LTV–Republic Steel agreed to the changes required by the Antitrust Division, and the merger went ahead, almost as planned. I'm sure Mac Baldrige thought it was all his doing, and that's fine with me. In fact what actually happened was that the companies followed the law.

❖ ❖ ❖

There were a number of *inter* and *intra* department and agency skirmishes during my time in office. A few of the more notable involved Treasury, Labor, the Office of Management and Budget, Transportation, and Agriculture.

Before getting into the specifics of these skirmishes, I should point out—even if I am somewhat reluctant to do so—that there may have been a certain amount of departmental chauvinism involved. I'd like to think that had I been the secretary of commerce, I would still have seen the merits of the position taken by the attorney general. But then again, maybe not. In any event, it is important for me to point out, early in this chapter, that the reason we "squabbled" was not because one individual cabinet member did not like another one, but because of the differences between the basic missions of our respective agencies.

Now for the examples.

One of our "contests" with Treasury had to do with who should operate the Glynco, Georgia, Training Center, the principal federal-level law-enforcement training facility. Logically, it should have been under the Justice Department, but Treasury had had it for years and refused to give it up. I finally had to conclude it wasn't worth the time and energy that would be needed to get it back.

We also wrestled with Treasury (and the Office of Management and Budget, or OMB) over a plan that would have consolidated the responsibilities of Customs and Immigration, or, to use their full names, the Customs Service and the Naturalization Service (INS). OMB wanted Customs to be the agency primarily responsible, at all airports and seaports, for handling passports and visas, inspections, and enforcements. INS would have the responsibility for land-border management.

Although everyone agreed it was a good idea to merge some functions, no one quite agreed with the overall plan. INS unions opposed shifting Customs' enforcement and investigative responsibilities at border crossings to INS. The Air Transport Association supported the idea of streamlining the movement of passengers and freight through the airports. Senator Dennis DeConcini (D–

Ariz.), while agreeing with the idea behind the restructuring, did not want drug enforcement, tariff assessment, or law enforcement shifted to the Immigration and Naturalization Service. In other words, SNAFU—"Situation Normal, All Fouled Up." The consolidation would have made sense, but it did not survive the Washington bureaucratic battle for territory, and fell by the wayside.

As for the Department of Labor, there, too, we were dealing with a serious question. Early on, I had felt that DOL had not been sufficiently diligent in pursuing corruption within the Teamsters' Central States Pension Fund. This corruption had been blatant for years, and yet the Labor Department had been almost nonexistent in trying to ferret out those responsible—possibly because of the strong influence the Teamsters had over the department.

In 1981, and thereafter, procedures for cleaning up this situation were being debated. I weighed in heavily for the strongest positions to be taken. My attitude was received with some alarm, but I believe had an impact that resulted in tougher approaches to this problem.

The need for more office space for DOJ personnel got us into a tussle with OMB. I had people spread all over Washington, and I very much wanted to get them all closer to "home." For example, the Tax Division was operating out of eight separate locations. We had our eye on the beautiful and newly renovated Old Post Office Building across Pennsylvania Avenue from Main Justice, but figured we would lose that choice location to the National Endowment for the Arts, which is exactly what happened.

Our search led us to a number of other buildings, but one thing or another always caused OMB to nix the deal—location, high cost of renovation, price. Gerald Carmen, then the head of the General Services Administration (GSA, the government's landlord), and later our ambassador to the United Nations in Geneva, was in our corner. OMB remained our chief antagonist.

Just before I was to leave office, which means after more than four full years, we found what was described to me as an excellent building for our purposes on New York Avenue in downtown Washington. I was told that it was new, unfinished, and in bankruptcy, which meant we could obtain it at or near cost. When I saw the building for the first time, however, I knew OMB would never okay its purchase, for the building had a lavish atrium that gave the whole building an air of luxury. I was right. Regardless of the building's bargain basement price, OMB said "no deal."

We got into it with the Department of Transportation over shipping conferences, those arrangements among international shipping companies that have been a way of life for years. Because the conferences in effect set prices and allocated markets in ways that are clearly in violation of basic antitrust principles, we wanted to look into them, with an eye to change. Again, "no way." We never made so much as a ripple in those waters.

Within Agriculture, we found marketing orders that were obviously anticompetitive. But they were so deeply ingrained that we, the Department of Justice, couldn't get the rest of the administration to support changes in the law that permitted them. As with the shipping arrangements, they maintained stability in their respective markets.

❖   ❖   ❖

None of these governmental entities caused the Justice Department as much trouble, however, as did one individual government *official*. His name was David Stockman.

Almost immediately after his inauguration, Ronald Reagan turned—with the zealous help of Stockman—to address one of his highest priorities, the reduction of government spending. With a single stroke, OMB required all agencies (except the Department of Defense) to reduce their spending goals by 6 percent, and personnel goals by 12 percent.

This created an immediate, and major, problem for the Justice Department.

During the Carter administration, DOJ resources had been sharply decreased. The number of FBI and DEA agents, for example, had been reduced by 10 percent between 1976 and 1980. But during that same period the crime rate was skyrocketing.

I believed that DOJ's resources needed to be increased, not cut, but we agreed it was important that all agencies participate in the deficit-reduction effort. We examined the budget in depth, determined where cuts could be made—in non-law-enforcement areas—and how certain functions could be performed more efficiently and with fewer resources.

As a result, we produced a budget of $2.3 billion and 52,655 positions, representing a decrease of $231 million and 2,114 positions. Some of this reduction had to be in areas affecting law enforcement, but most of it involved federal justice subsidies and research. The fact that we were actually decreasing, and not even holding our own, was of great concern to DOJ people.

It was readily apparent to me, but to few others outside the department, that law enforcement and the DOJ were different from other agencies of government. Society requires stability; without it government fails. Thus it is necessary to maintain that stability at all costs. In this fundamental sense, the function of the Department of Justice is much more akin to that of the Department of Defense than to other agencies, because defense is also necessary, no matter what it costs, to our national security. But if we don't have stability at home, the Department of Defense will have nothing to defend. The Department of Justice, in our opinion, was truly involved in *domestic defense*.

(Of course one should never forget that Justice's budget represents but 1 percent of that of the Department of Defense.)

This was the message that I tried to convey to the inner circles of the Reagan administration. As expected, however, it was greeted by hostility from Stockman and OMB, and not taken too seriously elsewhere. But the president was receptive, so I continued to pound away on that theme.

What complicated matters for me was that the overall budget as submitted to Congress required substantial cuts in the DOJ budget, and, being a member of the administration, I had to defend the overall budget.

Doing so was not easy. In 1981, I took a heavy beating in my appearances before the Authorization and Appropriations Committees of both houses, and not just from the Democrats. Proposing to cut back on our law-enforcement budget, rather than increasing it, was not popular anywhere. After all, we were the new "law and order" administration.

Despite that effort to reduce, we were consistently voted down, and OMB (without our knowledge) later agreed to restore the proposed cuts. The budget in that condition was voted into law.

Of course this produced the worst of all possible results. The supposedly strong-on-law-enforcement administration had proposed a reduction in law-enforcement resources, and the Democrats in Congress could—and did—take credit for preventing that from happening. Furthermore, the fact that no such cuts could be made was easily predictable.

In early 1982, the Department of Justice submitted its 1983 budget to Congress, asking for $2.67 billion and 54,104 positions, a significant increase over 1982. That requested increase did not come easily. During the budget process, OMB again strongly objected to our proposed increases. Apparently, it had learned nothing from its budget experience of the previous year.

It became clear to me that David Stockman was nothing but a numbers factory. He had no conception of policy, practical needs, political reality, or the proper differentiation of functions and responsibilities. I'm sure it is true that every agency that argues for an increase claims that it is "different," but as a matter of historical fact, DOJ, like Defense, *was* different.

In the part of the procedure known as the "passback," wherein OMB responded to our request for these increases, most of what we asked for was denied. Ed Schmults and I then met with Stockman himself to discuss this denial. We explained why these increases were critically needed for law enforcement, and then we spoke of the politics of the matter. The discussion produced little.

There was yet another step, however. The White House had established a Budget Appeals Board to review disagreements between OMB and the agencies and departments. The board had three members: Baker, Meese, and Stockman. If the "appeal" was denied on that level, then the cabinet officer could take his or her "complaint" to the president.

In December of 1981, I took the matter of our budget increase to the Budget Appeals Board. We met in the Roosevelt Room of the White House with Baker and Stockman and several others, including OMB deputy director Ed Harper, Bill Niskanen of the Council of Economic Advisors, and Dick Darman, deputy assistant to the president, among others. Ed Schmults and I were there on behalf of DOJ. Oddly, Ed Meese, who has a law-enforcement background and is considered to be quite interested in the field, absented himself for some reason.

At the meeting, I related, with some force, the sequence of events of the past year, and stated that I had no intention of going through the same process again—being beaten up by Democrats and Republicans alike, and putting the administration in a bad light only to have the budget passed as we'd really wanted it, *and* to have OMB, without our knowledge, cave in!

Stockman then stated *his* case: that we had to reduce the budget; that everybody had to cut; that we were doing fine (or should be) with what we had; and that, besides, law enforcement was a state and local responsibility.

It became all too clear that Stockman had little conception of what the Justice Department did. In fact, I doubt if he was ever inside the building. If you separated him from his charts and figures, his rote persiflage and badinage, he was helpless, especially in areas we knew and he did not. His main source of strength was that he had mastered the lingo and had dealt with figures on a governmentwide basis, something most of the rest of us had no need to do or interest in doing. Thus he was able to stay one step ahead of the group, and make a little knowledge go a long way. His economic and budget predictions were so consistently wrong, and by such wide margins, that it is remarkable he was able to maintain his credibility for as long as he did. Somehow he projected the image of "knowing" the budget and of being bright, and therefore he *had to* know what he was talking about. Not a bad image for Washington.

It is of course true, as Stockman so frequently stated, that law enforcement is a state and local responsibility, but that does not mean the federal government has no responsibility at all. Stockman ignored, or was unaware of, the role of the federal government in dealing with organized crime, drug trafficking, international crime, money laundering, terrorism, foreign counterintelligence, kidnapping, bank theft, white-collar crime, information services, enforcement of federal statutes, computer crime, training, and so on. All these are major efforts, and many have to do with crimes the states simply cannot handle by themselves.

Stockman then brought out his famous charts and graphs in support of his position, a blatant attempt to overwhelm one with statistics. I told him we didn't need charts, that they could be used to tell almost any story or support any desired result. What we needed were several rare commodities—pragmatism, reality, and common sense.

Baker said very little. Harper said more, but still not much. I think it was clear to them that if I did not get what I wanted I would go right to the president. And I suspect they all knew that he would give me what I wanted. Thus we settled, the Budget Appeals Board and DOJ, on figures that represented 95 percent of what we wanted originally.

None of this means that we were not in sympathy with the goal of reducing government spending. We were. But what was needed here was realism, and a sense of political reality. After all, Congress was going to give it to us anyway. And certainly the president was not going to veto it. So, our interest and desire to do everything we could to curtail spending was best realized through doing just what we were doing—but in less costly and more effective ways. As I said elsewhere, the crime rate was increasing dramatically and federal law-enforcement resources had been allowed to be depleted.

We continued to have problems with Stockman, and on another occasion I did have to go directly to the president. It was on January 3, 1985, and it involved the Comprehensive Crime Control Act of 1984. Just as I had figured, Ronald Reagan—who recognizes that law enforcement is crucial—gave us in essence what we wanted.

Overall, we did pretty well vis-à-vis David Stockman. During my time there, DOJ's budget for law enforcement doubled, going from $2.1 billion in 1981 to $3.7 billion in 1985, which represented the greatest percentage increase of any department or agency—including the Department of Defense.

By a happy coincidence, during this same period the national crime rate, as indicated by the FBI Index and by our own Office of Justice Statistics' Victims' Crime Survey, went down. Of course, we did not take total credit for this, but it was a most welcome change—and we did play a significant role.

Before leaving the subject of David Stockman, I have to mention that he was the cause of my, once again, having to formalize an internal Reagan administration dispute. Stockman had a bad habit of trying to usurp the functions of my office in determining what the law was and then acting on it, unilaterally.

Finally, I had to send him this letter:

> I am reluctantly forced to strongly protest the apparent practice and policy of your counsel to act as a roving attorney general within the executive branch. It is not his function and it has created considerable difficulties for me and for my assistants. I had hoped that this activity would cease before it became necessary to bring it to your attention, but it has not and I must request that you take some action.
>
> Just as your responsibilities cannot be efficiently or effectively discharged if the attorney general were to attempt to perform the functions of the Office of Management and Budget, we cannot represent the United States in the courts and with respect to legal questions if others attempt to do so for us.

I am pleased to report that things improved after that, even if the improvement was rather gradual. But I was often reminded of the comment made to the *Washington Post* by one of the career lawyers at Justice. He said, in reference to our displeasure at Stockman's trying to jump into the middle of DOJ business, that the budget director had been "just plain wrong, but after all, he went to divinity school, not law school."

❖   ❖   ❖

The problem of overlapping functions and responsibilities will always exist in Washington, and it will always result in "turf battles." Some of these battles involve an open fight over jurisdiction; others simply involve strong interest in what the other agency is up to. We, of course, had our share of all these battles.

The attorney general meets with the president in the Oval Office.
December 5, 1984. White House photograph.

A classic Washington turf fight centers on the question of who handles litigation before foreign tribunals that have the authority to render judgments binding on the United States. The Department of State says it does, and we, the Department of Justice, say, "No. That is the responsibility of the attorney general."

This question first arose, in the Reagan era, when Al Haig was secretary of state (in connection with the Iranian Claims Tribunal) and again under George Shultz (with respect to Nicaragua and the International Court of Justice at The Hague).

Under U.S. law, such representation is clearly the attorney general's responsibility. The State Department, however, bases its claim on the legal premise—which always struck me as very weak—of what it calls "past practice." As a practical matter, State is always able to act first because it is the first to know that there's a *need* to act. Therefore it can undertake representation, and has done so before the Justice Department gets word of the matter, and thus it can become entrenched before Justice is even able to raise the issue.

What is needed before these tribunals is, primarily, strong experience and expertise. Strong litigation skill is exactly what DOJ has—and the State Department lacks. A foreign-policy background is helpful, but there are issues being determined in what amounts to a court proceeding, and that is the Department of Justice's bailiwick. But because there's a foreign country (or countries) involved, State always feels that only *it* can be involved.

This was probably our most acute case of turf paranoia. If we needed an illustration of its seriousness we got one in the Nicaragua case (when that nation brought an action against us in the World Court); in our opinion just about everything the Department of State did in that case was wrong. For example, the issue of justiciability, a very important matter since it involved whether the Court could actually hear the case or not, was neither properly pleaded nor argued.

I had raised this issue in writing and in person with Secretary Haig and later also with Secretary Shultz, regarding the two issues mentioned earlier. I had even called Shultz in the latter case to advise him that we disagreed with the manner in which State was handling the matter. In a later conversation, he complained that State was not receiving support from Justice. (We usually do work together; the question is which one is in charge.) I responded by telling him that we couldn't help him when we disagreed so strongly with what he was doing.

Eventually, Secretary Shultz actually adopted our view and, to his credit, implemented it. But we took a pasting in the press and came in for quite a bit of foreign criticism.

It soon became clear to me that no secretary of state was going to surrender his turf *voluntarily*—even if the Department of Justice believed that turf to have been "improperly seized"—and that only the president could resolve this issue.

Toward the very end of my time in office, I did raise this issue with the president. Although I knew how greatly he disliked to have to take positions between two of his cabinet members, I felt that this was an issue that should be resolved, and I talked to him about it. Before I could pursue it further, however, my successor was confirmed.

I decided instead to take the advice of former Attorney General Herbert Brownell, and "just get through the day."

In fairness, it should be added, and here at the end of this chapter is as good a spot as any, that President Reagan has to bear some of the blame for the frequency of turf battles. Ronald Reagan has never, in all the years I've known him, displayed much interest in refereeing fights between the top-level people who worked for him. A top-level OMB person recently described this trait as "the president's unwillingness to tell his cabinet members they couldn't have what they wanted—to feel that these conflicts should be resolved without his attention."

According to this source, this reluctance on the part of the chief executive "allowed cabinet members willing to threaten to go all the way to the top the opportunity for extortion. Thus, there are significant weaknesses in the White House budget process that were heightened by the reluctance of the president to resolve disputes among his cabinet members."

I must say, and again I do so with a certain degree of reluctance, that there is more than a grain of truth in that observation.

6

IN RE CIVIL RIGHTS . . .

U NFORTUNATELY, WHEN LIABILITY FOR DISCRIMI-
nation has been found, some of the measures employed
to remedy its effects have been less than successful. In
fact, some remedies have not been remedial. Increasingly, many Americans—both black and white—view some types of remedial efforts as beneficial only because of the substantial and well-
intended commitment by government that they reflect.

After some twenty-five years of experience with various remedial devices, the time has come to test their effectiveness. We must not delay the
reevaluation necessary to the achievement of actual and not merely sym-
bolic progress. We cannot afford to pursue an ineffective course solely
because its intentions are good. Instead, we need to engage in practical
problem-solving and adopt measures that will realistically remedy the
direct results of discrimination. That means the nation must end its
overreliance on remedial devices aimed solely at achieving inflexible and
predetermined mathematical balance.

Those words come from a speech I gave on May 22, 1981. It was
only four months into the Reagan era, but I was announcing,
before a gathering of the prestigious American Law Institute, a
major departure from two decades of civil-rights policy in America.

In that speech, I declared an official end to the Department of
Justice's vigorous support of mandatory busing in school desegregation cases and racial quotas in employment discrimination cases.

Our approach, which was in keeping with conservative principles of both law and social policy, was simple—individuals should be treated as individuals without regard to race, creed, or religious background.

Over the next five years, we implemented that policy and enforced its underlying principles to a degree unsurpassed by previous administrations. We racked up a score that included 178 new *criminal* prosecutions for violations of civil rights; the filing of or participation in almost one hundred right-to-vote cases; and a record number of suits filed (and almost all of them won) in the area of employment discrimination against women and minorities. In the latter area, we also brought increased numbers of women and minorities into the work force based on merit, not "affirmative action."

To my way of thinking, we compiled not just a good record but an enviable one. Yet if one were to stop a passerby in the street—especially in Washington, D.C.—and ask his or her opinion of the Reagan Justice Department's record on civil rights, I am afraid that half of those respondents would give us a failing grade.

Why? Mainly because the civil-rights establishment and others who had fought hard for these rights were not about to compromise. They were not even interested in talking about, much less conceding, the fact that these remedies had been tried and failed. These changes provided ammunition for inflammatory attacks on the administration as "anti–civil rights." Political opponents and the media gladly joined in. We did not help much, either, by the way we handled a later matter called the Bob Jones case. Here again, we attempted to follow our basic premise that the best way to address a social problem also had to be the best *legal* way, and on that basis we opposed the IRS action denying Bob Jones University, a fundamentalist religious school, its tax exemption because it discriminated on the basis of race.

The account that follows is the inside story of the Bob Jones case *and* the Reagan administration's record in the field of civil rights.

❖ ❖ ❖

Ever since our nation first woke up to the undeniable fact of its long history of blatant racial discrimination, the Department of Justice has helped lead the struggle to achieve equal opportunity for all our citizens. Right from the beginning of my tenure at Justice, we determined to improve upon that effort by implementing new and different approaches—and by discarding remedies that had proved to be unproductive.

Our most controversial effort involved the rejection of quotas and busing as remedies for discrimination. Neither, in our opinion, had been successful and, in fact, had often been counterproductive. Nonetheless, we were well aware that any changes we would make in those two areas would alter the way things had been done around DOJ's Civil Rights Division and, in addition, would upset the vested interests of many civil-rights groups. Although Ronald Reagan had campaigned for years on the idea of new approaches to civil-rights enforcement, we knew that once the editorial-page writers of such papers as the *New York Times* and the *Washington Post* got wind of our proposed changes their objections would be violent. We were not disappointed. Nonetheless, we were also not deterred.

Guiding our efforts, as we forged ahead despite the brickbats of the press, was a single principle: Individuals should be treated as individuals, without regard to race, creed, or ethnic background. Freedom from discrimination consists of the right to participate fully in our society on the basis of individual merit and desire. That right engenders a guarantee that no one's path should be blocked because of race, gender, or ethnic background.

These issues manifested themselves in a variety of contexts: denial of rights (or the attempt to do so) by violence or intimidation; interference with the unfettered right to vote; freedom from discrimination in employment, in public education, and in housing; equal treatment of women and for the handicapped and mentally ill; also protection of religious freedoms.

During the next four years, and despite the verbal abuse and criticism and overreaction, this principle and these policies were implemented.

The level of activity in prosecuting those who used violence or intimidation to deny the civil rights of others exceeded that of any prior administration. Our 178 new criminal cases yielded a remarkably high percentage of convictions. They ranged from convictions for the brutal beating death of a black musician in St. Louis to the racially motivated murders of other black citizens to the enforced servitude of Indonesian farm workers.

In protecting U.S. citizens' right to vote, our Justice Department filed or participated in almost one hundred cases. We reviewed more than thirty thousand proposed voting procedure changes under the Voting Rights Act alone.

In employment matters, virtually all the enforcement effort was aimed at discriminatory conduct against women and minorities, but the principle was applied across the board.

We sued the Milwaukee Police Department for its treatment of black officers, and we opposed a quota remedy for the New Orleans Police Department because it would have discriminated against Hispanics, women, and all others not favored by the quota.

We brought more suits in this area than the previous administration, won almost all of them, and obtained the highest back-pay awards in history. Through affirmative outreach and recruitment programs we brought increased numbers of minorities and women into the work force—free of the stigma so frequently attached to those regarded as "affirmative action" employees unable to secure their positions on merit alone.

Throughout our enforcement activity we sought to promote the great goal of colorblind justice and restore the hope of an America in which race, gender, and ethnic background simply do not matter in the estimation of an individual's talents and abilities.

We filed an *amicus* brief (*amicus curiae,* or "friend of the court," for the type of brief a nonparty to a suit files when it feels so strongly about a pending issue that it wants a court to know its reasoning) in *Memphis Firefighters vs. Stott* arguing this principle of nondiscrimination, and the Supreme Court adopted our argument fully in the course of invalidating layoffs made on the basis of race. We argued before lower federal courts that a municipality may not allocate, or "set aside," a percentage of its business contracts for distribution according to racial criteria. The Supreme Court agreed with us in a child-custody case decided in 1984 that "race must be altogether stricken from consideration in custody determinations."

The *Memphis Firefighters* decision confirmed the administration's belief that the nation's commitment to the civil rights of all individuals was never intended to include a commitment to the use of numerical quotas. Quotas have never proven to be effective. More basically, they are contrary to our guiding principle of equal individual opportunity. Quotas are demeaning, and invariably they result in the establishing of employment ceilings, not floors. Support for quotas surrenders the individual right to a group remedy—which violates the most basic precept underlying the individual right. We were explicit in our opposition to this device from the very beginning. We believed that the country in general had come to understand, accept, and applaud the rejection of quotas as instruments of civil-rights law enforcement.

In the field of public education, the effort was to ensure that no individual be denied equal educational opportunity because of race. Even beyond the question of student assignments, we began investigations in several cases to determine if the quality of education offered in certain public schools was intentionally and illegally inferior to that offered in other public schools.

Either through settlements or court orders, we obtained relief in twenty-four cases involving school districts from Texas to Indiana. We reached favorable settlements in the North Carolina and Louisiana higher education cases and pursued similar cases in other states. Our efforts were to ensure equal educational opportunity regardless of race. We believed that no child should be assigned to a particular school solely because of race, and that no child should receive less of an educational opportunity because of race. That is the mandate of *Brown vs. Board of Education*, to which we were fully committed. That landmark decision vindicated the "personal interest" pupils have "in admission to public schools . . . on a (racially) nondiscriminatory basis."

Some, however, have focused not on this "personal interest," but on racial balance among and within schools. They advocate mandatory busing of students on the basis of race to "correct" any perceived imbalance. Experience has demonstrated, however, that forced busing does not guarantee equal opportunity; instead it often promotes segregation by encouraging many to leave the public schools.

Before the imposition of busing in Los Angeles in the 1970s, white enrollment stood at 37 percent. By 1980, it had dropped to 24 percent. After busing was imposed in Boston, white enrollment dropped from 57 to 35 percent; in Dayton, from 53 to 43 percent; and in Denver from 57 to 41 percent. Some of this was the result of normal demographic change, but much is clearly attributable to the public's reaction to busing.

A similar history is apparent in one community after another across the country: in Cleveland, for example, and in Wilmington, Delaware, in East Baton Rouge and Atlanta, in Memphis and Detroit. We did not consider it progress to act against one-race schools in a way that produces one-race school systems.

Our goal was a better education for all children. We therefore actively pursued remedies that furthered that goal more effectively. If specific remedies have not been effective, vindication of the underlying right requires resort to new and different remedies. Any other view perversely elevates the remedy above the right. And, what is most troubling, such a view may actually undermine the right itself by drawing racial distinctions.

We sought the following new remedies: We pioneered desegregation plans that rely on the voluntary participation of students in magnet schools, outreach programs, or careful structuring of school-district zoning, and on sound, long-range plans for school construction. In places as diverse as Odessa, Texas, Chicago, Illinois, and Bakersfield, California, these plans were put in place, and they work.

We were active in other areas as well, beginning thirty-six new investigations of state and local institutions under the Civil Rights of Institutionalized Persons Act; nineteen of these concerned institutions for the mentally retarded. One resulted in a court-approved plan by the Commonwealth of Pennsylvania to close the Pinehurst Institution. In addition, we vigorously protected the rights of the handicapped, successfully arguing before the Supreme Court, for example, that Section 504 of the Rehabilitation Act of 1973 forbids employment discrimination on the basis of handicap in all federally assisted programs. On a wholly different front, we successfully prosecuted a suit in Arizona under the Equal Credit Opportunity Act, stopping lenders from discriminating against Native Americans.

We also actively attacked discrimination in housing, restructuring the Civil Rights Division to enhance its enforcement capability in this area. We opened 283 new pattern-and-practice discrimination investigations, 20 of which resulted in our filing suit. In the *Havens Realty* case, we appeared as an *amicus* before the Supreme Court and took the position, with which the court agreed, that under proper circumstances "testers" have standing to bring housing discrimination suits.

Apart from traditional civil-rights enforcement activity, we also used the first term of our tenure at the Department of Justice to reestablish another civil right—the freedom of religion. Too often in recent decades the courts have seemed to think that freedom *of* religion means freedom *from* religion. Of course, government must adopt a crucial neutrality toward all manner of religious belief and nonbelief—but this should not position the state as an active opponent of religion.

Since the first Congress in 1789, legislative chaplaincies have been an accepted part of American life. Only in recent years have they been challenged as unconstitutional. In 1983 the Supreme Court decided to review whether such a chaplaincy (Nebraska's, in this case) did indeed violate the Constitution, since a federal appeals court had ruled against the practice. The Justice Department filed a friend-of-the-court brief urging the Supreme Court to reverse the court of appeals and uphold the chaplaincy. The Court did so, thus stopping the drive to expel religion from our public life at the door of legislative chaplaincies.

In 1984, the Supreme Court decided to review whether a traditional government involved in a religious activity—in this case a city's inclusion of a nativity scene in a Christmas display—violated the Constitution.

Here again a federal appeals court had ruled against the activity in question; here again the DOJ filed as a friend of the court, asking the Supreme Court to reverse; and, here again, the Supreme Court stopped the drive to eliminate religion from our public life short of another target.

As a result of the 1983 and 1984 rulings, it is clear that the public square need not be absolutely naked of religion. It is all right for a legislature to support a religious chaplaincy, and it is all right for a city to include the nativity scene in a Christmas display.

The need, however, is not only to repel the effort to strip the public square of every trace of religion, when it may constitutionally remain in that square. For example, thanks to previous federal court decisions, many believed that any tuition tax credit "scheme" benefiting parents of children attending church-related schools would violate the Constitution. But in 1983, the Justice Department, in an *amicus* brief, argued before the Supreme Court that such tuition tax credits do not necessarily violate the Constitution. In this case the Supreme Court upheld a tuition tax deduction plan adopted by the state of Minnesota.

The Justice Department's efforts to both protect and restore the rightful place of religion in our public life are inspired by the vision of a country in which citizens are free to worship and practice their beliefs free of government coercion. Government ought not to force belief of any kind on anyone. But neither should it force citizens to divorce belief from life, by requiring in effect that they shut off any visible expression of their faith whenever they enter a public place. Instead, government should find ways to accommodate, on a "neutral" basis, the religious beliefs of all its citizens.

Movement in this direction was evident not only in the Supreme Court but also in the Congress, which in 1984 enacted administration-supported legislation that provides for "equal access" to public school facilities for student religious groups. The equal-access bill perfectly reflected the idea of neutral accommodation. As a result of the bill, student religious groups now have the same access to school facilities as all other student groups.

I believe it is a telling—and favorable—statistic that the budget of the Civil Rights Division and the number of employees enforcing the civil-rights statutes of this country increased *significantly* every year we were there.

❖   ❖   ❖

Our critic-on-the-street would also do well to examine our record in relation to the Voting Rights Act, one of the strongest planks in the modern civil-rights platform. The Voting Rights Act expired in 1982. Before that expiration, the president charged the Department of Justice with reviewing how the act had operated. He also told us to make recommendations with respect to its renewal.

We researched that matter in depth, and had numerous meetings with representatives of all the civil-rights organizations and with other interested individuals and groups. Of course the act had to be renewed, but we concluded, tentatively, that certain administrative changes were desirable.

For example, almost all the thousands of voting-procedure changes that had to be submitted to DOJ for approval were approved. These included such changes as moving a voting booth from one location to another across the street. We felt that the administrative and bureaucratic costs involved could be greatly reduced by eliminating approval requirements that no longer served any real purpose or could be handled by the states or localities. It also seemed that states and localities that were covered by the earlier acts, and then definitely required coverage, had long since come into compliance, and now could be eliminated from this type of policing.

We were in the middle of this process, though a long way from any final conclusions (which were to be submitted to the president), when we learned for the first time just how much clout the civil-rights groups have in Congress. Without notice to the administration, without hearings, without debate, without consideration of how the administration thought the act could be improved or changed, the Subcommittee on Civil and Constitutional Rights of the House Judiciary Committee had reported out a bill that not only extended the Voting Rights Act, but also greatly expanded it. "In the public interest," this had been accomplished quickly and almost secretly. It was raw politics at work, and a classic example of special interests superseding the public interest.

Among other things, the new bill contained a provision that any state action that had the "effect" of diluting minority representation (as distinguished from "intending" to do so) was illegal. This together with other provisions was calculated to result in proportional representation—that is, members of a city council would have to be proportioned on the basis of race; if one-third of the constituency was black, one-third of the members would have to be black. This concept is repugnant to our system. Although a provision had been—very cleverly—inserted in the bill so as to make it sound as though this result were precluded, the provision in fact did not do so.

By the time the measure got to the House floor it had been packaged as a real "motherhood" issue: protecting the right to vote. Members of both parties were hard put to vote against it. The "con" arguments appeared to be merely technical—and, besides, why alienate the huge minority constituency over a matter of principle that smacked of nitpicking? This was Machiavellian politics, impure and simple—casting legislation in terms of motherhood, and denigrating substantial opposition as technical and minor.

It is often impossible to come to grips with the merits of proposed legislation in Washington. That was the case here.

Now the focus turned to the Senate, where we hoped procedural sanity would surely previl. No such luck—we were wrong again. We learned that over half the members of the Senate had become sponsors of (the essence of) the House bill. And then, for the first, but by no means the last, time we learned—*from the Hill itself*—that the White House had, in effect, already agreed to the Senate bill. Inquiries to Jim Baker and Ed Meese produced only fuzzy responses. I don't believe either man understood the real issues involved.

So, for the first time since I had become attorney general I went directly to the president. I pointed out that he was dangerously close to committing himself to signing a bill that could establish the foundation for proportional representation, with the only remaining bulwark being (one hoped) the federal judiciary. President Reagan agreed immediately, and instructed his staff to resist any such result.

Obviously, however, it would be impossible, from a political standpoint, for the president to veto an extension of the Voting Rights Act. All the senators, on both sides of the aisle, knew that. This left us little bargaining room, but bargain we did, and with some measure of success. After considerable discussion, including one extraordinary Saturday meeting at the White House with Senator Dole, me, Messrs. Baker and Meese, White House counsel Fred Fielding, and Brad Reynolds, my assistant attorney general for civil rights, we fashioned compromise language taken essentially from the earlier Supreme Court decision in *Wright vs. Register*.

As a result, with some changes to the congressional committee reports, we were able to make it clear that the purpose of the legislation's new "effects" test was not to mandate proportional representation. It was less than we had hoped for, but a result the president could accept.

What the courts will do—often a slender reed—remains to be seen.

By customary Senate standards, the Senate Judiciary Committee's action on the extended Voting Rights Act was "normal," yet still frustrating for someone who wanted to find the most fair and logical result. The drama was most instructive, but only for those who knew how to read between the lines. Senator Ted Kennedy was his usual self, skillfully delivering his standard line speeches (written by his able but misguided staff), which played beautifully to his civil-rights cohorts in the galleries.

Kennedy's performance was expected. That of Republican Charles Mathias of Maryland was not. Taking up the same theme, Senator Mathias argued earnestly for the same result as had his "distinguished colleague" on the other side of the aisle. Mathias's earnestness was compromised, however, by the fact that he cited case after case in support of his position, but when told that none of the cited cases stood for the proposition he claimed (and they didn't) he announced that whatever they held, he was going to vote for the bill. In other words, the facts be damned. Unfortunately, this kind of tortured "reasoning" is normal for the United States Senate, but frustrating to one attempting to get to the merits of an issue.

(Equally unfortunate is the fact that proof of this kind of "debate" is hard to come by, as neither body of Congress releases a verbatim transcript of its proceedings. Both in the Senate and the House, members are allowed to make ex post facto changes so that the "record" reflects what they preferred, in retrospect, to say, but not what they actually *did* say. One shouldn't be too surprised, however, for this is the same body that protects itself by exempting itself from the reach of practically all the major laws it has passed governing the conduct of others. For example, Congress has excluded itself from the coverage of such acts as the Fair Labor Standards Act, the Civil Rights statutes, the National Labor Relations Act, the Equal Pay Statute, the Freedom of Information Act, the Discrimination in Employment Act, the Ethics in Government Act, and the Independent Counsel Act, *among others*.)

❖   ❖   ❖

For the record, I should mention that there was also a good deal of internal Justice Department strife over the contents of my speech on civil rights to the American Law Institute. Several deputy assistant attorneys general in the Civil Rights Division, holdovers from earlier administrations, were vehement in their objections to the shift in policy I had announced. That shift, however, was not by me but by the voters in the election of the previous November.

Interestingly, the flap over the Bob Jones case resulted in the opposite situation—it was understood internally and roundly condemned on the outside. As things turned out, the whole affair was an object lesson in how *not* to handle a public issue of high potential volatility.

The simplest statement of the case is that in *Bob Jones University vs. United States* the Supreme Court ruled that the Internal Revenue Service, without prior congressional authorization, had the power to deny tax exemptions to private schools that practice racial discrimination. The simplest statement of the administration's position is that Congress could not legislate by acquiescence and, absent such authority, the IRS, an administrative unit, had no such power. Beyond that, nothing is simple.

As a religious, educational, and nonprofit institution, Bob Jones

University (in Greenville, South Carolina) clearly met the operative criteria for tax exemption. In 1981, however, when the IRS uncovered evidence of discrimination, it denied the school's tax exemption. The IRS was acting on an internal 1970 ruling (*which had never been challenged, enacted, or ratified by Congress*) that assessed to it the power to deny tax exemptions to educational institutions that practice racial discrimination.

The university sued and the case ended up before the highest court in the land.

The Supreme Court's decision to hear the case meant that the administration had to take a position concerning the authority of the IRS. It occasioned much debate within the administration on the somewhat esoteric issue of the authority of the IRS to make determinations on public policy issues not related to its primary mission. To some, including the president, it was an example of a regulatory agency's exceeding its mandate. Doing something about such excesses happened also to have been one of Ronald Reagan's main campaign promises. Thus it was decided that we would ask the Court to deny the IRS such power absent legal authority to do so.

Extensive debate took place within the department concerning the extent of the authority of administrative agencies and units to act without specific congressional enactments. Although the basic issue only peripherally involved the question of civil rights, much consideration was given to how a contrary decision could be misconstrued and distorted in the very sensitive civil-rights area.

On January 8, 1982, the Treasury Department and the White House, acting in concert, announced that the Justice Department had advised the Supreme Court that we did not believe the IRS had the power to deny tax exemptions to racially discriminatory schools. Accordingly, the Treasury Department had "commenced the process necessary to revoke forthwith the pertinent rulings."

Our position was classically the result of careful legal analysis. We did not feel the IRS had the legislative authority to deny, as the Treasury Department's announcement put it, "tax-exempt status to otherwise eligible organizations on the grounds that their policies or practices do not conform to notions of national public policy."

The outcry from the media, civil-rights groups, and critics of the administration was intense, and the legal issue that was the basis for the decision was totally ignored or obscured. The theme was that the Reagan administration was in favor of tax breaks for schools that discriminated—even to the extent of so arguing before the Supreme Court. That theme was extensively and repeatedly disseminated.

The matter was further aggravated by the fact that the administration did not handle the issue well. Although more than adequately warned of the potential firestorm—I personally advised Jim Baker and Mike Deaver, and Ed Schmults did the same with Ed Meese—the White House reacted to the furor as if in total surprise. At the time of the announcement, the administration should have sent proposed legislation to the Congress that would have given such authority to the IRS commissioner. It did not do so until five days later, when the media had already miscast the issue as a civil-rights statement. The matter was also complicated by the fact that a memorandum came to light with the president's notation on it raising the question of the IRS commissioner's authority.

The president dutifully took responsibility. Not so the secretary of the treasury, Don Regan. During the height of the controversy, the famous Alfalfa Club dinner took place at the Capitol Hilton Hotel. During the cocktail hour, Don, in front of a large group of dignitaries, said, in reference to the Bob Jones affair, "Of course, we all have to rely on our lawyers for advice in these matters."

Don's jibe was not mean-spirited, for we were good friends, but he nonetheless conveniently neglected to mention that he'd been in the middle of the decision-making on the Bob Jones matter (it was his IRS that had generated the issue).

On February 4, 1982, Professor Laurence Tribe of the Harvard Law School faculty, a leading liberal in a bastion of radical thought, rushed to testify before the House Ways and Means Committee. He said:

> High officials of the Executive Branch, including the Secretary of the Treasury, the Attorney General, and the President himself, have abruptly undertaken to accord favored tax treatment to certain racially discriminatory public schools, in derogation of the

basic duty of these officials faithfully to execute the Constitution and laws of the United States. These departures from the rule of law have, in turn, been both facilitated and aggravated by serious misrepresentations to the press, the public, and the Supreme Court.

Professor Tribe continued:

> Thus, if any action by Congress is called for, it is not legislative action to clarify or change the tax status of racist schools . . . but investigative and other corrective action to explore and remedy what appear to be grave abuses of office at the highest levels of the Executive Branch.

If Larry Tribe was worked up, some of the commentators—of the Anthony Lewis, Tom Wicker ilk—were almost apoplectic.

Our critics were supported by the decision of the Supreme Court—which went *against* us. And in case anyone thinks it was a close decision, I should add that the vote was eight to one.

The Court's decision, which was essentially sociological, turned on two factors. One was that the IRS ruling was acceptable in this instance because it was "in harmony with the public interest," and the other was that the Congress, in not objecting ever since 1970 when the IRS had first come up with the ruling, had "acquiesced."

Those reasons were contained in Chief Justice Warren Burger's majority opinion. Harsher treatment of the IRS ruling was to be found in the concurring opinion of Justice Lewis Powell (which one commentator called "a notably uneasy concurrence"). Powell felt that formulating national policy was the job of the legislature, not the Internal Revenue Service, and that acting in the public interest was simply beside the point—but he affirmed, nonetheless.

The lone dissenter was the future chief justice, William Rehnquist. In a very lucid opinion, the point of which was never really addressed by the majority opinion, Justice Rehnquist found that the IRS had no business passing on what was and what was not in the public interest in this area. That, he said, was the function of the legislature.

That last point was the same point we had decided to stand up and fight for. We did, and we simply lost. That was not the bad part, however. The bad part was the public *mis*perception that our

opposing the IRS's denial of tax exemption stemmed from anti–
civil-rights, antiblack attitudes on the part of the Reagan
administration.

It could have looked that way, especially to our philosophical
enemies. But that was not the way it was.

As an illustration of how differently the same Supreme Court
decision could be interpreted, consider these two excerpts from
newspaper editorials. The first is from the *Cleveland Plain Dealer*
and the second from the *Richmond News Leader*.

> The court's 8–1 ruling was a stinging repudiation of the Reagan
> administration's controversial endorsement of the school's posi-
> tion, a stand that threatened to undo some of the progress of the
> last 29 years.

> With this decision (to deny tax exemptions to segregated schools)
> no longer will national policy be made by those who parade their
> faces in front of the electorate. It will be made, rather, by a faceless
> tax collector. And we feel that somehow, centuries ago, the Foun-
> ders had something better in mind.

One last note—or, rather, two last notes. In early June of 1983,
I got a short letter from Charles Cooper, a lawyer at Justice who
felt strongly that, despite the bashing we'd taken from the media,
we had been right all along. He wrote:

> As the *Bob Jones* decision amply attests, we live in a time when
> the courts, including the Supreme Court, think nothing of cutting
> great roads through the law to get after what they perceive to be
> the Devil. Perhaps there has never been a time when they did
> not. But I am confident that there shall never come a time when
> the courts stop cutting roads through the law unless they are
> opposed on every swath. I thus hope that this decision serves to
> strengthen your resolve to vigorously criticize the Judiciary's wont
> to legislate.

The other note also involved a letter, but this one was not from
a supporter; it was from an early, and most vocal, opponent, the
aforementioned Laurence Tribe of Harvard.

Sometime after his congressional harangue against us, Professor
Tribe took a longer and more careful look at our position and the
legal reasoning behind it. To his credit, he changed his opinion;

in fact, he came around 180 degrees. In February 1984, he wrote to me, and said, in part:

> I have the highest regard for the quality of the brief finally submitted to the Supreme Court by the Department of Justice in the *Bob Jones* case. I thought it was a powerful and, in most respects, entirely compelling legal document. As I told Chuck [Cooper], I continue to think that the Fifth Amendment itself may well prevent all federal subsidies, even by way of tax-deductible status, of racially discriminatory public schools. But I do not think that the Supreme Court's use of congressional inaction to support the legality of the IRS policy was at all legitimate. If Congress wishes to legislate a tax rule, it must do so by action—not by silence. In this regard, you might find it interesting to glance at my enclosed article [from the *Indiana Law Review*] on the sounds of congressional silence. I mention the *Bob Jones* decision *in a disapproving way* at page 531, footnote 91.

Let the record reflect that the italics in the final line are my own.

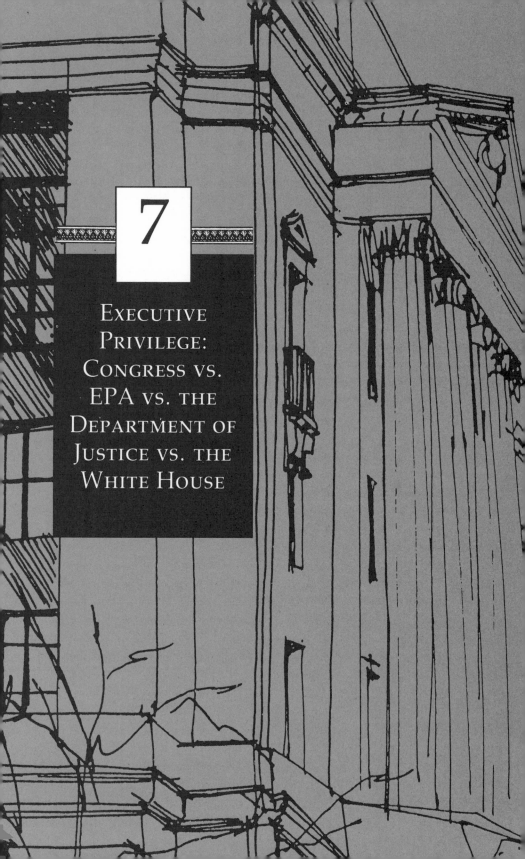

7

EXECUTIVE PRIVILEGE: CONGRESS VS. EPA VS. THE DEPARTMENT OF JUSTICE VS. THE WHITE HOUSE

CHAIRMAN RODINO HAS NOW ISSUED A REPORT WHICH *not only is a gross distortion of the role of the Department of Justice and its officials, but also accuses the department of purposely delaying or obstructing his inquiry. A detailed response to that report will be issued by the department soon, but I must go on record now as completely and unqualifiedly rejecting this report. Its premises and conclusions are baseless, and the motives of those who produced it are patently political. I am speaking at this time because the public deserves to know this fundamental fact now. It also should be apprised of the background of what has amounted to no more than a misguided vendetta against a department of the executive branch and its officials.*

The paragraph quoted above is from a preliminary draft of a statement I issued—in somewhat toned-down language—a few days later in response to the House Judiciary Committee's *long* overdue report on the highly publicized conflict between the Congress and the Department of Justice over certain Environmental Protection Agency (EPA) documents.

Actually, "conflict" hardly does justice to the intensity of the struggle or the extent of animosity it generated—not to mention the harm it did to the reputations (and pocketbooks) of a handful of people who had never before in their lives been involved in such an adversarial public scrutiny.

First, some history—both dusty and more recent. The framers of our Constitution were particularly sensitive to the propensity of Congress to enlarge its power at the expense of the other branches. James Madison warned, in *The Federalist Papers*, that the "legislative department is everywhere extending the sphere of its activity, and drawing all power into its impetuous vortex. . . . It is against the enterprising ambition of [Congress] that the people ought to indulge all their jealousy and exhaust all their precautions."

One area where Congress has increasingly intruded upon the executive branch is through the guise of what has come to be known as the "oversight" function. Interestingly, this curious process is not mentioned in the Constitution, and thus, as far as explicit constitutional language is concerned, Congress has no more business engaging in "oversight" of the executive branch than either the executive branch or the judicial branch would have conducting "oversight" of the Congress. The Constitution contemplated that "oversight" of the president would be exercised by the people, at the ballot box.

True, congressional committees do have wide-ranging fact-finding authority for purposes of legislation, to see how appropriated funds are spent, and for impeachment purposes. In recent years, Congress has—with the general acquiescence of the Supreme Court—expanded this function to a far-reaching, detailed, and ongoing general examination of virtually every action and activity of the executive branch. One consequence of this expansion is the frequent abuse of individuals (on a smaller, but no less damaging, scale of the type perfected by Senator Joe McCarthy).

Congress, which often gets so bogged down in the minutiae of government that it seems not to have time to deal with essential issues, does *not* have the authority to exercise executive functions or to intrude into the area of executive decision-making. Yet today's Congress has expanded beyond all expectations. There are now over three hundred committees and subcommittees in Congress, exercising overlapping jurisdiction, and providing jobs for tens of thousands of staffers. The tendency has been, more and more, under the guise of fact-finding, to attempt to engage in executive decision-making, second-guessing, and headline-grabbing demagoguery.

One of the more notorious instances of interference in executive decision-making occurs in the name of "legislative oversight," especially with respect to information contained in files of open criminal investigations (for example, the names of potential defendants, documents relating to litigation strategy, and the like). It has long been the policy of the Department of Justice not to produce such documents for inquiring members of Congress and their staff.

The reason for this policy is obvious: Such information would be of great value to people who are the subjects of investigations, and thus releasing it could seriously compromise law enforcement (to say nothing, taking the cynical view, of the potential value of such information to a congressman's constituents). Furthermore, the release of such information to the public can cause unnecessary and irreparable damage to the reputations and careers of the persons being investigated. Further, congressional pressure on DOJ to indict or to prosecute—or not to do so—interferes with the prosecutor's independence and may impermissibly taint a prosecution with political influence.

To be sure, there have been occasions where, upon a proper showing and with appropriate safeguards, such law-enforcement files (or portions of them) have been made available to Congress. But that has been by agreement and with the full consent of the president. Rarely has a congressional committee attempted, through the use of the subpoena power, to compel the wholesale and indiscriminate production of vast numbers of open law-enforcement files.

Once, when a special subcommittee of the House Judiciary Committee made such a demand on the Justice Department, President Truman firmly and categorically rejected it, saying, "I do not believe such a procedure to be compatible with those provisions of the Constitution which vest executive power in the president and impose on him the duty to see that the laws are faithfully executed."

Nevertheless, in 1982, two committees of Congress sought to subpoena more than three-quarters of a million pages of sensitive, open law-enforcement files relating to cases under development by the Environmental Protection Agency against companies that had deposited hazardous waste in dumps throughout the country.

Specifically, this is how it all began. That fall, with half a dozen congressional subcommittees looking into charges of mismanagement at EPA, a staffer for one of them requested permission to examine certain documents relating to Superfund (the money set aside by Congress for cleaning up the nation's worst toxic-waste dumps).

The people in EPA's Boston regional office gave him access, but not those in the office in New York City. The Hill staffer then appealed to EPA headquarters. When the request reached EPA's general counsel, he said no. But a lawyer who was the top aide to EPA administrator Anne Gorsuch (soon to become Anne Burford) reversed the decision. That put the matter squarely on the doorstep of DOJ, where it came to my attention shortly after I returned from an overseas trip.

Carol Dinkins, as head of Justice's Land and Natural Resources Division, was responsible for the investigation and litigation of EPA matters. Ted Olson, as head of the Office of Legal Counsel at Justice, provided the principal legal advice to the executive branch and to the divisions at Justice, as well as to the president. Bob McConnell, as assistant attorney general of the Office of Legislative Affairs, was responsible for the department's relations with Congress.

They—along with Deputy Attorney General Edward Schmults—advised me that then-Georgia congressman Elliott Levitas's Subcommittee on Investigations and Oversight (of the House Committee on Public Works) and the Subcommittee on Oversight and Investigations (of the House Committee on Energy and Commerce), chaired by Michigan's John Dingell, were demanding hundreds of thousands of open law-enforcement files in EPA investigations of companies having responsibility for scores of hazardous waste dumps.

EPA, which as I said had cooperated initially, now found itself at the mercy of congressional staffers roaming through EPA files at EPA headquarters and out in the field. Fearing—no, *knowing*—it would lose control over the information in those files if that material were relinquished to the legislative branch, EPA, accordingly, asked DOJ for advice. How can we, they asked, protect the integrity of our files?

After careful study we concluded that we should recommend to the president that he exert executive privilege to protect the documents in question from dissemination to these committees. (Only the president himself can claim, or exercise, executive privilege.) Presidential counsel Fred Fielding, and his deputy, Dick Hauser, concurred in our recommendation, as did EPA administrator Burford.

President Reagan followed our recommendations. He instructed the EPA administrator to assert her claim of executive privilege over that small fraction of the files—less than 1 percent—which contained particularly sensitive information having to do with tactics and strategy and delicate negotiations in certain other law-enforcement files. As for the rest of the files, he told her to get those over to Congress as fast as they could be copied.

What was the reaction of the congressmen who had asked for the EPA documents? Dingell and Levitas rejected the president's claim of executive privilege out of hand, and, to our great surprise, would not even open the boxes of documents actually produced. Evidently all they really wanted were the withheld files—typical behavior when the real motive is not fact-finding or the search for truth but politics and trouble-making.

As if that weren't enough, the two committees then convinced the rest of the House to cite Anne Gorsuch-Burford for contempt of Congress! It was the first time in history either house of Congress had voted to hold an official of the executive branch in contempt for implementing a presidential privilege the validity of which had been upheld by a unanimous Supreme Court.

Under the law, a contempt of Congress may be enforced by a proceeding initiated by the U.S. Attorney for the District of Columbia, who is an official of the executive branch appointed by the president. It seems self-evident that a subordinate to the president would not undertake to proceed criminally against another subordinate to the president whose only offense had been to assert, at the president's direction, a president's constitutional privilege. It had never happened before in our history, and any such prosecution would have been, in my view, unconstitutional.

The U.S. Attorney, acting entirely on his own, predictably declined to prosecute. (Had he been otherwise inclined, he would have been instructed to refrain.)

So we were at an impasse. The question was how to resolve it. Virtually every president, starting with George Washington, has asserted executive privilege at one time or another and, throughout history, disputes with Congress over such claims have been resolved by mutual agreement. But that did not seem possible here. Members of Congress rejected our every effort at compromise, with Dingell and Levitas continuing to demand unrestricted access to the law-enforcement files while rejecting any notion that the president had the power to restrict congressional access to them.

We decided that the best idea would be to turn to the third governmental branch, the judiciary, to resolve this dispute between the other two. We thought it important to demonstrate to the public that we would accept a judicial resolution of the controversy.

Unfortunately, two developments blocked our efforts at arbitration, and totally distorted the basic issue of the president's desire (and constitutional duty) to protect law-enforcement files from invasion by members of Congress and their staffs. One was the series of revelations, one after another, of the egregious management problems at EPA (which would rather quickly result in the resignation of the administrator); the other development was the discovery that a few of the subpoenaed documents bore handwritten notations that could be construed to give the impression that a low-level EPA staffer had been allowing political considerations to affect the timing of law-enforcement decisions. The latter was, obviously, an obnoxious and unacceptable development.

No one, congressional staff included, had noticed the notations during the first several reviews of the documents. When we found them, we ordered the questionable documents turned over to the Congress immediately. This development, taken along with the others, plus the confrontational attitude of the House leadership and the scandal-thirst of the Washington media, was enough to distract everyone from the centrally important question of the confidentiality of the most sensitive of the documents in the law-enforcement files.

Under other circumstances, the Court's decision not to hear our suit might have ended the standoff—but Congress had its back up. The House leadership was especially outraged that the Department of Justice would sue them, and that we would style the suit as we did, *"The United States of America vs. the House of Representatives of the United States."* (The caption of the case was merely a technicality.)

In any event, instead of letting the matter drop, the House leadership decided to seek a special prosecutor to undertake an "in-depth" investigation of the role of the Justice Department in the president's decision to claim executive privilege. Clearly, their goal was to prevent any future failure to obey their bidding.

The result of all of this was one of the most disgraceful programs of vengefulness in recent history. It disrupted the functioning of the Justice Department, cost the taxpayers millions, and violated elemental standards of fairness. After two and a half *years* of work by three full-time staff members, it produced nothing but the report I alluded to in the beginning of this chapter—in other words, *nothing* of substance or significance.

The principal villains were Tip O'Neill, Dingell, and Rodino (the chairman of the House Judiciary Committee), Elliott Levitas having been defeated in a recent election. This unholy trio let loose a team of three Judiciary Committee staffers whose sole function for two and a half years—and all at taxpayers' expense—was to probe the Justice Department's handling of the EPA investigation.

The extraordinary ground rules they laid down would have done justice to the Star Chamber: No interview subject was to have anyone else present (unless they wanted to retain a personal lawyer); the interviewee was not to discuss the contents of the interview with anyone else (even their DOJ colleagues); and so on in that same vein.

The interviews themselves were endless; in many cases they consumed *days*. They not only dissipated the ability of the DOJ personnel to do their jobs for long periods of time, but they also had a strong negative effect on morale—and this, as I mentioned, for a period of two and a half years.

When the report was finally finished it consisted of four volumes (printed by the Government Printing Office) and some 3,129 pages!

To make matters worse, more than two dozen officials—all of whom were scathingly criticized throughout the report—were notified that they had less than seven days (and over the Thanksgiving holiday, at that!) to read and review the entire report, and its thousands of pages of exhibits, in order to offer any factual corrections. (When Ed Schmults, who happened to be in Thailand on government business, asked for an extension of time, it was summarily denied.) When people did submit comments, they found they were subjected to a one-sided rebuttal by the staff. As for corrections, they were simply ignored.

Despite the fact that they were not supported by interviews or by the documents cited, the report's "findings" and "conclusions" were couched in sensationalized, journalistic language. Emotional, highly charged words—such as "misconduct" and "misrepresentation"—were used to describe behavior that was easily explained as proper.

According to the minority report (later submitted by the Republican members of the Judiciary Committee), its members didn't even know of the *existence* of the "investigation" until October 1985—*when the report was distributed*. There had never been either a subcommittee or full Judiciary Committee meeting to discuss the nature, direction, or objectives of the investigation, to say nothing of open hearings.

Then, to top off this heinous conduct, the executive summary of the report—which the "accused" were never allowed to see—was leaked to the press, thereby all but guaranteeing the publication of the most blatant, false accusations. And the victims of these accusations could not possibly expose the perpetrators. Since then, many people have assumed that, because they have been repeated so many times, the "facts" in the report are true.

The report was so vicious that I can say, without exaggeration, that about the only things *not* distorted are the title and the date. Every inference and conclusion is in favor of culpability, and the misstatements of fact and false conclusions are so pervasive that even the minority report could hardly mount an appropriate response. These liberals, who are so quick to bleat about human rights, are often the first to engage in character assassination without reason or due process, and for purely vindictive motives.

❖ ❖ ❖

Unfortunately, under the statute, it only takes a few members of the committee to request the appointment of a special prosecutor. Of course, doing so also tarnishes those inveighed against, even when there is no valid basis for the action. In this case, to add insult to injury, the "vehicle" used to trigger the request was the vapid report.

An example: One of the four principal charges against one Justice Department official—Ted Olson, then assistant attorney general in charge of the Office of Legal Counsel—was that when he was asked, at a hearing, "Do you think that the president read [the material]?" Olson responded that he had no firsthand knowledge that the president did. Of course, Ted was not there, and could have had no direct knowledge as to whether or not the president had read the documents. Nonetheless, this report states that he *should* have known (an impossibility under the circumstances) and that, therefore, he lied to the committee, which justified the appointment of a special prosecutor to investigate the matter. An absolutely outrageous conclusion!

The operative presumption of the House leadership was that there was no such thing as executive privilege, and that it would be an affront to the Congress for anyone to attempt to exercise it. This was a classic example of the arrogance of politicians who have been in office too long.

One of the many absurdities in the report is that impeachment be considered against the attorney general for recommending the claim of executive privilege be made, and then acting in accord with that recommendation. It should be remembered that the procedure of executive privilege has been exerted by presidents since the dawn of the republic. Its use is bound to cause tension between the branches, but in the past each dispute has somehow been resolved. Resolution, however, requires reasonable men who are not so blinded by partisanship that they fly into a rage when their demands are refused.

Another preposterous charge was that we, the Department of Justice, had indicted EPA's Rita Lavelle (who was later convicted) in order to prevent or at least to delay the subcommittee, because of the pending criminal proceedings, from obtaining access to documents and witnesses. That charge was totally irresponsible; there was not a scintilla of evidence to support it.

I knew the DOJ officials whose reputations the committee was willing to taint so gratuitously, having worked with them for many years, and I knew these were individuals of the highest integrity whose ability and dedication to public service were equal to that of anyone. Their performance had been exceptional. The charges against them were baseless, the so-called factual allegations distorted, and the process that produced them was the result of a true star-chamber proceeding. The only true crime involved was that of the abuse of public position and resources on the part of Tip O'Neill, Peter Rodino, and John Dingell. The three of them should have been investigated—for malfeasance of office.

Interestingly, at the same time that the House leadership was demanding that EPA open its investigation files, a federal district court in Baltimore, in the case of *Benford vs. American Broadcasting Companies*, issued a subpoena for the clerk of the House of Representatives to produce—in an active court proceeding, not a congressional subcommittee witch hunt—certain House investigative files.

And what did this "open" House do? It *refused* to comply. When the court denied the House's motion to quash the subpoena, that august congressional body then voted, 382–22, in favor of a resolution stating that the subpoena was "an unwarranted and unconstitutional invasion of [the House's] constitutional prerogative to determine which of its proceedings shall be made public." In other words, a clear case of whose ox is gored!

Yet while the House leadership was objecting because the judicial branch wanted to look at *its* investigative files, it was also voting, 259 to 105, to reject the executive branch's claim of executive privilege, and to hold EPA administrator Burford in contempt of Congress.

❖   ❖   ❖

I realize that the foregoing may sound like an extreme indictment. It is. And in *this* case, the facts fully justify the conclusions stated.

This episode brought together a vindictive, politically partisan House leadership group and an insidious statute called the Special Prosecutors Act (now "Independent Counsel"). The culprits were able to use this act to generate additional unwarranted publicity by demanding that the alleged conduct of four Justice Department officials be investigated by a special prosecutor, even though the factual basis for such a demand was specious, at best.

In fact, it was so weak that even the minimum facts necessary to trigger the act were insufficient with respect to three of the four officials named. In the case of the fourth, the act was triggered and its ponderous machinery put into motion even though the allegations were not necessarily related to culpability.

To put the shoe on the other foot for a moment, if the act had covered members of Congress, it should have been invoked in this case to investigate the blatant misuse of public resources. *But,* just as it has with every other major piece of legislation since the National Labor Relations Act of 1935, Congress has exempted itself from the Special Prosecutor Act. What makes this so unfortunate is that, in this instance, the true culprits were not the Justice Department officials but the House leadership itself.

On that point, and others previously mentioned, let me include the penultimate paragraph from my response to the Rodino committee report:

> For his part, the chairman has not displayed the same spirit of cooperation which has marked the department's efforts over the past 21 months. He has refused to allow department representatives to attend the interviews, thus preventing the department from assuring that these informal, unrecorded interviews were full and fair sessions. As a result of the chairman's unexplained, yet documented, refusal to permit such representatives to attend, the department determined to provide private counsel to those who wished it, in an effort to inject some measure of fundamental fairness into this process for the department's employees. This

has resulted not only in the expenditure of a considerable amount of time by a number of department employees, but also thousands of dollars in private counsel fees—all at taxpayer expense.

While on the point of legal fees, what about those fees that were *not* paid by the U.S. government? Anne Burford, who submitted legal bills of more than $220,000 had (admittedly, after a long wait) $198,000 of that amount paid by the government. As for Ted Olson, his legal fees totaled over $1.2 million dollars, of which the government paid only two-thirds.

The last paragraph of my response to the Rodino committee report is brief. It reads as follows:

In short, Chairman Rodino's report consists of baseless allegations that unfairly impugn the integrity and professional reputations of the department's employees and that present a distorted and inaccurate view of the actions of the department.

That conclusion was valid when I wrote it, and it is equally valid today, almost five years later.

I wish I could say, as I am able to in reference to the *Bob Jones University* case, that some of our most vocal opponents came, in the end, to understand and respect our point of view. Unfortunately, I cannot.

Not long after the Rodino committee's report came out, the *New York Times*, in an editorial, wrote, "A House committee demanded E.P.A. documents but received only multiple evasions and then a *bogus claim* [my italics] of executive privilege that was later abandoned." I wish I could report that I have seen evidence since then that the *Times*, which likes to refer to itself as "the paper of record," has corrected that utterly inaccurate view, but I have seen none—nor do I expect to.

Finally, what about Ted Olson? How successfully did he weather the ordeal?

He remains today, as he was when I tapped him for service in the Department of Justice, a highly valued and respected partner of Gibson, Dunn & Crutcher, the same firm of which I am a senior partner. In fact, he managed our Washington office until mid-1990. Ted has proven to be, in a phrase borrowed from Mrs. Burford's book, "tough enough."

This is what he had to say, recently, about the whole experience. "When I was at the Justice Department, there wasn't a day that went by that I didn't think about how important it was to do an honorable job, to act with integrity. What if," he added, "that's what you were doing, and someone were to come along and say: We're conducting a criminal investigation into everything that you have ever done, we have the power to take away your livelihood, to force you to spend resources you don't have, to destroy your life? It is an extraordinarily frightening feeling. It never, ever diminishes."

8

MEDIA
RELATIONS

ONE BIG DIFFERENCE BETWEEN MY LIFE AS A SENIOR partner in a large law firm and my life as the most senior partner in the largest "law firm" in the world, the Department of Justice, is that in private practice, I have more control over the timing of major initiatives and major developments. In the Department of Justice, however, it was not unusual for several large efforts to come to a head at the very same time.

For some odd reason, this often happened on a Friday. For example, on Friday, February 25, 1983, I received not one but three major news bulletins.

The first thunderbolt was delivered by an aide who told me that William Baxter, our assistant attorney general for antitrust, had made a most irregular public comment. In answering a question about a possible price-fixing case, he'd said that maybe the government should require all CEO's to *tape* their conversations with one another! Then all we'd need would be a poster saying, "Big Brother Is Watching You." I made a mental note to schedule a little woodshedding session with Bill Baxter.

Next, I got a somber phone call from William Webster, the head of the FBI, informing me that the bureau had just discovered its first traitor—Special Agent Richard Miller in California (who was later convicted of selling information to persons thought to be Soviet agents).

Finally, that same Friday afternoon, Tom DeCair, my usually unflappable director of public affairs, called, and in a highly agitated state reported that all three networks were going to run highly negative stories lambasting us for "Nazi-like" censorship of several Canadian documentaries. The truth of the matter was so far from "censorship" as to be laughable. But the way things worked out there was nothing to laugh at whatsoever.

Ironically, of the three explosions that landed on my desk that Friday afternoon, and despite the obvious seriousness of the FBI-turncoat matter, the one I recall most vividly—the one that still rankles—is the false accusation of censorship. The reason I continue to feel so strongly about it is that it symbolizes the whole problem of how the media operate.

Consider what happened in this case, and then decide for yourself if I'm seeing ghosts.

In a luncheon speech that afternoon, Senator Ted Kennedy made an inflammatory accusation that had absolutely no basis in fact. Playing it for the headlines, he stated that the administration had refused to allow three Canadian government-sponsored "documentaries" to be shown here because we disagreed with their content. "The book-burners of the 1950s have become the film black-listers of the 1980s," trumpeted the liberal senator from Massachusetts. "The attorney general," he continued, "has dropped his own iron curtain over the movie screens of America."

Had the senator been correct, our actions would certainly have qualified as censorship. However, he was not just incorrect. He was badly misinformed—intentionally or otherwise.

What had happened was this: After a routine review of three Canadian films, the Department of Justice, acting under the provisions of the Foreign Agents Registration Act, required that the films be labeled "political propaganda." It did so because the films—two on acid rain, and one on nuclear war—were clearly advocacy films—(meaning those that attempt to influence the opinion of viewers on the subjects in question) and thus fell under the purview of the act, which requires the disclosure of foreign government involvement in the dissemination of films—a truth-in-labeling measure. (I think it is fair to say, for the record, that the two acid-rain films made the United States their chief villain, and the antiwar film, which was narrated by Dr. Helen Caldicott, was also clearly antinuclear.) The act, forty-five years old, had been enacted during the Nazi era, and had been administered in the same fashion by all Republican and Democratic administrations during that period.

As soon as we got word of Kennedy's irresponsible statements, we rushed the facts of the matter to the three networks, but to no avail. All three networks chose to go with Kennedy's version of the story rather than check it out, despite the fact that doing so almost certainly assured doing damage to U.S.-Canadian relations.

The press also had a field day. The *New York Times* said the DOJ had "shamed America's democracy"; the *Washington Post*, in an editorial, wanted to know "What country is this? What decade?"; and *Times* columnist Anthony Lewis charged us with "Philistine ignorance." And on a television talk show, Jody Powell, once Jimmy Carter's press secretary, said that what we had done was "stupid."

The initial flak was bad enough. What was worse was that the media continued to play variations on that tune for days to follow, even though we had sent them irrefutable proof that the tale they were telling was wrong. Apparently, their version made a better "story."

Finally, a couple of responsible journalists came to our rescue. Chief among them, I am pleased to report, was the same Jody Powell who had labeled our actions as "stupid." Unlike his journalistic brethren, Powell had taken our suggestion and done his homework. When he found out that we were right and he—and they—were wrong, he was big enough not only to admit it, but also to admit it *in print* (in a column which the *Washington Post*, for one, headlined, "It Wasn't Censorship").

> By now the nation and a good portion of the world are familiar with the story of how the U.S. government has begun to censor films. As soon as news stories revealed that the Justice Department had "labeled" three Canadian films as "political propaganda," politicians, editorialists and commentators rose in righteous indignation. . . .
>
> Now, more than a week later, it is clear that the real story is that those cited above, and quite a few more, went off half-cocked.

Our rhetoric exceeded our knowledge of the facts by an embarrassing margin.

I wish I could report that Jody Powell's column set off a rash of apologies, but it did not. James J. Kilpatrick, in his syndicated column, did a piece entitled, "The Media Blew It," but these two journalists were a very lonely minority.

Guess what happened next. The whole "affaire de censorship" disappeared as quickly as it had materialized, and with no additional apologies, explanations, or—God forbid!—retractions. The courts ultimately approved our actions and rejected all claims that the department's conduct had violated the Constitution. As for Senator Ted Kennedy, who didn't care about the facts before he fired a broadside at the administration on purely partisan grounds, and who maintained his reputation for calumny, neither he nor his office issued any type of clarification.

I wish I could say that what happened in this matter was atypical. Unfortunately, it was not. What it was, was (media) business as usual.

❖   ❖   ❖

Having spent over four years as the attorney general of the United States, I have become well acquainted with certain aspects of our national life that might otherwise have escaped me. I say this somewhat tongue in cheek, for certainly I could have gotten along quite well without some of this knowledge. Near the top of the list of information I could have lived without very nicely is what I learned about the media in my own country.

Based on my own experience with the media, my most significant, if unsettling, observation is the "primacy of the story," the overbearing and arrogant need, for better or for worse, of getting the story—and getting it *first*.

This paramount need is exacerbated by the byline system in the print media and "air time," its equivalent in electronic journalism. Making the front page or garnering the highest TV rating becomes for the reporter the main thing, often the only thing, and its cause is this unholy interest in "getting the story."

The Canadian films fiasco is a good example of what so often happens even when facts exist to contradict the story, or to prove that there really wasn't a story to begin with. Another example, albeit a more mundane one, has to do with my "second dining room" in the Department of Justice. This episode likewise illustrates how the media's thirst for a story can push them beyond factual bounds.

Next to the attorney general's rather modest dining room is a small kitchen, on the other side of which was another small room that was not being used. We decided to make it a small auxiliary dining room—though "dining room" sounds rather grand for a room that would hold only two tables of four chairs each—by cutting a door through to the kitchen. The idea was to provide a space for the more senior people to have lunch without having to leave the building, a saving in time that would pay dividends to the taxpayers many times over. In other words, what we were making was a lunchroom, just like those in many office buildings all across the country, with access to the already-existing kitchen.

Unfortunately, the press room happened to be right across the hall from the new room, and as the work on installing the doorway progressed, the word spread, and grew, despite our disclaimers, that the AG was installing a "second dining room," with the implication being that it would be a grand affair, all mahogany paneling and chandeliers. At that point it had become a "story."

Soon the story was being flashed on all the nightly news and in all the major newspapers: The attorney general, not being satisfied with one dining room, was adding another, grander one. All accounts carried the same implication of big spending on unnecessarily plush furnishings. Once again, the truth was something quite different. The "dining room" was a small, plain room that, except for the new doorway, we did nothing to improve; we didn't even paint it. Even though we subsequently informed all of the newspapers and radio and TV stations of this fact, no one ever ran a correction or a clarification.

I was beginning to see a pattern, and it had nothing to do with the possible significance of the story. If it even *smelled* like a story, then it had to be one, no matter what the facts of the matter happened to be. The overriding goal, the unholy grail, was "the story."

As a chairman of the Board of Regents of the University of California (during the early 70s, a volatile period that encompassed the so-called free speech movement), I thought I knew the media. Certainly I'd had continuous contact with them. But the Washington press corps, I soon learned, was another animal altogether.

Joining the cardinal sin of the heedless pursuit of the story is the reliance on anonymous sources, such as "a high White House official." (Of course this kind of arrangement is a two-way street. The reporter could not quote his or her well-placed source if the well-placed source were not willing to be a well-placed source in the first place!)

Of the dozens of people who qualify as high White House sources, or "senior White House officials," there will always be some who have a personal or political or ideological ax to grind. A good reporter, or at least a persistent one, can build a small stable of such people. The danger—and unfortunately it is not a danger that the media seem concerned about—is that these "sources" are seldom close enough to have any real concept of what is going on in the department or agency about which they purport to speak.

Their "information" is almost always of a questionable accuracy, which *should* mean that reporters who want to use such sources will check with the agency or department or individual involved before doing so. But do they? Only occasionally. Too many do not, because if they did, they might learn there was no story—and that's a risk they are not willing to take.

During my years as attorney general, negative allegations about some Justice Department matter that found their way into print or made it on the air were often based on information provided by an anonymous source. Seldom did we receive calls from the reporter ahead of time asking if the story in question were true. A prime example of that kind of "don't-bother-checking reliance on an anonymous White House source" was a *Business Week* story on the department written by Lee Walczak.

I am not exaggerating when I say that almost every line was

either untrue or misleading. Verification or correction was but a phone call away, but no calls came to me or to my director of public affairs or to anyone in his office. After the article ran, I met with Mr. Walczak and pointed out his many errors to him; he never disputed any of my corrections, but he never straightened them out in print, either.

Business Week was a particularly egregious offender, and not just Lee Walczak but the whole staff of the magazine. In my four-plus years as AG, I don't think *Business Week* ever printed an accurate story on the department. At times I wondered if its reporters even knew where the building was; I know we hardly ever heard from them.

The practice of relying on unnamed sources was widespread. In his book *The Power Game*, former *New York Times* reporter Hedrick Smith, who is said to be highly respected by his peers, wrote:

> Some cabinet officials wangled private sessions with Reagan through subterfuges, to get around the Palace guard, the top White House staff. Attorney General William French Smith and CIA Director William Casey were especially aggressive, citing their need to report privately to Reagan on national security matters, though White House aides suspected them of doing other business, too. "It was important to them and their staffs for them to be seen meeting with the president as often as possible," one Reagan confidant remarked. "So they would think up inane reasons."

Talk about "inane"! How does one deal with the question of what is the factual basis for those statements when every line in Hedrick Smith's paragraph happens to be false? Only President Reagan and I knew the purpose or the content of our many discussions; and, except for isolated instances, no one on my staff knew. So how could some nameless "Reagan confidant" have sufficient (accurate) information to make the statements Smith ascribes to him or her? The answer is that he or she could not.

Did Hedrick Smith contact me or anyone on my staff to check out those statements? Nope. Instead, he chose to rely—despite the warning notes he sounds, in that very same book, regarding the use of "leaked" information—on anonymous sources.

Consider this observation on the same topic from *Newsweek* magazine, reporting on the book by former Chief of Staff Don Regan. Regarding "dependency [on high government officials who use the] cloak of anonymity to stab their enemies," *Newsweek* goes on to say:

> To keep the media attentive, officials need to come up with consistently juicy material. And to keep access open, reporters need to coddle their sources. In recent years, this cozy system of mutually assured seduction . . .

Now *there's* a good line!

> . . . has grown corruptive.

> The real danger is that good sources tend to win a measure of undeserving protection from reporters. Oliver North, a major leaker, benefited from this (*Newsweek*, January 19, 1987) as has James A. Baker III, whose failures as treasury secretary would no doubt be more fully examined if so many reporters were not indebted to him for leaks.

My own experience bears out the truth of Don Regan's observation regarding what is a not-so-minor form of press corruption. Among certain cabinet members it was common to hear the White House Troika of Baker-Meese-Deaver referred to as "the media sieve." It was generally assumed that whatever all three of them knew would be public knowledge within the hour. Which one, or two or three, did the leaking is a matter of speculation. (Another candidate for Chief Leaker, at least in the opinion of a number of people in my shop, was Dick Darman, then a deputy assistant to the president and now the head of the Office of Management and Budget.)

I had some firsthand experiences that proved to me people were not exaggerating when they called Baker-Meese-Deaver the media sieve. When President Reagan made his decision to name Sandra Day O'Connor to the Supreme Court, there were only four of us in the Oval Office with him—the Troika and I. Once the decision had been made, we agreed that it be kept secret until the president could officially notify her, and I could advise certain members of

Congress, according to the proper protocol and in the proper sequence, who had a need to know this historic news in advance.

All three nodded their heads in agreement. However, the very next morning, before I could do any of this, there it was on the front page of all the major papers. I know *I* kept the secret, as did the president; that leaves only the Troika.

Several years later, when I advised the president that I would be stepping down, I also asked that my decision be kept confidential so I would have time to advise my colleagues in the department, as well as certain people on the Hill. That was on a Friday, and I planned to spread the word, personally, on Monday. The only ones who were advised of this at the time were the president and the Troika.

My wife and I spent the weekend on Maryland's Eastern Shore with friends, and as we were driving back on Sunday, I happened to turn on the radio. To my chagrin, there was Rita Braver of CBS announcing my resignation. It took me two full days to explain to colleagues and close friends why they had to learn my news from the media instead of from me.

Is it any wonder why, after the first year, the only time I would discuss sensitive matters with the president was when we were alone?

The next item on my least-favored list, as far as the media are concerned, is what I have termed the "tyranny of the clips." By this I mean the infuriating habit of repeating stories or charges or claims about a person or topic simply because the information has already run in someone else's story and that story is available in the newspaper's, or the station's, "clip file."

For example, thanks to press repetition it is now an accepted fact that Ronald Reagan's Justice Department favored tax exemptions for private schools that discriminate, the abolition of abortion, the return of school prayer, and the elimination of affirmative action. But all those "facts" happen to be false!

Here's the truth. The department argued that the commissioner of internal revenue should not have the power to determine the tax exemption question unless Congress had given him that specific authority, which is a vastly different matter. As for abortion, the only position the DOJ took during my term was that, as a constitutional matter, this issue should be handled by the states, not the federal government. As for school prayer, the department's lawyers argued that a statute permitting a moment of silence in school did not offend the Constitution. Our position concerning affirmative action was, simply, that although certain types of it were an effective remedy, when it embraced racial preferences, it was actually counterproductive.

Nonetheless, the tyranny of the clips guarantees that the same inaccurate stories will run month after month, and year after year. I have been offered the excuse "time and space constraints," but that in no way justifies repeated falsification.

I *do* recognize that the world of the news media is fast-moving, and that time and circumstances do not permit anything even approaching perfection. However, at the same time, I also know that it is vitally important that the public know what they are getting—and what they are not.

❖   ❖   ❖

I should mention, before I begin to sound like a grouch, that I find news media people to be delightful individuals (of course, with the usual exceptions). I enjoy their company because they are witty, interesting, and bright. After one deals with them on a personal basis one becomes convinced that their "transgressions" are rarely the result of evil intentions. Perhaps the problem is inherent in the nature of the beast.

The late Joseph Kraft, many of whose columns were among those most critical of the Reagan administration, was a good friend. Over the years we had many good discussions, but I never convinced him of much, nor did he convince me of much. In fact, he was a hard man to get a concession from, even if the subject matter was totally noncontroversial.

I remember reading a column of his one morning in the *Washington Post* in which, after he had criticized a government official for having made a bad unilateral decision, he wrote that "all great decisions are made by consensus." That same night I happened to run into Joe at a reception, and I asked him how his consensus statement could be true in light of the accomplishments of Jesus Christ, Napoleon, and William Harvey (who insisted, while his peers laughed at him, that blood circulates in the human body). My friend Kraft changed the subject.

There are cases in which a columnist will either manufacture facts (especially quotes) or assume them with what can only be called a reckless disregard for the truth. *Washington Post* columnist Richard Cohen, having been at a farewell party for a White House official (or, more likely, having heard about it from someone who was), reported that my wife, Jean, was so insensitive to the plight of the poor that she wore diamond earrings that "cost more than a house." Apparently this was meant to typify the rich Californians who had descended on Washington.

This characterization was picked up by the Democratic policy committees of both the House and the Senate, and mentioned in their national television responses to President Reagan's state of the union address, which in turn created editorial interest. Fortunately, not all the commentators sided with the columnist or the Democrats. (The *Denver Post* accused them, in an editorial entitled "The State of the Earrings," of "low-road tactics.")

There was one other problem with Richard Cohen's valuation of my wife's earrings. It was all wrong. In fact, Jean had been wearing inexpensive costume jewelry. Having become used to this kind of "reporting," and having a sharp sense of humor, Jean responded by writing the following letter to the editor, which the *Post* promptly published:

> I am aghast that my taste in costume jewelry has so hoodwinked Mr. Cohen . . . that he thinks a pair of my earrings would buy a house. Well, maybe a small dog house, into which even he probably wouldn't fit.

One of the more unusual experiences I had with an individual journalist while I was attorney general involved Ben Bradlee of the *Washington Post*, whose "heroic" stewardship during the Watergate affair would later provide the actor Jason Robards with one of the meatiest roles of his career.

The experience had to do with an exchange of letters that I, in my naïveté, thought was a private matter. The letters concerned national security and Senator Jesse Helms, two volatile subjects.

In late May of 1984, I received this letter from Mr. Bradlee:

> Dear Mr. Attorney General:
>
> I have long had an interest in national security violations, as you must imagine. For more than 20 years in this city I have watched various people in the White House and in the Pentagon and in the State Department and in your office do battle with journalists and others on this subject.
>
> I am now trying to remember an apparent national security violation as significant as the recent revelation by Sen. Jesse Helms that the CIA had bought the election in El Salvador for Colonel Duarte.
>
> I wonder if you know of any in your time in this town. Your answer could be off the record, if you wish, although I would obviously prefer it on the record.
>
> Most sincerely,
BEN BRADLEE

My "answer" to his tongue-in-cheek letter was hardly what he had hoped for, but nonetheless provided a full explanation of my views on the subject he had raised. It must have come as no surprise to Bradlee that I did not choose to say anything about Senator Helms. Imagine *my* surprise, however, when I opened the *Post* a few days later to discover that Mr. Bradlee had seen fit to print both letters in his newspaper—without the courtesy of prior notice or a request for authorization.

The larger headline read PERFECTLY CLEAR? and the smaller, Smith "responds" on Helms' "leak."

What was his justification? I have absolutely no idea, except for the possibility that because he did not get the answer he wanted— the "story" he was after—he would make a story out of my response. (On the other hand, at no time in my experience has a reporter or editor who promised me information would be "off the record" or used only for "background" violated that pledge. So I guess that on balance, then, I'm ahead.)

Winston Churchill once wrote, "Man will occasionally stumble over the truth, but most of the time he will pick himself up and continue on." Before I went to Washington I thought of that comment as humor; now I consider it simple truth.

❖   ❖   ❖

I have now been away from the Justice Department for over five years. Still, I find it most unusual—no, I find it extraordinary—that sophisticated reporters gauged the significance of events by the style and tone in which they were reported by the administration official in charge. Evidently, pounding the table and yelling equals a better "story."

For a prime example, consider the civil-rights speech that I gave to the American Law Institute in Philadelphia in May 1981. The program I enunciated in that speech established the foundation for the Reagan administration's entire civil-rights policy. It had been advertised as such well in advance, yet only two of the three networks showed up, and no more than the usual smattering of reporters.

Frankly, I'm not sure that the contents of that speech and their import were fully understood. I know they were not fully reported. One of the reasons I say that is that three years later, William Bradford Reynolds, the high profile assistant attorney general for civil rights, gave a speech in New York City that reiterated part of what I had said in 1981 before the ALI. The *Washington Post's* front-page story made it sound like brand-new news!

Practically all the controversial changes in policy, from civil rights to antitrust—and some of them were revolutionary—were made during the first two years of the administration. And they were made and implemented with relatively little turmoil. (There were a *few* incidents. A significant number of people once threatened to resign *en masse* from the Civil Rights Division if we didn't make certain changes; we didn't, and they didn't.)

In each case, I would announce the policy change in a public speech, with copies widely available, and then hold a press conference. The substance would then be dutifully reported with the usual scattering of editorial comment, but to my surprise there was little sense of outrage or cries of alarm.

Some experienced reporters who knew their way around the DOJ—such as Ron Ostrow, who'd covered it for the *Los Angeles Times* for some fifteen years, or Steve Brill, publisher of *The American Lawyer*—attributed this rather unusual result to the fact that I was "low key," "nonconfrontational," or "bland." One reporter went so far as to say that I was a "'quiet' James Watt"—doing as much "damage," he said, but doing it "softly"!

Ostrow wrote:

> Many of the most important [policy] changes have attracted scant public notice—partly because AG William French Smith has a public style that spreads a blanket of blandness over otherwise controversial matters. "Blandness has its own rewards," said one department policymaker, referring to Smith's affable manner and flat style of delivering sharply worded speeches.

I still say that it is extraordinary that sophisticated reporters gauge the significance of things by the tone of voice in which they are announced.

In a similar vein, there's the tendency of the press to measure the success of a public figure by the number of press conferences he or she holds. Initially, I held very few, for the simple reason I was too busy—recruiting top-level personnel, reorganizing the department, getting used to the job, and in general waiting for things to shake down. It did not seem to me that until I had this done I should be holding many press conferences. The reporters who regularly covered the DOJ did not, however, like this, and they used it to form negative comparisons between me and my predecessor.

Were I to do it over again, and were I the type of person who valued the opinion of the opinion-makers, I would certainly do well to denigrate substance, elevate form, and hold more press conferences.

Finally, let me offer an anecdote that still makes me smile. I was having dinner one night with James Watt, the secretary of interior. Jim told me he'd read an article about himself in that morning's *Washington Post*, and he was disgusted at how inaccurate it was.

He went on to say that, next, he turned the page and read something—equally inaccurate—that was quite critical of me, and after reading it said to himself, "Now how could Bill Smith have done anything as stupid as that?"

Although the article about me was no more accurate or factual than the one about him, Jim Watt's point—which was extremely well taken—was that we instinctively use a different standard when reading about others in (public) print.

Apparently the old saw still holds true that "Everything one reads in the press is absolutely true—except for those rare instances in which one has firsthand knowledge of the facts."

Amen to that.

9

DRUGS, ORGANIZED CRIME, AND TERRORISM

AMERICA HAS ALWAYS DEMONSTRATED THE RE-
solve and ability to protect itself against threats from
without. In recent decades, however, American government has not succeeded in protecting its citizens
from predators within. It is not overstatement to say that an outbreak of
crime unparalleled in our history and unequalled in any other free society
has plagued this nation in recent years.

The perniciousness of crime has been fostered of late by two interrelated
developments. Crime has become increasingly organized and sophisticated. And organized crime has become especially lucrative because of the
enormous market for illicit drugs. Together, drugs and organized crime
wreak havoc on our communities, our lives, and our children's future.
Clearly, the combination of drug trafficking and organized crime represents the most serious problem facing this country today.

The Justice Department's new law-enforcement coordinating committees have underlined dramatically the gravity of organized drug trafficking. As you may know, I directed every U.S. Attorney to set up a law-
enforcement coordinating committee to assess the differing crime problems
in each district throughout the nation. More important, they are to act.
They are to bring a coordinated federal, state, and local effort.

from "Drugs and Organized Crime . . .
Alliance That Must Be Shattered"
New Directions, 1981–1983
"A Report to Employees from
Attorney General William French Smith"

As it had been years since the federal criminal law and its enforcement effort had been examined with a truly critical eye, during the period from my nomination to my swearing in I had made a point of discussing this subject with a number of state and local law-enforcement officials. I was particularly interested in their ideas on how the federal government could be the most helpful, keeping in mind the budget stringencies we all faced.

A couple of caveats are worth keeping in mind. One is that it is not the function of law enforcement to eliminate crime. Another is that it is not the function of law enforcement to destroy drug trafficking. As long as man is as he is, we will have both. The function of law enforcement is to maximize the risk to those who engage in criminal acts. Those who say that law enforcement is failing to do its job because drugs are still plentiful in this country simply do not understand the fundamental fact that law enforcement will not eliminate drugs any more than it will eliminate crime. Both are broad social problems.

That said, let me return to the fruits of my discussions with state and local law-enforcement officials.

Those officials, of course, would all have liked *additional* funds and resources from the federal government, but seeing as how the failed law-enforcement assistance administration was at that very moment being phased out of existence (a process begun by the previous administration), they knew we were going to have to be more, rather than less, frugal. Further, in this era of reduced funding it was incumbent upon us to find ways of doing more with less, which meant that significant changes in the federal law were badly needed. Given this background, almost all of the law-enforcement people I polled felt that the greatest contribution that could be made on the federal level was *leadership*.

Those were the principal reasons why one of my first official acts as attorney general was to appoint the Attorney General's Task Force on Violent Crime.

The first step in this ambitious undertaking was to name a distinguished bipartisan or, better yet, nonpartisan, panel. The second was to come up with fast and practical responses. To my great pleasure, Illinois governor James Thompson, a Republican who had been a U.S. Attorney and a prosecutor, and former

Attorney General Griffin Bell, a Democrat, agreed to serve as co-chairmen.

The other members were Harvard government professor James Q. Wilson; David L. Armstrong, the Commonwealth Attorney of Louisville (and president of the National District Attorneys Association); Frank G. Carrington, executive director of the Crime Victims Legal Advocacy Institute, an organization located in Virginia Beach, Virginia; Robert L. Edwards, director of the Division of Local Law Enforcement Assistance of the Florida Department of Law Enforcement; William F. Hart, the police chief of Detroit; and Los Angeles County's public defender, Wilbur F. Littlefield.

I gave the task force sixty days to make its recommendations for changes in the federal law-enforcement effort that would not require new legislation or additional resources, and another sixty days to recommend changes that *would* require either additional funding or new legislation. We also wanted specific, pragmatic results; we did not want yet another government report that would gather dust on the shelf.

The result of their efforts was the best and most useful government report I have ever seen.

Not only was it exactly what we wanted, but it was done *within the time allotted!* Perceptive, innovative, imaginative, aggressive, and practical, the report contained fifteen recommendations for Phase I and forty-nine for Phase II. Of that total number, we were able to begin implementing 80 percent of them right away.

One of the most significant recommendations was the establishment of the ninety-four local law-enforcement coordinating committees referred to earlier. The point of the program was to require each U.S. Attorney to take the lead in developing a "co-op" relationship with the various law-enforcement officials in his or her district—state authorities, local district attorneys, FBI officials, police chiefs, sheriffs, and so on. The purpose: to pool resources, develop common priorities, and provide for such effective procedures as the cross-designation of prosecutors (so that federal prosecutors can appear in state courts, and vice-versa).

Each U.S. Attorney was *directed* to establish these committees, and to provide me with specific reports as soon as they'd done so (plus periodic reports thereafter). With one or two exceptions, the committees proved to be very successful. They resulted in a more effective enforcement effort without requiring any additional resources—a highly desirable result in a time of tight budgets.

Interestingly, all but one district attorney ranked drug trafficking (and its attendant involvement with organized crime) as the number-one priority. The lone exception was Salt Lake City, Utah, which had a rash of white-collar crimes for a while. However, a later reading showed drug trafficking as number one there, too.

There were a few recommendations that we could not meet, such as a proposal for $2 billion in aid to the states and localities for prisons and detention centers. Instead, we adopted a recommendation that would aid the states but not involve significant additional expense—a program to make abandoned federal facilities (military bases, air force stations, and the like) available to localities as prisons. Another such modest-expense plan involved training state and local law-enforcement and correctional people through the National Institute of Corrections and National Corrections Academy.

Certain proposals that would have required changes in existing laws were deferred for a while, and most of them were included in the Comprehensive Crime Control Act of 1984. Three areas were not included, however: the death penalty, the exclusionary rule, and the reform of *habeas corpus* abuses.

These provisions were deleted from the legislation jointly introduced by Chairman Thurmond and Senators Laxalt, Biden, and Kennedy, and introduced as separate bills by Thurmond and Laxalt. We agreed to this procedural move upon a commitment from Biden and Kennedy that they would work to allow these "controversial" bills to be voted upon in the Judiciary Committee and on the Senate floor, and that they—Biden and Kennedy—would fight any effort to deny Senate floor votes on these proposals. We felt strongly that if these reforms could be wrenched out of committee they would pass overwhelmingly.

Senators Biden and Kennedy stuck to their bargain and the Senate approved all these proposals by a wide margin. It was always my opinion that the same thing would occur in the House of Representatives if one could find a way to extract these proposals from committees that were intent on burying them. Given public sentiment, it would take a brave member of Congress to vote against any of them in a recorded House vote.

The relevancy of this example can be seen in the fact that the task force on violent crime is one of the best illustrations of the value of this approach—that of bringing together the problems most urgently in need of solution and those individuals best able to recommend solutions.

As for the task force report, I commend it as an excellent example of private sector expertise and "highest-level" government utilization of that expertise.

❖ ❖ ❖

The Comprehensive Crime Control Act of 1984 was the most significant, far-reaching, and extensive reform of the federal criminal code in history, a landmark measure that fundamentally readjusted the balance between the forces of law and the forces of lawlessness.

The original idea had been to produce, out of the hodgepodge of laws passed over the years, a simplified, consistent, and uniform code. Most of the changes were procedural, but quite a few were substantive, and as a result the task was monumental, one that took years to accomplish, and resulted in a document that was thousands of pages long.

A document, however, is not a law. How it became one is an interesting story. Indeed, it could be called a cautionary tale.

As things turned out, and to the surprise of no one, both conservatives and liberals were suspicious of such massive changes in procedure. It soon became clear that we were not likely to get the procedural *and* the substantive changes, so we opted for the latter. We decided to put together a bill that would consist of just substantive, badly needed reforms.

To simplify the story, although we got the bill through the Senate with relative ease (only maverick Republican senator Charles Mathias voted against us), when it got to the House we encountered massive resistance. Congressman William Hughes of the House

Judiciary Committee announced that our bill was "dead on arrival," and Chairman Peter Rodino, another Democrat, swiftly parceled it out to various subcommittees, and it was never heard of again.

Nothing the Republicans could do was sufficient to revive it. The Democrats were adamant about keeping the bill bottled up in committee. So many measures had disappeared in the House Judiciary Committee that Congressman Henry Hyde (R–Ill.) had dubbed the committee "the Bermuda Triangle of legislation."

We had to come up with a plan to get our bill to the floor; we were convinced that if we did, it would pass overwhelmingly, despite the games the Democratic leadership was playing.

We reverted to the ploy of attaching a Crime Control Act amendment to the "continuing resolution" (meant to provide essential funding for government operation)—which for all intents and purposes the president *had* to sign.

Bob McConnell, my assistant attorney general for legislative affairs, set up a meeting of the Republican leadership, and we discussed our options. They ranged from attaching only the most important parts of the anticrime package (to the continuing resolution) to appending the whole thing.

My view, which I stated as strongly as I could, was that we should do everything possible to get the entire crime bill enacted. In addition to the substantive point—that this bill dealt with one of the major issues facing the country—there was the pragmatic reality that while the crime bill, if passed, would be a permanent piece of legislation, the continuing resolution by its nature covered only a single year.

Without even bothering to discuss this with him, I stated the president's approval of this course of action. Everyone there agreed. The only question was *how* to get it done.

What we came up with—without getting into all the details— was a brilliant procedural move by which we were able to get our crime bill, the same one that the Senate had approved ninety-one to one, onto the House floor and up for a vote.

We got Republican Silvio Conte to recognize Republican Dan Lungren (R–Calif.) at a unique and procedurally critical moment in the House floor consideration of the continuing resolution. The minute he was recognized, Lungren began to offer the *entire* Comprehensive Crime Control Bill as an amendment to the continuing resolution.

That brought the Speaker, Tip O'Neill, charging in from the cloakroom—but he was too late. Lungren had already offered the entire bill, which meant it had to be voted up or down on its *substance*. That put the Democrats right where we wanted them— on the spot.

The bill passed overwhelmingly.

It would be nice to be able to report that from there on out everything went smoothly—but of course it did not. We also had a big fight on the Senate–House conference level, where the Democrats tried to slip the knife past us. Bob McConnell realized what they were doing in a closed meeting and alerted Congressman Dan Lungren—who had to rush to the Hill at night and save the day.

The bill emerged unscathed from the conference, and when the president signed it, it became the law of the land.

❖   ❖   ❖

Strange as it may sound, prior to 1982, as I said earlier, the number-one federal law-enforcement agency—the FBI—was not being utilized in the fight against the nation's number-one law-enforcement problem, narcotics trafficking. To me, that made no sense. The Drug Enforcement Administration (DEA) was formally merged with the FBI, producing a truly unified federal investigative effort. For the first time we brought the "task force" concept into the war against drugs.

Beginning with the South Florida Task Force, all the federal agencies with responsibilities in this area were brought under a single entity, and began to cooperate in a comprehensive antidrug strategy. The administration also blanketed the country with thirteen organized crime and drug enforcement task forces. The 1,300 prosecutors and investigators, provided with totally new resources, targeted big drug rings and their top leaders for vigorous investigation, surveillance, and prosecution. By 1984, these teams had initiated more than seven hundred cases, and their work had resulted in the indictment of almost four thousand individuals, with over one-third in the "top leader" category, which means kingpins of the drug trade.

One case from the Southern District of New York, *United States vs. Badalamente*, illustrates how effective the task-force approach can be. In 1983, an investigation in New York City indicated that a group there appeared to be importing and distributing large quantities of high-grade heroin. The group was dominated by Sicilians said to be members of the Sicilian Mafia operating, it was alleged, as a faction of the Bonanno crime family of New York.

With the assistance of a task-force prosecutor in New York, a team made up of FBI, DEA, and Customs investigators worked together against this group of Sicilians. Their New York City wiretaps led to taps on phones in New Jersey, Pennsylvania, Michigan, and Illinois, as well as to Brazil and several other foreign countries. The FBI's wiretap expertise proved to be immensely helpful.

Based on the evidence gathered from the wiretaps, plus intelligence and information that came from long-running DEA investigations, customs agents were able to trace a huge amount of cash that the group had allegedly laundered through brokerage houses and then transferred into Swiss bank accounts. Eventually, through all these agencies, we obtained the help of police in Italy, Spain, Brazil, and Switzerland.

By early 1984, some thirty-eight members were arrested across the United States, as well as in Spain and Italy. The case was aided immeasurably by task-force personnel in ten U.S. cities. The people arrested were charged with running a multimillion-dollar heroin operation that we would probably never have been able to put out of business without the help of the task forces.

The case stands as a neat illustration of a key principle: We can dismantle major drug-trafficking organizations by using task forces that are as well organized as the drug traffickers themselves.

Of possible relevance to the drug wars of today, in 1984 we also brought the military (and its intelligence-gathering resources) into the antidrug war. This country's borders require a continuing surveillance against smugglers, a surveillance that is beyond the individual capacities of state and local law-enforcement agencies. A critically needed amendment to the *posse comitatus* law (a measure passed after the Civil War to prevent the armed forces from being used for the purpose of law enforcement) was pushed through Congress, which eased the restrictions so that the military could give some much-needed assistance to our federal agents.

By permitting the use of armed forces equipment and intelligence-gathering facilities in the drug-interdiction program, the amendment added enormous new resources to the antidrug effort but at little additional cost.

We also succeeded in repealing the so-called Percy Amendment, which prohibited foreign-aid funds from being used for the purchase and application of paraquat, a chemical used to destroy marijuana plants. In addition, new co-op deals were worked out with the Departments of Defense and Transportation (specifically, the Coast Guard), Treasury (Customs), and the CIA so that these same government arms could work effectively with the Department of Justice on the national antidrug strategy.

In March 1983 we established a brand-new initiative, the National Narcotics Border Interdiction System (NNBIS), under the direction of Vice President George Bush. NNBIS's job is to analyze the smuggling intelligence, coordinate resources available outside our borders, and assist in establishing interdiction priorities. Finally, we established a cabinet-level council to oversee the general antidrug effort. In 1984, Congress formalized the structure in the Crime Reform Act of 1984, and named the attorney general as the council's chairman.

By more than doubling the figures from 1982 to 1984, we authorized record levels of resources for the fight against drugs, especially notable in an era of general budget austerity. These dollars went right to the front lines of the drug wars, thereby allowing us to reduce such alarming trends as the downward spiral in the number of DEA agents. By the close of 1984, we had not only restored manpower totals to the previous levels but had also established record highs. There were more agents in place than ever before.

Of course drugs would not vanish, not then and not in the near future. But we had taken the initiative by developing a sound, coherent antidrug strategy, and thereby began to deliver a long series of body blows to the networks that deliver and distribute drugs.

❖   ❖   ❖

On October 23, 1984, I went to New York to make a statement before the President's Commission on Organized Crime. In my opinion, the ongoing work of the commission was so important that I wanted to make a personal appearance, to lend the prestige of the office I was privileged to hold to the vital task of the presidential panel. Three key points of my statement were as follows:

> My objective this morning is threefold. First, I am here to announce that the federal government has now achieved its greatest successes ever against the traditional organized crime families entrenched for so long in our major cities. Second, I am here to declare that the federal government has now, for the first time ever, developed a comprehensive response to the international dimensions of organized crime that is already proving extremely successful. Third, I am here to state that we must build upon the unprecedented successes achieved against organized crime both here and abroad by developing a solid base of information on the basis of which law enforcement can most effectively counter the new crime cartels emerging in the Far East and spreading to the West.
>
> Today, I am pleased to report that at no time in our nation's history have so many organized crime leaders in so many of the nation's largest cities been either indicted or convicted.

The very next day, back in Washington, the Department of Justice put out one of the longest press releases to appear during my tenure. It began:

> Attorney General William French Smith announced today that a federal grand jury in Manhattan has indicted the entire leadership of a major organized crime "family" for massive racketeering

offenses that include widespread extortion in the construction and restaurant industries in New York City.

Attorney General Smith said the indictment charges extortion and payoffs, mob control of labor unions, embezzlement of union funds, trafficking in heroin and other drugs, multimillion-dollar thefts, illegal gambling, loansharking, and bribery.

The 51-count indictment, returned in federal district court in Manhattan, named 11 leaders, members, and associates of the Colombo family of La Cosa Nostra, one of five organized crime families in New York City.

The defendants include all of those who have controlled and directed the Colombo family since the early 1970s.

"It is one of the very few times in the history of law enforcement that an entire top echelon of a major organized crime family has been charged in a single federal indictment," Attorney General Smith said.

New York was hardly the only city to feel the "sting" of an organized crime task force. During that four-year period we hit the leaders of crime families in New Orleans, Kansas City, Detroit, Milwaukee, Denver, Philadelphia, Los Angeles, and Cleveland. The many families involved were largely immobilized by arrests, convictions, and heavy prison sentences. In no fewer than ten cities the syndicates were reduced to relying on secondary leadership. This decimation of the organized crime leadership in the United States, a direct result of the outstanding work of the organized crime strike forces, was very important. The jewel in the crown was the 51-count indictment against the Colombo family in New York.

The job of the task force and the strike forces was aided greatly by the work of the President's Commission on Organized Crime, to which I referred earlier, a part of the president's crime program. Chaired by United States circuit judge Irving Kaufman, the commission was charged with illuminating the ways organized crime worked in the eighties. In doing so, the commission highlighted the need for crucial reforms in the area of banking as one way to end money laundering by the syndicates. It also developed much-needed information on the striking changes in the organization and operation of the nation's crime cartels.

To pursue organized crime properly in the modern era required recognizing that it was a new era for the syndicates, too. They had become true multinational operations. For example, a drug crop might be grown in one country, processed in a second, shipped through yet another, and then, eventually, arrive in the United States. The profits generated by the trade would often then undergo the complicated international account-switching used to cleanse the money of its origins. Largely as a result of the drug trade, the relationship between New York and Palermo is now no different than that between New York and Chicago.

DOJ's reaction to this "internationalization" of crime was to develop an international enforcement response. In pursuit of effective drug-control policies (and to negotiate modern extradition and mutual assistance treaties) I traveled to Pakistan, Thailand, Bolivia, and Peru, among other countries, and conducted negotiations that led to precedent-setting agreements on the control of narcotics. Treaty-making efforts yielded progress on new and innovative mutual assistance pacts with thirteen countries. We also began a process aimed at modernizing treaties with nations—such as Thailand and Colombia—that we expected would be of long-range interest as far as our pursuit of drug traffickers was concerned.

In an attempt to minimize the disruptions that can accompany transnational legal disputes, we increased consultations with friendly nations as well. For example, we worked closely with British and Swiss authorities in a number of high-profile cases to avoid unnecessary friction between our nations. We concluded an accord with the British regarding the Cayman Islands that preserves the Islands' desire for confidentiality in the banking community but also accommodates our legitimate needs for information that may reveal elaborate money-laundering schemes.

Signed on July 26, 1984, the accord followed months of feuding and litigation between federal prosecutors and Great Britain (which represents the Cayman Islands, a former British colony). Under the terms of the accord, the Islands agreed to turn over business records of suspected drug traffickers and money launderers. We estimated that 20 to 40 percent of the $76 million generated annually by illegal narcotics trading is laundered through offshore jurisdictions, mainly Caribbean banks, which are attractive because of their countries' strict secrecy laws. (In the past, investigations have been frustrated by launderers who move money from one anonymous account to another before bringing it into the United States.)

In 1982, we began serving the Cayman Islands, the Bahamas, and other Caribbean nations with subpoenas for business records that we felt were related to narcotics transactions. These efforts met with increasing success as federal courts issued huge contempt-of-court fines for banks that did not produce the requested records. Not too surprisingly, these actions had triggered a diplomatic row with Great Britain, Canada, and some U.S. corporations that used Caribbean banks for investing in foreign markets. Finally, worn down by the constant litigation over the subpoenas, and desirous of easing tensions, the British and Cayman Islands officials signed the new pact.

Under the agreement, bank and business executives who fail to produce records within fourteen days of a request from the attorney general of the United States would be subject to a prison sentence and fines, and the Cayman officials could seize the documents.

If the foregoing sounds a bit abstract and dry, here is a living example of the type of effort that resulted in this much-needed agreement.

One day I received a call from Allan Gotlieb, the Canadian ambassador to the United States, who said he wanted to talk to me about a matter of great concern to his country. We met, and he told me that the United States had involved a Canadian bank—the Bank of Nova Scotia—in a proceeding that was proving to be very difficult for Canada.

We had subpoenaed the Bank of Nova Scotia at its Florida operation, but the records we were after were located in the Cayman Islands; under the Caymans' secrecy laws in effect at that time the Bank of Nova Scotia could not produce the records we wanted. Ambassador Gotlieb said that, as a result, his country's bank was being fined $50,000 for every day it failed to produce the records. I told him I would look into the matter.

I did, and learned that this was all part of a large drug-trafficking and money-laundering investigation we were conducting, and although the Bank of Nova Scotia was not involved, large amounts of cash *were* being transferred through its accounts. It was a bit hard to believe that the Canadian bank did not even have some suspicions about the situation—just as some large and prominent U.S. banks, which were also fined, should have known what was going on and should have been complying with the law that required them to report cash transactions of $10,000 or more.

As a matter of policy, I had determined that we should apply the maximum pressure on banks and other financial institutions within our borders that were, knowingly or unknowingly, participating in sustaining our number-one crime problem by aiding in the processing of its essential ingredient, money.

I had a second meeting with Ambassador Gotlieb during which he was quite insistent that this was a major issue that could affect the relationship between our two countries. He requested, urgently, that we reconsider our action against the bank because it was only complying with the laws of the country where the records were. By this point, the State Department had also weighed in, urging me to respect the importance of our relationship with Canada and defer to their wishes.

I reminded the ambassador, as I did the State Department, that drug trafficking and its allied evils (including money-laundering) was our number-one crime problem, that those who helped in the laundering process, wittingly or unwittingly, were aiding and abetting, and that it was hard to believe that no one, especially in Florida, was suspicious regarding these large amounts of cash. I added that the bank-secrecy laws in various Caribbean jurisdictions were being heavily exploited in this terrible acitivity. Finally, I reiterated that we were going to apply every pressure we could, including the subpoenas and the contempt process, to stop it.

(I was not exaggerating when I said the situation was becoming very grave. Not too many years later, it came out in the trial of a Colombian drug kingpin that he had spent $205,000 just to have a bank in the Bahamas *count* his cash!)

There was little negotiating room in our position, and it seemed to me that the Canadians understood our stand. In the meantime, the Bank of Nova Scotia appealed the contempt order. The order was upheld on appeal, and a fine that totaled millions of dollars was enforced. Finally, the treaty referred to earlier was successfully negotiated.

Once the agreement had been signed, I made several requests for documents in important cases, and they were all promptly produced. The agreement has worked well, and it may well prove to be one of the most significant breakthroughs in international evidence-gathering in a long time.

❖   ❖   ❖

Another area that received much needed attention during the first term was this nation's fight to protect itself against terrorists.

An open society such as ours is particularly vulnerable to the political extremism of the crazed ideologue. What's more, protection from terrorist atrocity is more difficult to gain when it must be achieved without harm to a political landscape known and admired for its freedom. I believe we succeeded in establishing the necessary vigilance without undue cost to the nation's high standards of individual privacy.

The United States has always been a tempting target for terrorists. Since 1968, 40 percent of all international incidents have been attacks on United States citizens, diplomats, military personnel, or public institutions. Sometimes the target was a U.S. citizen, sometimes the citizen of another nation.

Some of the terrorist groups were entirely home-grown in their origin, funding, and fields of operation. These included the May 19 Communist organization; the FALN from Puerto Rico; and, on the right, the KKK and the Posse Comitatus. Other groups that struck within our borders had international connections. These included the Omega Seven, a fanatical anti-Castro Cuban exile group that, under the guise of fighting communism, has committed numerous murders and bombings, and, on the left of the political spectrum, the Armenian Secret Army for the Liberation of Armenia, a pro-Soviet organization that has left a worldwide trail of violence.

When the administration took office in 1981, it was apparent that we needed a more effective response to domestic terrorism. DOJ took the early lead. We elevated terrorism to one of the FBI's four national law-enforcement priorities, and as a result more funds and more agents were assigned to the investigation of terrorist acts. During four years, the number of agents employed in these investigations increased by 25 percent.

With these additional resources, we were able to strengthen our ability to prevent *and* respond to terrorist acts. For example, in 1982 the FBI decided to form a specially trained fifty-person hostage rescue team that would be capable of responding to a terrorist incident anywhere within our borders. The team became fully operational in 1983. The FBI also established a Terrorist Research and Analytical Center at FBI headquarters to compile and computerize data on terrorists and terrorist groups in the United States.

Meanwhile, at DOJ, we also made greater use of available law-enforcement tools and techniques. Whenever possible, our agents went undercover to identify informants and to conduct surveillance of terrorist groups. Under the authority of the Foreign Intelligence Surveillance Act, and Title III of the Omnibus Crime Act, we substantially increased the use of electronic surveillance against terrorist groups. Title III authorizations had rarely been sought in the past. We used this law-enforcement tool whenever necessary.

The enhanced effort against terrorism also required a careful examination of the guidelines under which FBI agents conduct their investigations, the so-called Levi Guidelines (promulgated by President Ford's attorney general, Edward Levi). An unfortunate consequence of Watergate and its progeny was the imposition of too-stringent limitations upon the FBI's means of acquiring knowledge about domestic terrorist groups. In 1976, the attorney general had issued intelligence guidelines covering domestic security investigations that sought to clarify and circumscribe the rules for conducting these investigations. Seven years of experience under these guidelines demonstrated, however, that they were overly restrictive and hampered the FBI unnecessarily. Domestic security investigations had, in fact, declined drastically during this period,

Press conference featuring Attorney General Smith and Italian minister of the interior Oscar Luigi Scalfaro following a meeting of the Joint Italian-American Working Group on organized crime and drug trafficking. October 1984. Official Department of Justice photograph.

in part because of what the guidelines required (or, at least, seemed to require).

Therefore, reemphasizing the importance of the FBI's domestic intelligence role in the fight against terrorism became one of my top priorities. After a careful and lengthy review, we issued new domestic security guidelines in 1983, designed to prevent abuses by government without preventing or discouraging government from combating the abuses perpetrated by terrorist groups.

Our efforts in this area were vitally important, for even a single terrorist attack is an unacceptable assault on an open society. In four years, the program for fighting this domestic threat was conceived and put in place. I am proud to say that Americans will enjoy its protection for decades to come.

❖   ❖   ❖

By 1980, the needs and concerns of our citizens who suffered at the hands of criminals had been ignored for too long. When this administration took office in 1981, we announced a commitment to the victims of crime—their plight would be recognized by those of us on the federal level. *And*, we would do something about it. We would honor that commitment.

Some of the help came from reorganized in-place resources. In 1982 we established the President's Task Force on Victims of Crime, headed by Assistant Attorney General Lois Herrington, which, among other things, studied the issue with the charge of coming up with some recommendations for helping such people. DOJ took the lead in pushing both the Federal Victim/Witness Protection Act of 1982 and the Victims of Crime Assistance Act of 1984. Both acts help assist, by monetary compensation, the victims of crime.

In mid-1983 we also established an Office for Victims of Crime, which had the twofold mandate of facilitating information and referral services for victims, and of developing model victims' legislation for states. A Family Violence Task Force was also set up, to focus needed attention on the victims of domestic violence.

In addition, we succeeded in passing the Missing Children's Assistance Act. Under this act, the DOJ established the first-ever national toll-free telephone line for reporting information and assisting in locating missing children. We also set up the first National Resource Center and Clearinghouse on Missing Children, and pushed, successfully, for passage of the Child Pornography Act, which allows for easier prosecution of child pornographers and tougher penalties for convicted offenders.

All these efforts go to show that the scope of the federal law-enforcement effort is truly global. It ranges from the work of a DEA agent in northern Thailand who helps in the substitution of coffee plants for poppy plants, to the concern shared by various federal law-enforcement arms that organized crime is muscling into gambling on American Indian reservations, where so-called

Indian Bingo and other gambling activities are not covered by state law.

Given that the aim of the Reagan administration was "to make a difference," I truly feel that an excellent example of our successful effort was our assault—our all-out assault—on drugs, organized crime, and terrorism.

10

INTELLIGENCE, FOREIGN AND DOMESTIC BRANDS

I T IS HOPED THAT THIS BOOK WILL MAKE ITS APPEARANCE
shortly before the 50th anniversary of the Japanese bomb-
ing of Pearl Harbor, an event that stands alone in our
national history as a monument to inadequate intelligence-
gathering. Fifty years ago on December 7, we awoke to the reality
of that inadequacy, our surprise entry into World War II. Despite
the fact that the war's end was hastened by a much-improved
American and Allied intelligence system, for those of us of a
certain age, the attack on Pearl Harbor will remain in our con-
sciousness as the symbol of the need for proper intelligence.

This book will also make its appearance at a time when the
political structure of Eastern Europe and the so-called Communist
world has been radically altered. No one who entered government
when I did could have predicted the truly amazing events of the
final months of the 1980s. Yet, while we now frequently hear such
terms as the "end of the Cold War" and the "peace dividend," that
does not mean there has been any lessening of intelligence-gathering activities on the part of the USSR. Nor does it mean there
should be any such lessening on *our* part.

In fact, as the events of the Persian Gulf so dramatically proved,
from our standpoint intelligence-gathering continues to be a critical
need—especially in regard to the early diagnosis of potentially
unstable situations, as well as the threat of political, terrorist attacks
in third world countries. Indeed, in the areas of economics and

technology there may well be an even greater need for hard intelligence data. The legacy of the recent changes should definitely not be a relaxed watchfulness.

❖   ❖   ❖

The importance of intelligence-gathering to this country is as old as the country. In 1777, George Washington, who personally supervised such operations during the Revolutionary War, noted "the necessity of procuring good intelligence" and the "secrecy" upon which that effort depends. From that day to the present, effective—and secret—intelligence-gathering has enhanced the security of the United States. In the nuclear age, it has become essential to our preservation.

At the same time, secrecy, in a democracy, cannot be unrestrained. Ours is a nation of laws because we recognize the dangers inherent in exercising power in secret, even when it is done by well-intentioned officials. Just as the preservation of our national security requires effective intelligence-gathering, the preservation of our national principles requires accountability and obedience to the law in the exercise of governmental authority, *especially* when secrecy is necessary.

The faces of terrorism are easy to recognize, but terrorism itself is difficult to combat. Consequently, it has occurred all too frequently in recent years.

Everyone recalls the tragedy of the 1972 Olympics in Munich when eleven Israeli athletes were massacred by the Palestinian group Black September. Five years later, West German industrial leader Hanns-Martin Schleyer was kidnapped and subsequently murdered by the Baader-Meinhof Gang. In 1978, Italian statesman Aldo Moro was kidnapped, and later killed, by the infamous Red Brigades. In the summer of 1979, Britain's royal war hero Lord Mountbatten was assassinated when a bomb blew apart his fishing boat.

In none of these examples of international terrorism was a U.S.

citizen the target, but the United States has suffered at the hands of terrorists.

Between 1968 and 1983, 40 percent of all international terrorist incidents were attacks on U.S. citizens, diplomats, military personnel, and public institutions. The seizure of our embassy in Teheran and the kidnapping of our countrymen there remain a vivid memory. So does the car bomb attack on the U.S. Embassy Annex in East Beirut, and on the Marine barracks, which took more than two hundred lives.

Terrorist incidents have also occurred within our own borders. Sometimes the target was a U.S. citizen, sometimes a citizen of another nation. Some of the terrorist groups were entirely "homegrown" in their origin, funding, and field of operation.

The Department of Justice has primary responsibility for countering the clandestine intelligence activities of foreign powers and international terrorist activities within the United States. The threat that we have faced is real.

Before 1975, however, intelligence matters only occasionally received public exposure. U.S. intelligence remained an iceberg with nine-tenths of its substance below the surface. During the 1970s, a number of improper activities by our intelligence agencies were disclosed in the Congress, and in the press, resulting in an emotionally charged public reaction.

Among the excesses were "Operation COINTELPRO," aimed at "disrupting" certain domestic groups and "neutralizing" individuals deemed to be threats to domestic security; "Operation Chaos," also aimed at domestic dissidents, involving indexes and files on both groups and individuals; alleged involvement in assassination plots and unethical drug tests on American citizens; and mail openings, electronic surveillance, and physical searches within the United States (of citizens) without regard for Fourth Amendment standards.

In response to the perfectly understandable public outcry against these excesses, President Ford, by executive order, reorganized the National Security Council decision-making structure, defined the functions of each of the intelligence agencies, and prescribed limitations on the use of various types of intelligence collection techniques in the United States or against its citizens abroad.

President Carter added another level of detail. The attorney general was directed to develop or approve procedures governing virtually every aspect of intelligence-gathering in the United States or affecting its citizens abroad. As a result, over thirty discrete sets of procedures and guidelines, and scores of interagency directives and regulations, were created.

During this period of national soul-searching, Congress also responded by setting up permanent House and Senate Select Committees on Intelligence to oversee the activities and budgets of the intelligence agencies. In 1978 it went further by enacting the Foreign Intelligence Surveillance Act, which established new administrative and legal requirements for electronic surveillance.

By January 1981, there had been six full years of revelation and condemnation, as well as an ever-increasing body of new regulations and budget restrictions for U.S. intelligence agencies. That the men and women of the intelligence community continued to function ably in that atmosphere of suspicion and distrust is a testament to their dedication and professionalism. At the same time, there were negative effects on our intelligence efforts during that period. For example:

- Intelligence agencies and their employees became cautious and reluctant to undertake perfectly legitimate activities.

- Cooperation among agencies was discouraged by rigid rules about the jurisdiction and powers of particular agencies, and by prohibitions on the flow of information among agencies.

- Massive leaks and the exposure of legitimate intelligence matters compromised many secrets and called into question our ability to protect classified information from unauthorized disclosure.

Unfortunately, during this same period, our need for a reliable foreign intelligence capability was increasing dramatically. Communist takeovers in Indochina—as well as the loss of pro-Western governments in Central Asia, the Middle East, Central America, and the Horn of Africa—posed new dangers. When the Soviet Union invaded Afghanistan and the Iranians took our diplomats

Smith interviews refugee candidates at Kamput Refugee Camp, Thailand, with Immigration and Naturalization Service commissioner Alan Nelson and U.S. ambassador to Thailand John Gunther Dean. October 1982. Smith family photo collection.

hostage, the need for more effective foreign intelligence was glaringly evident.

In 1976 Attorney General Edward Levi issued intelligence guidelines covering domestic security investigations that sought to clarify, and circumscribe, the rules for conducting these investigations. Seven years' experience under these guidelines had demonstrated, however, that they were overly restrictive and unnecessarily hampered the FBI. In fact, domestic security investigations had declined drastically during this period, in part because of what the guidelines required (or at least seemed to require).

Therefore, one of my first priorities as attorney general was to reemphasize the importance of the FBI's domestic intelligence role in the fight against terrorism. After a lengthy, careful review, we issued new guidelines in 1983. They were designed to prevent abuses by government without preventing or discouraging government from combating the abuses perpetrated by terrorist groups.

The basic thrust of the new guidelines was to give the FBI considerably more discretion in deciding at what point to institute an investigation of suspect organizations or individuals as well as what investigative methods to use. Under the Levi Guidelines, the principal concern involved the high threshold necessary for the FBI to initiate effective preventive domestic security investigations of groups advocating criminal conduct—having due regard, of course, for First Amendment rights.

The new guidelines were integrated with the existing General Crimes and Organized Crime Guidelines that governed FBI investigations. They governed general crimes, racketeering enterprises, and domestic security and terrorism. The purpose was to enlarge the scope of circumstances warranting the initiation of domestic security investigations, and to make the choice of investigative techniques more flexible and subject to the discretion of the FBI.

Perhaps the most controversial provision was the one that concerned advocacy. Of course, the exercise of First Amendment rights would not in any way trigger an investigation. However, under the Smith Guidelines, advocacy of criminal activity, force or violence, or statements that created an apparent attempt to commit a crime, could do so. For example, if somebody threatened to kill the president, that is something the FBI could then look into; incredibly, under the Levi Guidelines, the FBI could not do so. It could not even collect information that was *publicly available*!

As for information regarding racketeering enterprises, the pre-existing standards would apply under the Smith Guidelines— namely, whether the facts and circumstances reasonably indicated that two or more people were engaged in an enterprise to further political or social goals in whole or in part through the use of force or violence in violation of federal law. That standard is considerably below probable cause, but it does establish what the law calls a "criminal nexus."

Although these guidelines created concern among certain groups, they were carefully crafted to preserve individual liberties while

Smith relaxes at lunch break during Justice Department's retreat for senior staff in Leesburg, Virginia, April 30–May 1, 1982, with Ted Olson, assistant attorney general, Office of Legal Counsel. Department of Justice photograph.

at the same time allowing the FBI to be an aggressive law-enforcement agency.

In August 1984, in a six-to-one ruling, the U.S. Circuit Court of Appeals for the Seventh Circuit (in Chicago) upheld what was perhaps the most controversial aspect of the guidelines. It confirmed that the FBI could properly investigate domestic political groups that advocate violent acts, even if the groups have not actually committed violence. Under the previous guidelines, the FBI could not have done so. (Although it is not generally known, the FBI operates under a host of other guidelines, most of which are also the progeny of Watergate.)

Although the terrorist's motive is not primarily financial, terrorists seek to achieve their goals through covert criminal alliances of like-minded individuals who rely on violence and intimidation. Based upon a realistic recognition of the way terrorist alliances in fact do operate, the new guidelines drew a close parallel between investigations of organized criminal groups and terrorist groups. Because of this change of focus, the new guidelines enlarge the arena in which our agents may lawfully conduct investigations of terrorist groups.

❖   ❖   ❖

The department's greatly intensified effort against terrorism has borne fruit. In 1983, there was almost a 40 percent *decrease* in terrorist incidents in the United States. There were fifty-one incidents in 1982, but only thirty-one in 1983. In 1984 there were but eight, which represents the greatest percentage decline ever recorded in a single year.

What makes this figure so impressive is that we know it could have been higher.

In 1983, the FBI prevented six terrorist incidents. FBI agents foiled the plans of the FALN, the left-wing Puerto Rican group, to free one of its members from Leavenworth Penitentiary, to rob and murder a Chicago Transit fare collector, and to bomb both the Marine and the Army Reserve Training Centers in that city. FBI agents prevented these incidents through outstanding surveillance work and the use of Title III wiretaps.

In Philadelphia in 1984, the FBI intercepted two Libyans before they could carry out their acts of terror. One Libyan bought two bulletproof vests and ordered four .45-caliber handguns (equipped with silencers) from an undercover FBI agent. Immediately after three of these weapons were delivered, the two Libyans were arrested. In 1985, we were able to detect and thwart twenty-three terrorist missions, perhaps the most notable being a failed attempt by a group of Sikhs against Indian prime minister Ghandi on the occasion of his visit to the United States.

With respect to terrorism abroad, the story is not as favorable. From January through November of 1985 there were 695 terrorist incidents worldwide. Over 40 percent of these were directed against citizens or facilities of the United States. As we develop better relationships with other countries, our intelligence capabilities improve, but it remains far more difficult to deal with terrorist events that occur outside our borders.

Improved legal tools, among other things, were needed to do the job more effectively. To meet this threat, we proposed to Congress in 1984 a legislative package designed to assist in the attack against terrorist organizations and to protect our citizens abroad. We did secure enactment of the part that provided, among other things, new and stronger federal penalties for aircraft sabotage and the taking of hostages. Furthermore, we developed a coordinated plan that drew on the resources of a number of federal agencies and departments, with the focus being to take *preventive* action. Clearly, however, much remains to be done in the international arena.

All our work in this regard was done without endangering the rights of Americans, but there is no question that as an open society we were at a distinct disadvantage, especially vis-à-vis the Soviet Union.

Had I been attorney general when the Foreign Intelligence Surveillance Act was being debated in 1978, I would probably have opposed it as being an undue interference with the working of the executive branch. I would have been wrong. As a practical matter, the act has worked very well. Our investigative agencies have been able to do their work, which otherwise would have been the subject of constant congressional and ACLU-type carping, subject to the approval of the courts.

The act established legal standards and procedures for the use of electronic surveillance to collect foreign intelligence and counterintelligence within the United States. It was the first legislative authority for wiretaps, radio intercepts, monitoring devices, and other forms of electronic surveillance for intelligence purposes against foreign powers and their agents, including Americans in the United States. The court, known officially as the Foreign Intelligence Surveillance Court, is composed of seven federal district court judges who review and approve requests that have been appropriately proposed and submitted.

Applications prepared by such intelligence agencies as NSA, FBI, or the Defense Intelligence Agency are reviewed by the Office of Intelligence Policy and Review of the Justice Department. If approved, they are signed by the attorney general and submitted to the court.

The fact that not a single application has been denied has caused some raised eyebrows in Congress, but that result is expected when one considers how thoroughly each application is prepared.

The attorney general must also give personal approval to all physical searches, initiation of mail covers (the photocopying of the exterior of mail) on U.S. persons, operational support to other agencies, and disclosures under the Freedom of Information Act in federal proceedings, among other activities. Given this fact, it should not be surprising that an attorney general may spend 10 to 15 percent of his time on intelligence matters.

❖　　❖　　❖

A further word on the importance of dealing with terrorism abroad:

Prior to 1984, the threat to our government and its citizens from hostile intelligence services and international terrorist groups increased dramatically. As a result, the activities of two Soviet intelligence groups in particular, the Soviet Committee for State Security (or KGB) and the Chief Intelligence Directorate of the Soviet General Staff (or GRU), were more widely recognized.

Foreign agents operated under a number of guises and disguises. Their most favored cover was that of a diplomat. At least one-third, and possibly more, of the 2,500 Soviet-bloc personnel in the United States assigned to embassies, consulates, and the U.N. or other international organizations were believed to be full-time intelligence officers. Over the last dozen years, the number of official representatives of governments with hostile intelligence activities in this country has increased by over 400 percent.

Their second most favored cover has been as trading-company representatives. There are some four hundred corporations in the United States that are largely or exclusively owned by Soviet-bloc countries. The third-place cover category includes students, scientists, and reporters. Over the last decade, Soviet-bloc–United States exchanges increased dramatically, and their ranks were packed with intelligence operatives, both full- and part-time. Indeed, every person from the Soviet Union granted a visa was expected to respond if called upon to do so by a Soviet intelligence agency.

The fourth most popular cover was that of an immigrant or refugee. Although it was virtually nonexistent before 1973, immigration from the Soviet Union to this country grew to more than 150,000 by 1984. Finally, we learned that hostile intelligence services continued to infiltrate agents under assumed identities. For example, KGB colonel Rudolph Hermann, who entered this country with his wife and son many years ago, thereafter posed as a free-lance photographer living in a New York City suburb. That cover lasted for eighteen years.

At one time the FBI could match suspected hostile intelligence agents in the United States on a one-to-one basis, but in time their number had grown so much that our FBI counterintelligence agents were greatly outnumbered. However, by 1983 we were able to close the gap significantly.

Between 1966 and 1975 there were five federal prosecutions for espionage. From 1975 to 1984, there were thirty-seven cases, of which twenty-seven involved the Soviet Union or its allies. There was much more espionage going on in the early 1980s, and as a result we got much better at detecting it. It is also true that there were more secrets to be kept, with our vastly expanded technological advance—and thus there were more Soviet spies. Another difficulty is that today's spies are motivated by financial gain and not by ideology: People are selling secrets for cash.

Hostile intelligence services have placed a high priority on scientific and technical data. The acquisition of Western technology is an important aspect of Soviet foreign policy. Access to our advanced technologies has enabled Soviet-bloc countries to improve their armament and communications systems in a short time—and without the substantial research and development investment that made our achievements possible. It allowed them to employ components in their weaponry that they were unable to manufacture at home, and gave them the opportunity to analyze our systems and determine their weaknesses. The Soviet effort to acquire strategic technology was massive, well planned, and well managed. And it was directed from the highest levels of the Soviet government.

Parenthetically, I might say that the microchip, which introduced the age of instant information, may be more important than any device in modern history. Indeed, political observer Leo Cherne advances the proposition that the microchip may ultimately prove more powerful than nuclear weaponry. The quick and unfettered availability of information and the existence of total political control are incompatible. That raises a question as to whether the Soviet Union had another motive in stealing Western technology. Soviet power was based in large part on controlling access to information. Computer technology development requires the opposite—intellectual freedom and exchange and a scope of inquiry and investigation unknown in the Communist world. The Soviets, therefore, may well have wanted to acquire rather than develop such technology. In fact, to maintain political control it would have been safer for them to do so.

In many instances, the Soviet Union acquired Western technology through legal means. Soviet assurances that legally purchased strategic technology will be used solely for civilian applications, however, must be judged with suspicion. The Soviet Kama River Truck Plant was built with massive imports of U.S. and West European automotive production equipment and technology. Large numbers of trucks produced there were used by Soviet forces in Afghanistan and by Soviet military units in Eastern Europe.

Improvements in the accuracy of Soviet ballistic missile systems were aided during the 1970s by the legal purchase, by the Soviet Union, of U.S. precision grinding machines for the production of small, high-precision bearings. These purchases enabled the Soviet Union to manufacture the bearings that are an integral part of high-quality guidance components in the latest generation of Soviet ICBMs.

The Soviets also acquired military-related technology through various covert and illegal means. The sophistication of their illegal schemes to acquire our technology was impressive. They knew what they wanted right down to the model numbers of specific items. Their boldness was astonishing, too.

Not long ago, it was discovered, based on information provided by a company in California, that a computerized processing system designed to enhance photographs taken from reconnaissance satellites had been illegally diverted to the Soviet Union from its lawful destination—a firm in Great Britain. The equipment was subsequently returned by the Soviet Union to the company in the United States through Great Britain for upgrading and modification—and was scheduled for shipment *back* to the Soviet Union, when it was seized by American authorities. This brazen incident illustrates the confidence, indeed arrogance, that the Soviet Union had developed in this activity. It also underscores the dependence of federal countermeasures on support from the U.S. business community. Without the alertness of the U.S. firm, the equipment would probably not have been seized and would have found its way back to the USSR.

❖   ❖   ❖

The techniques used by foreign agents should be made known to every American who works in our technology industry or who is exposed to classified information. First, there is a chance social meeting followed by what in some cases could be months or even years of careful cultivation of that social relationship. Next, there is a deliberate sounding-out of the target for information that indicates his vulnerability and his access to valuable data. Then, the sometimes unwary person is "involved," through gifts, loans, or a personal favor. Finally, the moment of truth arrives—the hook is firmly set, and confidential or classified information is requested.

Often, even after uncovering such a scheme, it is not possible to bring a criminal prosecution against the foreign agent because many of these people are protected by diplomatic immunity. When caught, they can only be deported. In other cases, we had to make a very difficult judgment call—whether to leave a known intelligence officer in place so that he could be used, or at least neutralized, in various ways. If we did not, he could well be replaced by someone we did not know.

Equally insidious is the threat posed by "active measures" in this country, aimed at influencing public opinion and the political process through "disinformation" and "agents of influence."

The Soviet boycott of the 1984 Olympics in Los Angeles was an attempt to discredit the United States and to retaliate for our boycott of the 1980 Moscow Olympics, which had been a result of the Soviet invasion of Afghanistan. The Soviet Union, nonetheless, alleged that their boycott was made necessary by some kind of security threat to their athletes posed by anti-Soviet groups in the United States.

With this background in mind, we were especially concerned by reports in the press that the Ku Klux Klan had allegedly mailed threatening and abusive letters to some twenty Asian and African countries that were planning to take part in the 1984 Olympic Games. Fortunately, none of the nations that received these letters succumbed to the attempted intimidation.

Even more reprehensible than the letters themselves, however, was what we learned about their actual origin. They were *not* produced or sent by the KKK—instead, they were manufactured and mailed by another terrorist organization, the KGB. The letters were a classic forgery and disinformation operation. Apparently, they were intended to aid the Soviet Union in justifying its Olympic boycott, and to gain the support of the non-Communist-bloc countries.

This type of plot is what the intelligence community refers to as an "active measure," or one intended to influence or affect the policies of another country. In the intelligence context, an active measure is distinguished from espionage and counterintelligence, and includes, among other things, manipulation or control of the media, use of foreign front operations, economic warfare, disinformation, and forgery. Active measures such as these must be approved by the Soviet Politburo itself.

To counter these aggressive and expanding Soviet activities, major steps were taken during my last several years as attorney general to revitalize the intelligence efforts of the United States. Significant organizational changes were made, personnel levels

FBI director William Webster, Deputy Attorney General Ed Schmults, Attorney General Smith, and Associate Attorney General Rudy Giuliani hold the first satellite video teleconference between the Department of Justice's Washington office and representatives from field offices in six southeast cities to improve opportunities for "face-to-face" communication across the United States. September 15, 1982. Official Department of Justice photograph.

rebuilt and expanded, and morale was reestablished. Substantial new and increased resources were made available to the intelligence community, and the gap between Soviet efforts and our ability to respond was narrowed significantly.

The president's Foreign Intelligence Advisory Board (to which I was named upon leaving office) was reestablished and given broad authority. And the president, by executive order, simplified and redirected the authorities, responsibilities, and limitations of the U.S. intelligence agencies.

Legislation was proposed that exempted CIA operations from the requirements of the Freedom of Information Act, and other amendments improved our ability to protect our sources and methods of intelligence. Criminal penalties were imposed on those who make a practice of ferreting out and exposing the classified identities of our intelligence agents. In addition, substantial effort was made to bring about some balance between the size of the Soviet presence here and our presence in the Soviet Union.

Legislation was enacted imposing the death penalty for military personnel who spy during peacetime, and legislation was proposed that would confirm greater use of the polygraph (which has been successful in this area). Communication and computer security have become priority matters. National security legislation, including laws prohibiting unlawful export of advanced technology and munitions, was vigorously enforced.

❖　　❖　　❖

As I mentioned, after I left office the president named me to his Foreign Intelligence Advisory Board, the same body I had dealt with while in office. That group, which was made up of such distinguished Americans as Henry Kissinger, Jeane Kirkpatrick, Caspar Weinberger, Dr. John Foster, Dr. Zbigniew Brzezinski, Albert Whelan, Professor Albert Wohlstetter, Leo Cherne, and chaired by Ambassador Anne Armstrong, oversees (in a nonoperating sense) the functioning of all the intelligence agencies, and reports directly to the president.

Its breadth and range are fascinating, and it can review practices, procedures, and occurrences in a way that no operating agency can. This is particularly true of problems, failures, and breakdowns in the system that are better for an outside agency to deal with.

Of course all of its work is highly classified. However, there *are* times when we do wish we could speak out. For example, when Secretary of State George Shultz testified before Congress's Iran-Contra hearing that he felt some of the intelligence he had received had been altered for political purposes, we investigated to see what had happened (so as to correct the situation, if what Shultz had said was in fact true). However, we found no basis for the statement. It turned out to be an undeserved—and very serious—charge against our intelligence agencies, especially as it had come from such a high-level government official.

❖   ❖   ❖

Whenever I think of our work on this subject, I am reminded of a statement that Bill Casey gave to *Time* magazine the year before he died:

> We are well protected against another Pearl Harbor. I am confident we are not likely to miss any such major preparation. We have learned the lesson of Iran and established a team of people who study the factors of instability in various countries. We look at the world on a daily basis. It is hard work, but we are doing fine.

11

THE (MUCH TOO) INDEPENDENT COUNSEL

AFTER A CAREFUL REVIEW OF THE *[Special Prosecutor] Act within the Department of Justice and an analysis of its practical effect over the past few years, I have serious reservations concerning the constitutionality of the act. In some or all of its applications, the act appears fundamentally to contradict the principle of separation of powers erected by the Constitution. The power to enforce the law and to prosecute federal offenses is committed by the Constitution to the executive branch. Indeed, the courts have generally recognized that the prosecution of federal offenses is an executive function within the exclusive prerogative of the attorney general, and, ultimately, the president. For that reason federal prosecutors must be accountable to the president or the attorney general.*

The Special Prosecutor Act removes the responsibility for the enforcement of federal criminal laws from the executive branch and lodges it in an officer who is not appointed by or accountable to, or save in extraordinary circumstances, removable by the attorney general or the president.

The above opinion, which no one could possibly call vague, was part of my response to a letter sent to me, as attorney general, by the Senate legal counsel, who wanted to know my views on the Special Prosecutor Act (as it was then still named.) My point in including the quote here is that the date of my letter is April 17, 1981. Thus it reveals that less than three months into my tenure as attorney general, I already held a strong negative opinion of the

Special Prosecutor Act. Did that view change over the years since then? Yes. It got stronger—and more negative.

Let me hasten to add one caveat, in the form of another quote from that same letter. Its final paragraph reads:

> If the department's position is sought in future litigation, we would espouse views consistent with the above and addressed to the specific facts of the case.

And then I added the caveat:

> I should also, however, make it clear that until there is a statutory change or a judicial declaration of unconstitutionality, the Department of Justice will continue to comply with the current requirements of the Special Prosecutor Act.

Which, like it or not, is exactly what I did.

❖　　❖　　❖

Part of the congressional overreaction to Watergate was the passage, in 1978, of the Ethics in Government Act, the father, so to speak, of the Special Prosecutor Act. Part of the Ethics Act established a mechanism whereby a defined group of the highest-level officials in the executive branch, including the president and vice president, would be treated differently from all other citizens if allegations were made that they had engaged in wrongdoing. Under the provisions of the mechanism, all it takes to trigger further investigation and possible prosecution (which is removed from the executive branch's normal law-enforcement process and transferred to the judicial branch) is a very low evidentiary threshold not necessarily related to culpability, namely, a finding that there are "reasonable grounds to believe further investigation is warranted."

What happens next is that a three-judge panel of circuit court judges in Washington then appoints an independent counsel— which is the current name for the post, yet it is universally referred to by its old name, "special prosecutor"—who then proceeds to investigate as he or she sees fit.

This independent counsel is, as a practical matter, beholden to no one as to how the immense powers of investigation are employed. These powers include the ability to empanel grand juries, issue subpoenas, confer immunity, and so on, and then to prosecute without the approval of any accountable officer. Nor is the independent counsel restrained with respect to the resources used, the money spent, or the time period within which action must be taken.

Consider this: With no budgetary restraints, Lawrence Walsh, the long-standing independent counsel in the Iran-Contra matter, organized a staff that in 1990 consisted of twenty-nine lawyers, seventy-three administrative staff members, thirty-five FBI agents, eleven Internal Revenue Service agents, and six agents from Customs. In less than a year he spent some $4.7 million, not counting the "cost" of the IRS, FBI, and Customs agents.* Compare that whopping expense with the $2.35 million annual budget of the DOJ's Public Integrity Office, which has the responsibility of investigating and prosecuting public officials in the entire United States. This gross imbalance says volumes about the wisdom of this politically inspired law.

❖   ❖   ❖

Despite the 1988 decision of the United States Supreme Court affirming the constitutional validity of the Independent Counsel Act, I continue to believe that the U.S. Court of Appeals for the District of Columbia Circuit was correct when it held the act to be an unconstitutional invasion of the powers of the executive branch.

In any event, there has been insufficient attention given to whether the legislation, constitutional or not, is *good* legislation or good public policy. It is not—and I say that as one who had the

---

*Ed.'s note: As of May 1991, Walsh's investigation had cost $25.9 million.

responsibility for administering the act longer than any other attorney general. Not only is the scheme established by the act an unsatisfactory and unwise response to a perceived problem, but it is also a serious threat to the fair, evenhanded administration of justice.

Everyone agrees that the law must be enforced in an impartial manner, without bias and without politicizing the process. This legislation has not served the ends of justice. It is cruel in its operation. Its application to individuals can be, and has been, devastating, falsely destroying reputations and forcing one to incur great personal debt. Moreover, it has applied artificial standards often unrelated to culpability, and to that extent has prevented the use of normal standards of prosecutorial discretion. All in all, the act has been used more for political purposes and the satisfaction of media appetite than to achieve justice, has been a nightmare to administer, and has caused a substantial (and needless) waste of the taxpayers' money.

Other than that, I have no objections to the act.

Seriously, the act remains a massively flawed and totally unnecessary piece of legislation. Because of the high-profile nature of the cases involved, the independent counsels selected have felt it necessary to undertake massive investigations. These have resulted in the establishment of legal and investigative bureaucracies, and have caused the process to be drawn out from six months to over six years—with the result being great cost to the public, and tremendous personal anguish for people even when they are ultimately vindicated. In some cases, independent counsels have tended to roam beyond the scope of the matter originally assigned to them, converting investigations into endless microscopic examinations, and in the process running roughshod over both individuals and national interests (as illustrated by the remarkably outrageous conduct of Whitney North Seymour with respect to Canada's ambassador, Allan Gotlieb).

Certainly, over the years there are cases in which, because of the magnitude of the situation and the high position of those involved, a special prosecutor should be appointed. When this is the case, *it should be done by the president.* There is no historical justification for the legislative morass created by this act. When, in the past, a special prosecutor has been needed, one has been appointed. Examples range from Teapot Dome to Watergate.

The triggering event for the passage of this legislation was the firing, by President Nixon, of Watergate special prosecutor Archibald Cox. This event was an aberration, however, and was quickly corrected by the designation of a successor to Cox. Those particular special prosecutors fully accomplished what their role was intended to do and what the public expected: the indictment, prosecution, and conviction of those who broke the law. This process has happened before; whenever an investigation or prosecution had to be handled differently from the normal process, a special investigator or prosecutor has been designated, and the results fully satisfied the public in terms of the fairness and thoroughness of the investigation.

President Nixon's firing of Watergate special prosecutor Cox was a politically costly move. No one has ever suggested that Cox's successor, the respected lawyer Leon Jaworski, or his successor, Henry Ruth (Jaworski's deputy), favored the man who appointed them or otherwise conducted themselves in their office in a manner suggesting that the appointment power should be removed from the executive and bestowed on a three-judge panel of the D.C. Circuit Court.

Another major reason why I dislike the act is that it establishes artificial standards that require the attorney general to set in motion a cumbersome and expensive process that thus far has damaged reputations but produced little else that could not have been handled in the usual process. The principal vice of this required process is that it precludes people charged with enforcing the law from doing what they normally do, and that is to use what is known as prosecutorial discretion to determine, based on the exercise of their professional opinion, whether or not proceedings should be undertaken.

What this means is that once the act has been triggered, a case that would normally have been dismissed out of hand (after appropriate inquiry) now *must* run its entire interminable course irrespective of ultimate vindication. Furthermore, virtually every inquiry under the act results not only in high intensity, but also in publicity that is seriously damaging to the person under investigation—publicity against which there is little, if any, opportunity for response.

Virtually all the cases that have been handled so far by special prosecutors could have been conducted by the Criminal Division of the DOJ, the division that would normally handle such matters. In my experience as attorney general, I never saw any of the career investigative people in Justice put forth anything other than a strictly professional effort regardless of the rank of the person they found themselves called upon to investigate. In fact, if there is any tendency one way or the other, it is to lean over backward to check out everything the higher the "rank" of the person involved. And this applies equally to politically appointed officials.

The first two cases in which independent counsels were appointed—during the Carter not the Reagan administration—are worth considering. Both involved allegations of drug use, but in neither case under the standard operating procedure of the Department of Justice would there have been such an intensive, resource-draining investigation.

It is extremely rare for the federal government to conduct a full-scale grand jury investigation to determine if a person used marijuana or cocaine on a specific occasion, particularly in cases where the allegations are received well after the fact, are of dubious credibility, and will not lead to the seizure of any drugs or of money related to the purchase and sale of drugs.

In both of these Carter administration cases, however, the Special Prosecutor Statute mandated full preliminary investigations and the appointment of a special prosecutor (who virtually duplicated the preliminary investigation). And in both cases the targets were subjected to great expense and damage to their reputations—only to be cleared in the end. People should not be subjected to this sort of treatment merely because they hold public office. On the contrary, our system of justice is based on the premise that all citizens are to be treated equally. Yet it is that very premise that in both of these cases was turned on its head.

Although I realize many people feel that even when there is no actual conflict of interest, the *appearance* of a conflict is enough to justify triggering the independent counsel mechanism, my experience has been that in almost all such cases the dangers of conflict turned out to be more apparent than real. Thus, I don't believe there is any basis for assuming that DOJ personnel cannot or will not investigate crimes by public officials fairly and thoroughly, especially considering the huge cost of independent counsel investigations. Where a reasonable danger of conflict might exist, it can always be handled by individual disqualification or, in the most egregious cases, by resort to nonmandatory temporary independent counsels, such as were used in the Watergate and the Carter Warehouse cases.

The effect of removing normal prosecutorial standards has been to subject public officials with extremely vulnerable reputations to the stigma and expense of criminal investigations in circumstances where such an investigation would not be warranted absent the statute. Even when it results in a decision not to prosecute, a person can never emerge whole from a criminal investigation.

Perhaps this is the price society has to pay for having a free press and an open criminal justice system that provides due process at all its stages. Where normal standards of prosecutorial discretion are eliminated for a certain class of cases, however, and then one adds the stigma of a special prosecutor, the cost to innocent people becomes greater than necessary, and serious questions of fairness and justice are raised.

Some people argue that anyone who has been subjected to this process and been vindicated should be grateful—because the mechanism was there to clear them. That argument is of course specious, because it assumes that they would not have been cleared under the (far more efficient) normal procedures. It also ignores the fact that they might well not have been caught up in the whole process in the first place had it not been for the act's artificial standard. The most important fact to keep in mind is that if their case had been handled under the normal process they would not have come away with the impossible-to-remove tarnish that attaches to any "vindicated" victim of a special prosecutor.

Another specious argument that is nonetheless often heard is that the target of the investigation has *asked* that a special prosecutor be appointed so as to clear his name, and that it has been done as a direct response to his wishes. Again, this simply is not true. In the first place, the wishes of the "target" are entirely irrelevant to the operation of the act. Furthermore, where such a request *has* been made, it has been made—in my opinion—because the potential target knew the act was about to be triggered, and a public request for its implementation was a way of putting the best face on the situation. That is the only situation in which I can imagine any rational person would submit himself to this gruesome process.

❖   ❖   ❖

I am hardly the only person with an interest in law enforcement who dislikes the Special Prosecutor Act. In fact, I have a lot of interesting company in my camp, and it includes such seemingly different folks as former Attorney General of the United States Edward Levi and Steven Brill, founder and editor of *The American Lawyer*.

Testifying in 1976, when this legislation was proposed, Attorney General Levi stated, "It would create opportunities for actual or apparent partisan influence in law enforcement; publicize and dignify unfounded, scurrilous allegations against public officials; result in the continuing existence of a changing band of multiplicity of special prosecutors; and promote the possibility of unequal justice."

Attorney General Levi was right then and he is right now. In enabling the criminal investigative process to be transformed into a media event each time high officials are involved, the act casts aside one of the most decent traditions of our criminal law system. This procedure for spreading improper charges contributes to a public attitude of cynicism and distrust of government officials— again a problem the act was intended to help solve.

Given the fact that he is a journalist, Mr. Brill, whose irreverent publication, *The American Lawyer*, is now not just accepted but required reading, *might* be expected to favor the act (after all, it does foster headline-making events). But Mr. Brill does not like the act; he does not like it at all.

In March 1981 he wrote, in reference to the naming of former

U.S. Attorney (in New Orleans) Gerald Gallinghouse as the special prosecutor to investigate whether Carter aide Tim Kraft had possessed cocaine on two ocasions:

> All the evidence thus far indicates that Gallinghouse, a former Republican U.S. Attorney, has conducted himself with probity and in a non-partisan manner. But you can't read [(Kraft's lawyers'] motion and accompanying memorandum without concluding that the lawyers among the members of the House and Senate, who voted 370 to 23 in the House and 74 to 5 in the Senate for the act that created the special prosecutor, must have been on a post-Watergate binge that robbed them of all ability to think or even to read. . . .
>
> Several witnesses, including Watergate stars John Doar and Leon Jaworski, testified against special prosecutor legislation. In 1976, Doar, for example, said of the proposal that eventually passed in 1978 that, "It is difficult to rationalize the abuses of power with this solution that grants so very much power."
>
> I am not among those who generally believe that we've overreacted to Watergate; the abuses of the Nixon era should not be easily forgotten, and they deserve the continuing vigilance of government through financial disclosure laws, vigorous congressional oversight, a robust press, and other such checks on government wrongdoing. But the law *is* an overreaction. It has damaged the reputation and bank accounts of two honest public servants—[Hamilton] Jordan and Kraft—and in the process it has created a real, though unrealized, potential for corruption by forcing the two to seek loans and contributions from private parties to pay enormous legal fees. . . . The very act of announcing the appointment of a special prosecutor and giving that person a full-time job investigating these petty allegations hurt Kraft's and Jordan's reputations far more, and cost them far more in legal fees, than a simple and probably secret investigation of these allegations would have.
>
> Yet, as the post-Watergate argument goes, a special prosecutor may exact a high cost from honest public servants, but it's worth it because a non-special prosecutor can't be trusted to investigate these charges impartially.
>
> Even if that argument is true, appointing a totally independent

prosecutor who has license to run amuck with his high-visibility assignment is not the answer, especially since a dishonest attorney general can short-circuit the law simply by not applying for a special prosecutor.

Brill closed his long article by offering me some advice:

[Attorney General Smith] should push for the repeal of the special prosecutor act, assuming the district court in Washington where Kraft's injunction motion is pending doesn't repeal it for him. Smith should similarly forget all those warnings about staying clear of the White House. If he or his colleagues are dishonest, no pious organizational chart and no special prosecutor law will help us. If he's honest, special prosecutors and elaborate protective structures will only get in the way.

I could not agree more.

❖   ❖   ❖

Some supporters of the act expected that it would rarely require the appointment of special prosecutors, but what has happened thus far, and what is likely to happen in the future, indicates that just the reverse is true. The existence of a multitude of special prosecutors, each with only one case to pursue, creates the inevitability of unequal justice under the law. Individual rights are clearly undermined when the special prosecutor is charged with focusing on one person, and almost by definition has an incentive to prosecute. Each prosecutor is beholden to no one and, having no central authority, applies his own brand of justice. The entire concept of "equal justice for all" becomes a fiction.

It is true that under the 1982 amendment the independent counsel is supposed to follow Department of Justice prosecutorial policies. But that is such a general standard that in many cases its de facto effect could be minimal. Independent Counsel Walsh in the Iran-Contra case has indicated that he would seek indictments if he believed he had evidence to establish probable cause that a crime had been committed. The prosecution manual of the Department of Justice states that fundamental fairness requires that an indictment issue only if the prosecutor believes that an unbiased jury would convict. Even then, a federal prosecutor should be cautious about seeking an indictment if no substantial federal interest would be served by a prosecution. Those are not the same standards announced or followed by Mr. Walsh.

Although not responsible to anyone, the independent counsel has enormous investigative powers. We have already seen situations develop in the Iran-Contra and Michael Deaver cases where the independent counsel has tangled with our foreign-policy interests and procedures. But with an independent counsel, who would resolve such disputes? Normally, it would be done, if need be, by the president. Would it be the three-judge court that appointed the independent counsel? If so, does that mean that the judicial branch would not only have become enmeshed in the prosecutor's function but our foreign policy as well? Could the independent counsel have the last word, thus overriding the State Department?

That this is far more than mere speculation can be seen in the following exchange between Walsh's chief deputy and a judge on the United States Court of Appeals for the D.C. Circuit, which was considering the constitutionality of the act.

COURT: So if the president and the independent counsel have a disagreement over foreign policy and its implications for a prosecution, then the independent counsel has the last word?

DEPUTY: That's right, that's right. If I understand the hypothetical, I think in principle the answer has to be yes.

An effort was made by the independent counsel in the Michael Deaver case to subpoena the Canadian ambassador. It should not come as a major surprise to anyone that the State Department strongly objected to this effort. In the Iran-Contra matter, an effort was made to obtain information from four Israelis, amid objections from the Israeli government.

In response to the charge that the independent counsel is responsible to no one, some of the act's proponents refer to the fact that he is removable by the attorney general for good cause. However, as almost everyone knows, it would be impossible, politically, for the AG to exercise this power unless the independent counsel's conduct were so egregious that he or she would have to resign anyway.

Defenders of the current regime also refer to provisions requiring reports to Congress and to the special court that appointed the independent counsel; to grand jury, judicial, and other relationships; and in given cases to efforts to comply with DOJ policies and to seek guidance from appropriate officials. However, none of these affect the independent counsel's power, only his modus operandi.

Equally bothersome is the continuous tendency to use the act for purposes that are essentially—in some cases blatantly—political, by members of Congress and others. In the administration of criminal justice, an area where politics should play absolutely no role, this act provides a convenient mechanism for politicians to practice their trade. There is no indication that this practice will lessen. It seems that some members of Congress stand poised, whenever they sense any vulnerability on the part of an official in the executive branch, to cry for an independent counsel. And that cry is usually worth a headline.

As subcommittee chairmen (and there are many of them) know all too well, this is the kind of juicy "news" the media delight in covering, and the damage to the individual is secondary. The act has become a political weapon.

The grossest example of the act's politicization is the outrageous, years-long "investigation" conducted by the Democratic majority of the House Judiciary Committee regarding their running dispute, in 1983, with DOJ over producing documents, and invoking executive privilege in an ongoing investigation of the Environmental Protection Agency (the details of which I provided in Chapter Seven).

These and other applications of the Independent Counsel Act have turned the entire act, and its original purpose, on its head. As a result, the act that was supposed to take the politics out of law enforcement has itself become one of the favorite weapons of political attack.

❖   ❖   ❖

What follows are several personal examples of why I oppose the act.

For one thing, the act has the effect of causing public officials to behave in ways they would not if the act did not exist. Early in the first Reagan term, the press—without any basis in fact—alleged that a substantial (board of) director's fee I had received before I came into office was an attempt by the corporation involved to augment, unlawfully, my government salary.

As absurd as the charge was, it nonetheless triggered an investigation by the DOJ's Public Integrity Office. Only in order to minimize the possibility of triggering the Special Prosecutor Act, I returned the money to the company—something I never would have done without this threat. Months later, following an extensive investigation, the fee was confirmed to be entirely proper, and a subsequent unanimous Supreme Court opinion made it absolutely clear once again that the severance fee was completely legal.

Something similar happened to me with respect to an oil and gas investment that had afforded me some financially beneficial deductions on my income tax. Up to that year, this type of investment had been perfectly legal and proper. But, using a hypothetical case based on that investment, and obtaining some information from an anonymous tax "authority," the press and some politicians proclaimed it an "abusive tax shelter." Since the DOJ was supposed to prosecute these, I therefore had an "automatic" conflict of interest.

What the press had done was to adopt a stated *position* of the IRS and treat it as settled law. Up to that point, the IRS had not raised a question about my particular investment; needless to say, they did so after that. The technical legal issue involved has yet to be resolved. Once again, to prevent the triggering of the Special Prosecutor Act, I resolved not to take the deductions in question.

I took these actions because I believe that it is absolutely essential for the public to have the fullest confidence in the attorney general. However, I think it is a sad commentary that I would not have had to take these actions under the perfectly adequate protections of the normal DOJ procedures. As an old D.C. hand is fond of saying,

"The fact that one is right does not matter—the important thing is to stop the story."

❖   ❖   ❖

My feelings for the act notwithstanding, during my tenure as AG I authorized a number of preliminary investigations under its provisions, and of these four received wide media attention. In each case, the question was, of course, whether or not we had received enough information to require going further with the investigation—a very minimal finding, and one not at all necessarily related to culpability.

The two cases that did not even meet the minimum standard were those of Richard Allen (President Reagan's first national security adviser) and "Debategate" (the infamous Carter briefing-papers episode).

In Allen's case, an inquiry was initiated because ten one-hundred dollar bills had been found in a safe in an office that had been occupied by Allen. During the inquiry, we also learned that Allen had received two watches from Japanese business interests. In "Debategate," a majority on the Subcommittee on Human Resources of the House Committee on Post Office and Civil Service had asked for an independent counsel to look into how the Reagan camp came up with briefing materials belonging to President Carter.

In the Allen case, the media did its best to indict, try, and convict. But neither in the Allen incident nor in "Debategate" was the minimum standard met—we found no evidence that any federal laws were violated—and no special prosecutor was named.

One *was* named, however, in several other cases while I was attorney general, including those of Secretary of Labor Ray Donovan and Ed Meese, then counsellor to the president. Donovan was alleged to have had Mafia connections while an officer of a construction company in New Jersey, and Meese was said to have helped people who had helped him financially to land government jobs. In both cases there was an extensive investigation, and in both cases there was no indictment. No charges of any kind were brought against either one of them based on these investigations.

As I mentioned, I did not like being involved in these matters, but because of my position it was my responsibility to do so, and thus I did. It has been my experience—and almost every other former attorney general I have spoken to about it shares my view—that the legislative scheme established by the act is simply not necessary. Our predominant experience has been that this law not only raises serious constitutional questions, but is also not in the public interest.

One last non-surprise. In case you had forgotten, let me remind you of one interesting fact: Congress, in its "wisdom," exempted itself from the provisions of the Independent Counsel Act. Given the small amount of criticism over this point, I suspect the public really does not realize that our representative body has given itself this preferred status. One should not be surprised at this. Congress also exempted itself from coverage by the Ethics in Government Act.

I began this chapter with a quote from a letter I wrote about the Special Prosecutor Act in 1981. As I said, I did not like it then, and my opinion did not soften. Here is part of what I had to say about it in a 1987 letter to Senator Carl Levin, who had had the courage to ask me for my views on proposed changes in this law.

> In my opinion, this legislation has not served the ends of justice, is cruel and devastating in its application to individuals—falsely destroying reputations and requiring the incurring of great personal costs—has applied artificial standards unrelated to culpability and to that extent has prevented the use of normal standards of prosecutorial discretion, has been used more for political purposes and media appetite than to achieve justice, has been a nightmare to administer, and has caused a needless and substantial waste of taxpayers' money. Because of the high-profile nature of the cases involved, the independent counsel selected have felt

it necessary to undertake massive investigations, delving into minute detail and wholly irrelevant trivia. This has required the establishment of legal and investigative bureaucracies and has resulted in the process being drawn out from five months to almost a year—and this at tremendous personal anguish to individuals and great cost to the taxpayers.

As I said at the beginning of this chapter, over time, my opinion of the Special Prosecutor–Independent Counsel Act has changed. It has gotten worse.

Smith with Jimmy Stewart at a private going-away dinner in Los Angeles in 1981. Bill and Jean's faces replaced Jimmy Stewart's and Jean Arthur's on the movie poster from the 1940s. (An early draft of book was titled Mr. Smith Went to Washington.*) Smith family photo collection.*

Playing golf at Sunnylands, home of Ambassador Walter Annenberg, on New Year's Eve day December 1986 are George Shultz, secretary of state, the attorney general, Charles Price, U.S. ambassador to Great Britain, and the president. White House photograph.

Attorney General Smith with President Reagan and Myra Tankersley at the Justice Department, October 14, 1982. Official White House photograph.

First Cabinet meeting of the Reagan administration, January 21, 1981. Official White House photograph.

Attorney General and Mrs. Smith at surprise birthday celebration given by his hometown of Wilton, New Hampshire, in 1981. Smith family photo collection.

The attorney general visits an inner-city business area of Newark, New Jersey, to assess the impact of crime and fear on neighborhoods. From the left: Patrick Murphy, president of the Police Foundation; Kenneth Gibson, mayor of Newark; Tom Kean, governor of New Jersey; James ("Chips") Stewart, director of the National Institute for Justice, Department of Justice; Attorney General Smith; Hubert Williams, Newark police director; Charles Knox, captain of police; and two unidentified Newark police officers.

At a meeting on the crime bill with the president are, from the left: Robert McConnell, assistant attorney general, Office of Legislative Affairs; the attorney general; Congressman Dan Lungren; Congressman John Conyers; Senator Ted Stevens; Senator Arlen Specter; Chairman Strom Thurmond; the president; Congressman Hamilton Fish, Jr.; Congressman William Hughes. March 14, 1983. Official White House photograph.

Signing the United States Prisoner Exchange Treaty with Thailand in Bangkok are Attorney General Smith and Thailand foreign minister Siddhi. October 1982. Smith family photo collection.

Signing the U.S./Thailand Extradition Treaty, Attorney General Smith and Thailand foreign minister Siddhi. December 14, 1983. Official Department of Justice photograph.

Smith announces his resignation at a press conference on January 23, 1984. He was not to leave for another year, however. Official Department of Justice photograph.

Garlands are presented to Attorney General Smith by tribesmen at the Khyber Pass. Home Secretary Jamshed Burki is on the right. November 2, 1982. Smith family photo collection.

Attorney General Smith and John Gavin, U.S. ambassador to Mexico, along with Mexican officials and federal judicial police, inspect a mountain site outside of Zihuatanejo for opium poppies and marijuana fields. April 6, 1983. U.S. Embassy photograph.

Attorney General Smith, President Reagan, Sandra Day O'Connor, and Vice President George Bush at the press conference at which President Reagan announced O'Connor's nomination to the Supreme Court. July 15, 1981. Official White House photograph.

Attorney General Smith presents the Presidential Commendation to the University of California at Los Angeles (UCLA) debate team and Tom Miller, director of Forensics, Speech and Debate Program at UCLA, in honor of their national championship. May 21, 1982. Smith actively supported the UCLA debate team, which has won six national championships. Terry O'Donnell, Associated Students of UCLA photograph.

Biweekly meeting with heads of offices, boards, and divisions of the Justice Department. From the left (at the table): Edward C. Schmults, deputy attorney general; Rudolph W. Giuliani, associate attorney general; William H. Webster, director of the FBI; Alan C. Nelson, commissioner, Immigration and Naturalization Service; Myra Tankersley, confidential assistant to the attorney general; Carol Dinkins, assistant attorney general, Land and Natural Resources; William F. Baxter, assistant attorney general, Antitrust Division; Francis M. Mullen, Jr., administrator, Drug Enforcement Administration; Stanley E. Morris, director, U.S. Marshals Service; Kenneth W. Starr, counselor to the attorney general. From the left (against the wall): Theodore B. Olson, assistant attorney general, Office of Legal Counsel; Glenn L. Archer, assistant attorney general, Tax Division; J. Paul McGrath, assistant attorney general, Civil Division; David Stephenson, pardon attorney (acting); Mary C. Lawton, counsel, Office of Intelligence Policy and Review; Catherine L. O. Anderson, special assistant; Jonathan C. Rose, assistant attorney general, Office of Legal Policy; Rex E. Lee, solicitor general; Robert A. McConnell, assistant attorney general, Office of Legislative Affairs; Jane Evered, secretary. January 21, 1983. Department of Justice photograph.

Attorney General Smith conducts a press conference with President Reagan and Secretary of Transportation Drew Lewis concerning the air traffic controllers' strike. August 3, 1981. Official White House photograph.

Meeting in the attorney general's office after President Reagan's nomination of Sandra Day O'Connor as associate justice of the United States Supreme Court are, from the left, Ken Starr, counselor to the attorney general; Fred Fielding, counsel to the president; Bob McConnell, assistant attorney general, Office of Legislative Affairs; Attorney General Smith; Judge O'Connor; Ed Schmults, deputy attorney general; Jonathan Rose, assistant attorney general, Office of Legal Policy. July 14, 1981. Department of Justice photograph.

12

REFORM: IMMIGRATION AND THE CRIMINAL CODE

MY FIRST IMPRESSION WAS THAT ALL 1,200 IN-mates were screaming and yelling at the same time. The sound, which was the initial assault on my senses, seemed to come from every-where and cover everything in waves of painful undulation. I was not at all surprised to notice that the guards were wearing ear plugs.

It was 1981, and I was visiting the federal prison in Atlanta, where some 1,200 of the Mariel boat prisoners had been housed, 1,200 of the (mostly) hard-core residue for whom there seemed to be no solution. In March, the president had appointed me to head the cabinet-level Task Force on Immigration and Refugee Policy, and I had come to Atlanta to see for myself what had been de-scribed to me as the worst immigration problem imaginable. That description turned out to be right on the money.

The Mariel boatlift of 1980 saw 125,000 Cubans flocking over water to get to the United States. In that number, thanks to the fiendishness of Fidel Castro, were his country's least desirable inhabitants. Castro had simply opened his jails and his mental hospitals and asylums, and allowed the dregs of his society to come ashore on the coast of southern Florida alongside the hordes of law-abiding humanity seeking a better way of life in the United States.

Simply housing them had become a huge problem, and one of

the solutions was to put them—and especially the most obviously troubled—in the prison in Atlanta. Because of Castro's vicious cynicism, we could not send them back, nor could we, on legal grounds, incarcerate them indefinitely. The cost of what we were already doing was a major burden to the taxpayers.

I had come to Atlanta to see for myself if the conditions—and some of the inmates—were as bad as I had been told they were, and indeed they were. The "detainees" had ripped fixtures out of the walls of their cells, destroyed their beds, and were potentially so dangerous, to themselves as well as to the prison guards and the regular prison population, that they were not allowed to exercise as a group.

My sole consolation was the immediate realization that no other immigration problem I might have to face could be as bad as this one.

❖　　❖　　❖

I welcomed the challenge of chairing the Task Force on Immigration and Refugee Policy. The United States is a nation of immigrants, and we want to preserve that proud heritage—witness the recent renovation of Ellis Island as an immigration museum. The 50 million men and women from other shores who have arrived since colonial times have enriched this country in every way—socially, politically, culturally, and economically.

Today, however, we are a nation swiftly approaching 250 million in number, and in just the past few decades or so we have lost control of our borders. As a result, we risk the economic well-being and the faith in our laws on which the very welfare of the country depends.

Today there are between 3 and 6 million persons living illegally in the United States, a number that is probably increasing by 500,000 each year. The existence of this hidden fugitive class is unfair to our citizens, who must compete with the illegal aliens for jobs, and whose schools, hospitals, and other social services are thereby burdened. The situation is inhumane for the aliens themselves, too, as their constant fear of deportation makes them easy to exploit.

The problem, however, is hardly new. For years we have pursued unrealistic and failed immigration policies. Finally, the people of the United States were insisting, justifiably, that something be done. One poll showed 91 percent of the respondents wanted "an all-out effort" to stop illegal immigration.

Congress had recognized the problem for a long time, but had done little about it. During the Carter administration, a commission on immigration and refugee policy was appointed to grapple with the complex human problems involved. Although this very distinguished commission—headed by Father Theodore Hesburgh, then the president of Notre Dame—did produce a comprehensive report, the matter seemed to end there. Indeed, it is not unreasonable to conclude that Congress created the commission rather than dealing with the problem itself at that time.

We were determined that our task force would not suffer the same fate.

Made up of the cabinet departments involved—State, Justice, Commerce, Defense, Labor, Treasury, Transportation, and OMB—our task force reported to the president in July 1981. As a result, the administration announced a comprehensive program of administrative actions and legislative reforms designed to restore control over the nation's immigration policies. This program was the result of almost four months of intense work by the task force—consultations with concerned parties in the Congress, with affected states and localities, and with the public.

Parts of this program could be initiated by the administration, but the principal goals had to be accomplished through new legislation.

We also sought and obtained substantial budget increases in the law-enforcement resources of the Immigration and Naturalization Service—most of which Congress appropriated. These funds provided for

- More border patrol personnel
- Helicopters and other needed equipment

- Expanded efforts against alien smugglers, the despicable "coyotes"
- More efficient processing of alien records

We also sought and received additional funding to step up the Department of Labor's fight against sweatshop conditions that victimize illegal aliens as well as other workers.

We took firm but fair steps to curb illegal immigration by sea from the Caribbean. As mentioned above, the 1980 Mariel boatlift brought 125,000 Cubans to the beaches of South Florida. Most of them were seeking a better life, but also coming aboard were criminals and mentally ill people expelled from Cuban prisons and asylums by a hostile and cynical dictator. The effects on some U.S. communities had been devastating. The United States must never again permit its immigration policy to be set in Havana—or any other foreign capital.

The criminals and mentally ill who came to this country courtesy of Fidel Castro in the Mariel boatlift created major problems for U.S. authorities. They have cost the U.S. taxpayers over $30 million a year just to house. Most were kept at the federal prison facility in Atlanta, and it required a continuous effort by the Department of Justice to keep them there.

An equally continuous program to release them was conducted by a group of immigration lawyers. They were aided by a federal judge who, in my opinion, was indifferent to society's concerns. This judge—in order to impose his own system of values—determined to invade the province of the executive branch and in effect perform the functions of the INS. He was finally reined in by the United States Court of Appeals, thereby preventing even more people from being released to prey upon the public.

The dangerous residue of the Mariel boatlift could not be released to the public; but because of Castro's policy, they could not be returned to Cuba. Nor was permanent incarceration the answer. Meanwhile, the cost to the taxpayers was staggering.

How to send these sick and dangerous people back to Cuba was given in-depth consideration by the various agencies involved. The National Security Council, the Joint Chiefs of Staff, and even the president all wrestled with the problem.

Various proposals were advanced: take them to Guantanamo (the United States naval base) and release them on Cuban soil; put them on board a ship and sail it toward Cuba, or release them in rubber boats at an appropriate distance from the island, and so forth. For various reasons, particularly humanitarian (to others as well as to themselves), all these proposals were rejected.

Furthermore, attempting to accomplish any of this in secret was highly improbable. Among other things, to move such large numbers of violence-prone individuals forcibly would create major logistical problems—and in the process there would undoubtedly be some lawyers who would try to prevent it by seeking an injunction. Our experience with some judges had been such that we knew there would be, at a minimum, a prohibitive delay.

In 1984, a committee consisting of representatives of the DOJ, the State Department, and others did succeed in negotiating an agreement with the Cuban government under which a small number would be returned to Cuba each month. The quid pro quo was the reestablishment of the processing of visas in Havana for those who wanted to come to the United States. Shortly after this agreement was reached, Radio Martí (a Florida-based effort to reach Cubans by radio, much like the Voice of America) was put into operation by the U.S. Information Agency. In protest, the Cubans canceled the agreement, after only some two hundred of these people had been repatriated.

❖   ❖   ❖

Pressure to migrate to the United States from the Caribbean basin is not limited to Cuba. Political instability and poverty throughout this critical region drive illegal immigration, and these pressures could increase in coming decades. Increasing numbers of illegal immigrants have arrived by land and sea, from all the Central American countries.

Through the president's Caribbean Basin Initiative, the effort has been made to work with the countries of this hemisphere to address the root causes of immigration—economic underdevelopment and the poverty and instability it breeds. We could no longer afford to ignore the fact that illegal migration is an international problem and requires international solutions.

The plight of the Haitians was particularly tragic. In their homeland many faced poverty and hunger. Economic opportunity in the United States seems to them a concrete hope for a better life. Obviously we cannot open our doors to all the poor people of Haiti, any more than we can accept all the poor in the rest of the world. No nation, however great or prosperous, can take *all* who would come.

The fact of life has been a part of our laws since 1921, when numerical limits on immigration were first set. Realistic limits are as much or more necessary today, in fairness to our own citizens.

Any line, no matter where it is drawn, will seem harsh to those denied the opportunity to come here, but lines must be drawn. As presently drawn by our laws, the lines are rational and fair. Each country has an equal share in legal immigration and each person must wait his or her turn. Any who come in violation of these simple and just rules will be sent home, unless they have a well-founded fear of persecution based on political beliefs, race, or religion.

To enforce these laws fairly and firmly, the administration restored the policy of detaining undocumented aliens as they arrived. The detention of excludable aliens, with limited exceptions, is mandated by our immigration statutes. That policy was applied evenhandedly to undocumented aliens regardless of nationality or race.

The problem of where to locate detention centers for the Mariel boat people was extremely difficult. No one wanted one in his own backyard, and the reaction of politicians to proposed sites in their areas was strong. The Republican governor of Arkansas had even made a campaign promise that he would see that the Mariel Cubans who were detained at a military base in that state would be moved elsewhere, and when elected he was determined to accomplish that result.

As it turned out, only two areas welcomed such a facility. One was in Oklahoma, and the other in Louisiana, both in areas of high unemployment with a great need for jobs. The Louisiana site,

Oakdale, selected in February 1983, was the scene a few years later of riots by the detainees, principally the Cubans again.

We also took firm action against the seaborne smugglers who traffic in Haitians. The program of interdicting boats smuggling illegal aliens from Haiti was intended to stem the then-large illegal traffic in human lives, and to avoid the often tragic consequences of permitting these perilous voyages to continue unabated.

Together, the interdiction program and the policy of detention reduced the opportunities for preying on undocumented arrivals to less than ⅟₂₅th of what they were in 1981.

❖   ❖   ❖

Our administrative initiatives represented a new and important beginning. Equally important were legislative reforms. Congress very nearly enacted the Simpson-Mazzoli Immigration Reform and Control Bill in 1984. In the 97th Congress the bill had passed the Senate by a vote of seventy-six to eighteen; in the 99th by eighty to nineteen. As always the problem was in the House. The 99th Congress finally did pass the legislation in 1985. Embodying proposals submitted to Congress (over my signature) in October 1981, the bill produced the most thorough reform of our immigration laws in more than thirty years.

The core of any rational and comprehensive reform of our immigration laws must have four elements:

■ Imposition of sanctions on those who knowingly hire illegal aliens, with safeguards to prevent discrimination against Americans

■ Reform and speeding-up of our procedures to return home those who come here illegally

■ Realistic dealing with illegal aliens who are now here by granting many of them a legal status

■ Reform of our procedures to admit foreign workers for temporary employment where there are not U.S. citizens to fill needed jobs.

Of these, the most important is the first. The immigration problem at bottom requires an end to illegal immigration. Since illegal aliens come here to work, it must be made unlawful for them to do so, and for employers to hire them. Otherwise, illegal immigration will not be stopped or even slowed. The bill is now in the process of being implemented.

The nation owes a debt of gratitude to Senator Alan Simpson in particular and Congressmen Ron Mazzoli and Dan Lungren for the persistence and hard work required to bring this legislation to passage. It would never have happened without them. This was legislation in the long-term public interest but which cut against a host of short-term special interests. There was no political benefit, only travail for the sponsors. The immigration bill had passed the Senate on three occasions by overwhelming majorities. It was finally passed in the House despite, and not because of, the leadership there. Indeed, the handling of this important legislation—the delays and lack of leadership particularly of the Speaker and the chairman of the House Judiciary Committee—was very disappointing.

Shortly after I had been given the assignment to develop an administration immigration reform program, President Jose Lopez Portillo of Mexico visited Washington. It was the first visit of a foreign head of state in the new administration. The president and the interested cabinet officials spent the weekend at Camp David, where several meetings were held.

At one of those meetings I outlined the basic elements of our program for immigration reform. I had expected some opposition and a lively discussion. On the contrary, the Mexican officials had very little to say, neither agreeing nor disagreeing. Indeed, it was not easy to determine which of the officials had the responsibility for this area. It was probably the minister who would be the equivalent of our secretary of labor.

The official position of the Mexican government was that our immigration policies were an internal U.S. matter in which the Mexican government should not interfere. It was obvious that

Mexico had a great interest in this subject, both economically and politically, but it did not show during our several meetings.

This attitude continued during my visit to Mexico in 1983. That trip dealt with drugs and drug trafficking, but I was prepared to discuss immigration should the occasion warrant. But in my meetings with then-President de la Madrid, Secretary of Foreign Affairs Sepulveda, and other officials, not a single word was mentioned on this subject.

❖   ❖   ❖

At the state dinner in President Portillo's honor at the White House, the two presidents exchanged very friendly toasts and clearly "hit it off." As I listened to President Portillo deliver his remarks I had to recall attending the second state dinner held outside the White House. It was in honor of the then-Mexican president, Gustave Diaz Ordaz, who was just completing his term as president (1964–1970). The dinner was held at the Hotel del Coronado in San Diego, California, on September 3, 1970, and hosted by President Nixon.

President Nixon had always enjoyed doing things in surprising ways and holding a state dinner elsewhere fit that pattern. All the trappings were there, including the receiving line and the Marine Band.

At the conclusion of dinner it had been planned that each of the principal dignitaries present—President Nixon, former President Lyndon Johnson, and then-Governor of California Reagan—would bring greetings to the Mexican president and he would respond in the usual fashion. The first three did exactly that. (There, for the first time, President Johnson told the story about his response to what he was going to do now that he had retired: "First, I am going down to my ranch in Texas, then I am going to sit on my rocking chair on the front porch. And a couple of years later, I will start rocking." That was the hit of the evening.)

Then the Mexican president commenced his response. It turned out to be a major policy address and not one particularly friendly to the United States. To those of us there that night, even more important was the fact that it consumed an hour and a half in Spanish *plus* an hour and a half in translation. That was three hours of speech! Both Governor Reagan and I had to be in Sacramento for a 7:00 A.M. breakfast the next morning, where he was to speak to what is called the Sacramento Host Breakfast, prior to delivering the traditional state of the state address. To compound matters, when we returned to the San Diego airport all take-offs had been halted for security reasons until the Mexican president's plane took off—another hour!

Senator Barry Goldwater, who sat at our table at the dinner, is not known as a patient man. He also has an extensive vocabulary and had had a few martinis. His description of his view of things as that speech droned on would have elected him president if his only constituency were those who attended the dinner that night.

❖   ❖   ❖

My other most memorable example of reform during my time as attorney general of the United States is the Comprehensive Crime Control Act of 1984.

A landmark measure that realigned the historical balance between good and evil, so to speak, the enactment of this law was the product of four years of hard, hard work. Originally, we had wanted to enact a total revision of the federal criminal code in order to make out of this mish-mash of laws a much-needed, consistent, uniform, and simplified code. That turned out to be too ambitious a task, for a variety of reasons. Many of the proposed changes were procedural, but many were changes of substance, and the result was thousands of pages long. The total package of reforms and recodification was just too much to push through the legislative process. We decided to concentrate on the most substantive and badly needed reforms.

The product was a bill that incorporated many of the recommendations of our Task Force on Violent Crime. It consisted of over fifty critically needed changes in the federal law, including the reform of the bail law to allow the courts to consider for the first time the danger to the community posed by a suspect free on bail, the tightening of the criteria for post-conviction release, increasing the penalties for bail-jumping, the abolition of parole and establishment of a system for uniform punishments, the strengthening of the rules of forfeiture requiring that criminals give up the profits of illegal enterprises, the reform of the insanity defense, and so on.

To ensure passage by the Senate, we had agreed to exclude four of the most controversial issues: the death penalty, the Fourth Amendment exclusionary rule, the reform of habeas corpus procedures, and the insanity defense. In addition, as mentioned earlier, the agreement included the commitment of Senators Biden and Kennedy that if we removed these items from the bill they would support Senate floor votes on these four items as individual bills, *and* they would oppose any effort to avoid a vote. They kept their end of the bargain, and eventually the insanity defense was put back into the comprehensive bill. These were to be processed as separate legislative matters. Part of this agreement with the Democratic members of the Senate Judiciary Committee was that when each of the excluded items was introduced they would oppose any filibuster when it reached the Senate floor. Each then did pass the Senate as individual bills. Nothing more was heard when they reached the House, however.

The act as thus agreed upon passed the Senate by a nearly unanimous vote, on two separate occasions (the only dissent each time was from Republican senator Mathias of Maryland). The four principal players were Senators Thurmond, Laxalt, Biden, and Kennedy.

On occasion the Democrats on the House Judiciary Committee would produce a bill that contained changes in the criminal law that they could label "crime control," and advertise as evidence of their concern and commitment to the issue. In substance these bills never contained language that addressed major issues.

In 1982 the House did pass a small bill dealing with supervision of federal prisoners in release status. This House legislation was then sent to the Senate. The Senate considered and passed the much larger and more significant bill with one amendment that we had strongly opposed. This amendment would have established an "Office of Director of National and International Drug Operations and Policy"—Senator Biden's "drug czar." It was an effort to create an unneeded new bureaucracy under the guise of purporting to bring together under a single entity all the various agencies of government that dealt with drug enforcement. The reason this was a redundancy was that there already was such an entity, the president.

Senators were as impatient with the House's inaction on meaningful anticrime legislation as we were, and once the Senate passed its bill, Thurmond moved to attach the entire Senate package to the little bill the House had passed. He also requested a Senate conference to reconcile the differences in the versions passed by the two bodies. This was intended to force the House to deal with the real anticrime legislation.

Chairman Rodino and the House leadership were so strongly opposed to treating this important issue that, at Rodino's request, they stripped all the Senate's crime legislation (on the supervision of federal prisoners) from the House bill and sent it back to the Senate hoping that since the session was almost over that would be the end of it. The Senate was not so easily swayed. It again attached the substantive bill to the House's proposal, and send it back with a request for a conference. This move forced a conference.

With adjournment looming, Rodino argued that the House did not have sufficient time to consider the major changes we had proposed and the Senate had passed. Promising consideration of these issues in the next session, he used the leverage of adjournment to get the conference to produce what came to be called the "mini crime bill." It contained some Justice assistance programs, a provision making product tampering a federal crime, a career criminal provision, as well as a few other items *and* the drug czar proposal (which the House had learned about in conference).

This last provision, included despite knowledge of the White House's strong opposition, was a political move by House Democrats. If the president signed the bill, they could say they had passed a crime bill; if he vetoed the bill because it contained the drug czar provision, that would give the Democrats the basis for charging the administration with vetoing a "crime control" bill.

And that's just what happened—the mini-crime bill was sent to the president, he did veto it, and those charges were made.

During the time these charges were being hurled about, Congressman Bill Hughes suddenly became a great advocate of the drug czar idea. In fact, he began to act as if it were his own idea. But clearly, from the beginning it had been a Senate, not a House, idea.

This House Judiciary Committee maneuver of reporting legislation that "appeared" to be substantive crime legislation continued into the next session. The most active practitioner of this strategy was Bill Hughes. In 1984, when pressure from the administration and the Senate began to build for the House to do something before the election, on more than one occasion Hughes took the name of one of the titles in our bill and used it in labeling a bill that he would introduce that contained little, if any, of the substantive provisions of our proposal. He would get his bill reported out of his subcommittee to get his version reported to the House floor.

All these maneuvers were intended to show movement by Hughes and his subcommittee, and give Democrats legislation to vote for while not allowing the House to work its will on meaningful reform of the federal criminal justice system. There never was any doubt that if our crime bill could reach the floor of the House it would pass overwhelmingly. Rodino and the House leadership knew that, and that is why they kept it bottled up in committee.

Our task therefore was to somehow get it to the floor.

During my time in D.C., Congress never passed, as it should have, a single appropriation bill for the Justice Department. Instead, it utilized blunderbuss "continuing resolutions" to provide funding for government operations. A continuing resolution is a "must-pass" piece of legislation, and therefore the temptation is to attach all kinds of special interest amendments to the bill. The administration, on the other hand, knowing that, absent extraordinary circumstances, the president must sign such legislation, wants a "clean bill," one without such amendments. Nevertheless, it occurred to some of us that we might consider attaching the Comprehensive Crime Control Act of 1984 to the continuing resolution then being considered by the House, and in this manner get it to the House floor.

To develop this possibility, Bob McConnell, my assistant attorney general for legislative affairs, set up a meeting on September 20, 1984, with certain members of the Republican leadership and House Judiciary Committee. Among them were Henry Hyde (Illinois), Dan Lungren (California), Bill McCollum (Florida), Trent Lott (Mississippi), and Hamilton Fish (New York), in whose office the meeting was held. Bob Michel, the House minority leader, could not attend, and sent in his place Bill Pitts, the very able Republican House parliamentarian. Representing the department in addition to myself and Bob McConnell was Associate Attorney General Lowell Jensen.

Ham Fish chaired the meeting, at which I strongly urged that the crime bill be added to the continuing resolution. I had the support of Hyde, McCollum, and especially Lungren. But Pitts said the White House had told Michel it wanted the bill "clean," with no additions allowed. That got to me, so I reached for the phone, saying I would be happy to call the president himself on a matter of this grave importance.

No, no, they all said, and soon we were discussing strategy.

When the continuing resolution came up for a vote, Lungren moved to add the crime bill, and was voted down. That was procedural, however, and not an up-or-down vote on the crime bill itself. Bill Pitts then came up with the idea of what to do next. After an appropriations bill has been considered on the House floor there are certain sacrosanct traditions. One is that the chairman of the committee that has managed the bill acknowledges the diligence and hard work of those involved, and then recognizes the ranking majority member. At that stage, the bill's having been voted out of committee to the full House for final vote, it is the practice that neither the committee chairman nor the minority member acknowledge anybody else, except possibly another member of the Appropriations Committee who can praise the chairman for great diplomacy in managing the bill.

Bob Michel, who was very familiar with this practice (before becoming the minority leader he had been a member of the Appropriations Committee), met with Silvio Conte from Massachusetts, the ranking Republican on that committee, and made an extraordinary request. He asked that Conte recognize Dan Lungren of California, and Conte agreed to do so.

When he did, everyone knew what was about to happen, and terror struck some Democratic hearts. Speaker O'Neill, getting wind of what was transpiring, came charging in from the cloakroom, but by then Lungren offered the entire Comprehensive Crime Control Bill as an amendment to the continuing resolution. That action forced an up-or-down vote on the substance of the crime bill (not, as before, just on the procedural question of whether he *could* offer it).

The Democrats were now confronted with whether to vote for or against a major strengthening of the federal criminal law.

At that point, one speaker is allowed on each side. Dan Lungren spoke for the bill, and William Hughes of New Jersey spoke against it (the only one who did). The bill passed overwhelmingly, as we knew it would if we could ever get it to the floor.

The matter was far from over, however. Appropriation bills originate in the House and then go to the Senate. At an all-night session in the Senate, Congressman Hughes sat on the Senate floor with Senator Mathias, the only senator to oppose the bill, doing everything possible to defeat or stall or (hopefully) to separate the crime bill from the continuing resolution, which, with the crime bill attached, passed the Senate unanimously—except for Mathias.

The bill then went to the Senate-House Conference Committee. Normally, the conference committee for an appropriations bill consists only of Appropriations Committee members (though when there are significant unrelated attachments to the appropriation bill, members of other committees may be permitted to attend). In this case, with the conference scheduled from 7:00 to 8:00 P.M., the senators on the Judiciary Committee (which certainly had an interest in the crime bill attachment to *this* continuing resolution) had been advised in the afternoon that only Senate Appropriations Committee members would be allowed to attend. Relying on this representation, the Senate Judiciary Committee members therefore went their separate ways.

Later, signals changed and the Appropriations Committee conferees told the available Judiciary Committee members to join them. Senator Warren Rudman, who was to chair this portion of the conference—the one considering the crime bill—told Thurmond, Rodino, and Hughes to settle their differences in two hours, and he left.

Thurmond and his chief of staff (Vinton Lide) came out of the room and told Bob McConnell what had been said. Rodino and Hughes were busily trying to get allies to the conference room. Biden was at home in Delaware and Kennedy was away—and both were furious at the change in signals.

Thurmond needed help. The best and brightest was Lungren, but he was also at home.

McConnell called Dan Lungren right away. Lungren was not just "at home," but had a priest there saying a private mass for the Lungrens and a couple of their very close friends. McConnell (who had been a Catholic high school classmate of Lungren's) emphasized the critical nature of the situation on the Hill, and Lungren came back to the Capitol immediately—and saved the day.

Apparently, Rodino and Hughes had been telling the conference things that had gone on in the House in connection with adding the crime bill to the continuing resolution, things that may or may not have been accurate. They did everything they could do, to the bitter end, to defeat the bill. They did not succeed. The bill emerged unscathed from the conference, and with the president's signature it became law.

Postscript.   The very next day, Congressman Hughes attempted to take full credit for the passage of the crime bill—as though he had drafted it and shepherded it through Congress! And he tried this despite the fact that he—more than anyone except Rodino—had done his best to defeat it at every stage.

Unfortunately, the press, including Stuart Taylor, Jr., of the *New York Times*, who covered the department, bought his story! Taylor, in an action (or *in*action) so typical of the media, even when confronted (by Bob McConnell) with overwhelming evidence to the contrary, refused to relent.

Hughes's role here is hard to diagnose. Generally, he is a good legislator. But he is known, even among his Democratic colleagues, as one who, if chairing a committee or subcommittee, will take a good bill drafted by someone else, and then, instead of submitting the bill *by* the original sponsor with amendments, will resubmit it under his own name.

I am still puzzled by the strength of Hughes's opposition. It must have been political—he didn't want the Republicans to get credit for such an extensive (and much-needed) change in the criminal law.

What a shame.

13

THE POWER-HUNGRY CONGRESS

A LTHOUGH THERE IS MUCH TO CRITICIZE ABOUT THE activities and conduct of various members of Congress, as always the good outweighs the bad. Most congressmen and senators are dedicated individuals, industrious and hardworking, both for their constituents and in the public interest. Because of our more common legislative interest, during my time as attorney general I worked more closely with Republicans than I did with Democrats, although except for ideology the characteristics and the disparities existed on both sides of the aisle.

The closest working relationship that an attorney general will have with Congress is with the chairman of the Senate Committee on the Judiciary. For one thing, the attorney general proposes to the president the appointment of more presidential nominees requiring Senate confirmation than any other cabinet member (excluding military commissions)—all federal judges, U.S. Attorneys, U.S. marshals, DOJ officials. Second, Judiciary is the Senate committee whose jurisdiction coexists with that of DOJ; and, third, a great deal of the legislation in which DOJ is interested is within the orbit of that committee. Therefore the relationship is vital to getting things done.

I could not have been more fortunate than to have had Strom Thurmond in this position. He was patient, understanding, sympathetic, helpful—and he knew the political process. We worked extremely well together. He was friendly, if intense, articulate but sometimes preachy, and on occasion even somewhat pious. Before the committee, his prefatory remarks were usually so extensive that the person being interrogated did not have to spend much time answering questions—not, I felt, an unhappy result. But he was affable and cooperative, and I think we developed a good relationship with him, which was primarily the work of Ed Schmults.

Happily, Senator Kennedy was usually busy elsewhere. Now and then he would make an appearance and deliver endless pronouncements—often far removed from the facts—whenever he had a constituency to please. My principal encounter with him had to do with the extension of the Voting Rights Act. This was fairly early in my tenure, but it confirmed how irrelevant the facts or merits of an issue can be if the subject matter is controversial enough.

Congressman Dan Lungren, in my opinion, was one of the best and most effective of all the members of the House. He knew the political process, how to get things done, and was a genuine leader for the Republicans. I worked with him on a variety of matters, but in particular on what became the Comprehensive Crime Control Act of 1984 and immigration reform. As mentioned earlier, he played a leading role in the latter, and a crucial role in the former.

Not infrequently, a legislator's ties with his institution override his ties with the administration, party, and even his ideological loyalties—to say nothing of his common sense. Senator Charles Grassley, to choose an example not quite at random, was one of the four new senators we Republicans had worked so hard to elect in 1980. He was the chairman of the Senate Subcommittee on Administrative Practices and Procedures.

Grassley, through his subcommittee, and Senator William Proxmire, the Wisconsin Democrat and co-chairman of a Subcommittee of the Joint Economic Committee, had investigated the Department of Justice's decision not to prosecute certain shipbuilding companies for overcharging the government. They requested a ream of documents, which were given to them, except for sensitive ones that were part of an open DOJ investigation including grand jury materials. Our people had refused to supply such documents, and I supported their decision.

Words were exchanged, letters were exchanged, but we refused to comply. Later in 1984, after the usual public charges, including "cover-up," Senator Grassley wanted to hold a hearing and require me to testify and to bring the documents he wanted. He could not get permission from Senator Strom Thurmond, the chairman of the full committee, for a hearing room in which the subcommittee could meet. He then teamed with Senator Proxmire to hold a joint hearing of their respective subcommittees in a room arranged for by Proxmire. They requested my attendance—and the documents. Steve Trott, assistant attorney general for the Criminal Division, who had overall supervision of the case in question, was the department's designated witness.

Neither Grassley nor Proxmire was pleased that I did not attend the hearing and that our witness was someone who knew a great deal about the issues they claimed to want to address. No other member of either subcommittee attended the hearing. After a lively exchange between the senators and Steve, a lifelong prosecutor of exceptional ability and now a judge on the United States Court of Appeals for the Ninth Circuit, Grassley announced that his subcommittee would, then and there, consider a resolution holding the attorney general in contempt of Congress for not appearing and providing them with the requested documents. Grassley purported to have the proxies of other subcommittee members.

It was a subcommittee action that, if valid, had to be agreed to by the full Committee on the Judiciary before it could be presented to the entire Senate. Chairman Thurmond had never authorized the subcommittee, and would not schedule Grassley's resolution for consideration by the full committee.

It was an invalid effort that I ignored, but the senator got his publicity. I refused to comply and the matter died quietly. There was a certain irony, however, in the situation: A Republican senator had taken a very public action against a Republican attorney general just shortly before the national election to reelect the president whose first election effort had originally swept that same Republican senator into national office.

❖   ❖   ❖

Incredible as it may seem, Congress, which has 535 members and a remarkably skimpy record of dealing with the major issues of the day, has a total staff of over 31,000, which is vastly larger than that of any other democracy in the world (for example, the British House of Commons, which has 650 members, employs about 1,000 staff members).

During the past fifteen years, the staff of the U.S. Congress has *tripled* in size, yet anarchy, particularly in the House, has made Congress so unproductive that, while we were there, it not only failed to deal with the budget and trade crises, but it also passed very few appropriations bills during all the Reagan years. As one man with fifteen years of Hill experience said, "These . . . staffers have become agents of conflict and impasse." There is no way their bosses can know what they are up to, nor can a congressman comprehend the total product of their effort. Congress's attitude seems to be that the way to handle a problem is throw more staffers at it, much like the New Deal philosophy of solving a national problem by throwing more money at it.

There are now 150 subcommittees, each one of which has to create the façade of being engaged in meaningful work. Of course this evil is magnified by the fact that more and more executive branch officials come before these committees—in a long, duplicative effort of no discernible social or economic value. However, if an appearance can attract a little media attention, then that becomes a goal in itself.

❖   ❖   ❖

During my years as attorney general three very important legislative matters of particular concern to us required urgent attention. The Senate had acted on all three by large majorities. None was a partisan issue, but each required action in the public interest. Each had been stalled in the House Judiciary Committee, and every effort to get the committee to act had failed. The three matters were reform of the federal criminal law, immigration reform, and the need to reestablish stability in the nation's bankruptcy system as a result of the June 1982 Supreme Court decision that declared the current system unconstitutional.

For some time, my assistant attorney general for legislative affairs, Bob McConnell, had been urging me to meet with the Speaker and stress the public-interest significance of these matters, their nonpartisan nature (as demonstrated by the Senate's action), and the high priority placed on them by the administration—not to mention the need to jar them loose from the Judiciary Committee.

Because I suspected that Speaker O'Neill was more likely part of the problem than the solution, I had a dim view of my chances of success in such a meeting, but I agreed to see him (on the basis that I had nothing to lose and everything to gain). McConnell made the arrangements, and we met in the Speaker's office one day near the end of September 1983.

Sitting in a room with McConnell, O'Neill, and O'Donnell (Kirk O'Donnell, the Speaker's chief of staff), I felt like the odd man out. Unfortunately, this did not turn out to be as cheery an affair as most gatherings where Irishmen predominate.

The Speaker was cordial enough, but it was immediately obvious that he was not interested in discussing the merits of these issues.

Bob had suggested I open the meeting by telling an O'Neill story, which I did. The story involved his first run for Congress. O'Neill had campaigned all over the district, and when the election was over, the woman who lived right next door to him mentioned she had not voted for him. A surprised O'Neill asked why not, to which the woman replied, "Because you never *asked* me to." I told the Speaker that I did not want him to be able to say that I had never asked him to act on these three pressing matters we considered high-priority items.

Then we exchanged pleasantries regarding our respective Boston and New England ties. At that point I thought we were ready for business.

I brought up the crime legislation first, then the bankruptcy situation, and, finally, immigration reform. In reference to immigration reform, I noted that it was hard to enact because, although it clearly was in the long-term public interest, it cut across so many short-term special interests. Then I referred to the polls, which showed overwhelming support for the immigration reform.

To my amazement, at just that point O'Neill cut me short. He said, "I don't deal in polls or public interest here. I deal in *politics.*"

I wasn't quite certain I understood him, so I began again. But he interrupted me again.

"Mr. Attorney General," said the Speaker, "you don't follow me. I deal with votes on the House floor—pure politics—not these other matters. Floor politics is all I do here."

Then, for the first time to my knowledge in more than five years of work toward immigration reform (an effort that started with the Carter-appointed commission), naked partisanship was injected into the issue. O'Neill stated that the Reagan administration wanted Congress to pass an immigration reform bill so the president could veto it, thereby ingratiating himself with Hispanic voters just in time for the 1984 election!

Not only was this astounding statement absolutely false, but it revealed a startling lack of information on the subject, because all the polls showed that Hispanics *supported* reform. O'Neill's comment was the first time I had ever heard this charge.

You can guess what happened as a result of that meeting—absolutely nothing! Afterward, I was sorry I had requested it (or let myself be talked into requesting it) and felt depressed and actually a little unclean. I am not naive as far as government process is concerned, but here was the all-powerful leader of the U.S. House of Representatives *disinterested* in discussing, much less acting on, three important nonpartisan issues that were clearly in the public interest and that the U.S. Senate had strongly supported.

Instead of statesmanship and leadership we got political posturing and outrageous charges.

Eventually, all three measures were enacted into law, but not because of any help from Tip O'Neill.

The crime reform bill passed (as described earlier) despite the Speaker's opposition, and immigration reform got to the fifty-yard line in 1983, to the five in 1984, and finally made it into the end zone in 1986. As for the bankruptcy reform bill, it too was finally made law for the simple reason that the system was collapsing without it.

As I left that meeting with the Speaker, I thought of how disillusioned the man on the street would be if he could have seen how some of the nation's leaders deal with the public's problems.

O'Neill's attitude was not simply a matter of disinterest; the administration had been too persistent for that. It had to be political but, if so, it seemed bad politics to me.

On the crime reform program it had to be the desire to prevent a so-called law and order administration from succeeding in enacting strong crime legislation. The bankruptcy reform program involved the appointment of judges, and the Democratic leadership did not want to give the administration more appointees than it had to. (It is also true that there was a bona fide issue as to whether the judges should be "Article III" judges—appointed for life with no pay reduction ever—or "Article I" judges, not so protected. At issue also was the *number* of judges, in either case.) With respect to immigration reform, the motive must have been his misreading of the politics of the situation, or an astounding degree of "un-information." Another strong possibility was O'Neill's deference to certain very vocal special interest organizations that were opposed to any changes in the immigration laws. Furthermore, O'Neill had asserted that the only people who were in favor of immigration reform were the editorial writers, despite overwhelming poll (and other) information to the contrary.

The Speaker announced that he could find "no constituency" for reform. This despite the fact that everyone from AFL-CIO head Lane Kirkland to former Presidents Ford and Carter to a cross-section of the community were in favor of it. I found it incredible that a politician considered to be so "savvy" could be so far removed from the reality of public sentiment. I believe this was the case because he was so influenced by the relatively few but nonetheless noisy special interest groups that he could not see the forest for the trees.

Somehow, some way, a message seeped through: In October 1986, O'Neill let the immigration reform bill get to the floor of the House where it was, finally, enacted into law.

❖   ❖   ❖

I was hardly the only one appalled by O'Neill's performance. Nor did the criticism come down along strictly party or ideological lines. Carl Rowan, the columnist, wrote:

> I don't understand why the press has made so little of House Speaker O'Neill's imperious, blatantly political decision to deny Congress an opportunity to deal with the important issue of immigration reform.
>
> On the flimsy ground that President Reagan intended a "double-cross"—faking support of the Simpson-Mazzoli bill to get Democrats to pass it, and then vetoing it to win Hispanic votes—O'Neill played "pre-emptive" politics. His ploy is to keep Hispanic voters loyal to Democrats by refusing to let the immigration bill go to the House floor.
>
> This is a blunder that could cost the Democrats far more votes than can ever be delivered by the Hispanic politicians O'Neill was trying to placate.

And Kentucky Democratic congressman Romano Mazzoli, obviously a strong supporter of the bill that bore his name, said:

> I came back to Washington to the smoking ruins of three years of labor. The Speaker's abrupt, unnecessary, thoroughly unfounded action deprives the Congress and the country of the right to deal with an issue that has plagued us for years. This is sad.

❖   ❖   ❖

One of the most significant cases—some would say *the* most significant case—decided by the United States Supreme Court during my tenure was *INS vs. Chada*. That case invalidated the legislative veto. Pursuant to this device Congress would pass a law in general terms with the provision that if it disagreed with the manner in which it was enforced by the executive branch or an independent agency, that action could be invalidated—vetoed by a joint resolution of both houses, or one house, or action by a committee, or even a subcommittee. It in effect permitted Congress to avoid its responsibility, pass general legislation and then veto actions taken to enforce it that it did not like. It would do so without following the constitutional mandate that requires that for Congress to act, both houses must concur, and its enactments must be presented to the president for signature or veto.

Republicans as well as many Democrats over the years had generally been in favor of the legislative veto because they believed that it provided a check against excessive government regulation. Indeed, the 1980 Republican platform contained a provision supporting the veto, and the president in at least one campaign speech had also endorsed the device. In addition, OMB director Stockman had backed the veto in his confirmation hearing and several prominent Republican senators including Laxalt, Schmitt, and Grassley were advocating generic veto bills. Many other congressmen were strong advocates of this practice.

Under the Immigration and Nationality Act the AG had been given authority to suspend the deportation of aliens for specified reasons. After granting a suspension of deportation the AG was required to notify Congress of the decision. Under the legislation, either house might then veto the suspension during the session in which the report was received or during the following session. A veto meant the alien was subject to deportation. On December 14, 1975, the House included Jagdish Chada's name on a list of those whose suspension was vetoed. Chada, an East Indian, had been living and working in California and did not wish to be deported.

In subsequent litigation in the federal courts the constitutionality of this action—and of the legislative veto—was squarely presented. A decision of the United States Court of Appeals for the Ninth Circuit, written by Judge Anthony Kennedy, now a justice of the United States Supreme Court, found the legislative veto invalid. An appeal had been taken to the Supreme Court and the administration position was required by May 1, 1981.

Our Office of Legal Counsel, the premier legal group in government, was strongly of the view that the veto was an invasion of the president's prerogative under the Constitution. Larry Simms, who had long been in that office, Ted Olson, the assistant attorney general in charge of the office, and Ed Schmults all concurred. Upon reviewing the issue, I fully agreed.

But convincing the president, the vice president, and the White House staff to change such a long-held and publicly advocated position was not an enviable task. To advocate that position was a formidable undertaking. It would involve taking a position contrary to the campaign statements of the president and the strongly felt views of many senators and congressmen. If successful it would invalidate over 300 laws enacted during the past fifty years, including those dealing with war powers, consumer, health and environmental regulatory matters, arms sales, budget impoundments, and numerous others. Such a decision would nullify more legislative enactments than had been overturned by the Supreme Court in all its history!

Furthermore, it had always been the policy of the DOJ to defend acts of Congress. Not only did we preserve consistency in this way but we had our parochial interests in controlling such litigation. There were, however, two exceptions to this policy and this case fit into one of them—namely, when the legislation intruded upon the function of the executive branch. (The other was if the legal arguments in support of the act were patently frivolous—a rare case.)

A review in depth of this issue convinced me that we had no other course than to deal with the veto head on. I was also convinced from meetings at the White House that over the years the argument that this device should be supported as a means of keeping a check on government agencies had been accepted at face value without analysis. I therefore sent a decision memorandum to the president recommending that he take this position. I doubt if the president ever saw this memo, but it shocked the White House staff into recognizing that this was a major issue. Indeed, talk then surfaced concerning a compromise—because there was a recognition that presidential powers were adversely affected but also a desire to placate both congressional veto advocates and White House staffers who continued to believe that this device was a hedge against government regulation. On April 1, 1981, James C. Miller, director of the Office of Information and Regulatory Affairs in OMB, publicly stated that although the president opposed legislative vetoes over cabinet-level departments he would not oppose vetoes over independent agencies such as the Federal Communications Commission or the Federal Trade Commission. The matter was discussed at a cabinet meeting on April 20, 1981, at which I presented our position that the veto was invalid. Following that meeting we proceeded upon the basis that we had been authorized to take the position we desired before the Supreme Court.

This did not conclude the issue, however. We learned that a White House meeting scheduled for June 10 was to lay the groundwork for an announcement by the vice president that the administration position vis-à-vis Congress would be to support a veto for independent agencies. At that meeting I strongly pointed out that as a constitutional matter the issue could not be compromised. We had to meet it head on.

Furthermore, as a simple matter of politics it made no sense to support a device that transferred power from the executive branch to the legislature. I pointed out that the Republicans had controlled the presidency for one-half the time since 1952, but had controlled both houses of Congress only two years during that period. Why then sacrifice executive power for legislative power? That argument, in addition to those stressing clear separation of powers, made a dent, I believe. It did not, however, still the voices.

That necessitated a direct appeal to the president. I did not use that "chit" often, and thus when I did it worked. (In fact, I used it so sparingly that it worked every time.) This was an issue of great importance, and thus it was justified.

Justified, too, by the Supreme Court: In a seven to two decision, the Court found the veto to be an invalid device under the Constitution. It was one of the most significant cases decided by the Court in many years. "The encompassing nature of the ruling," wrote Justice Powell, "gives one pause." Probably no other recent decision of the Supreme Court had such an extensive and direct effect on existing statutes.

❖   ❖   ❖

If there was one area in which the White House was deficient during my years in office, it was in the protection of presidential power. Decisions there were made on the basis of the substance of individual issues. There was no effective concern or review of the impact that issue or the position taken with respect to it would have on presidential power. Nor was there any effort to identify governmental activities elsewhere that, if developed, would adversely affect the province of the executive. Nor, to be candid, was the bully pulpit used to provide leadership or defense of that vital institution.

The following is a list, and not even a complete one, of examples of the congressional appetite for involving itself in functions that are properly part of the executive branch: the so-called Ethics in Government Act; the Special Prosecutors Act; the Boland Amendments; the alleged oversight function; the legislative veto; the War Powers Resolution; the continuing demand for records and documents in open committees; the disregard for the principle of executive privilege; the creation of independent agencies; the many actual and attempted interferences with and restrictions on the president's appointment and removal powers; the attempts to remove prosecutorial discretion; the concurring reporting requirements; the attempts to restrict access; the hybrid and bipartisan commission requirements; the dispersal of litigating authority; the attempts to participate in executive decision-making in both domestic and foreign affairs; and the injection of the General Accounting Office, an agency of Congress, into the process of awarding contracts.

As stated elsewhere, Congress has nicely exempted itself from almost all regulatory legislation applicable to the executive—and everybody else. Just try to obtain a record or document from Congress that it does not want to give up. Just try to breach *its* equivalent of the executive privilege!

Indeed, a federal district court in Baltimore tried to do just that (by way of subpoena) at the very time that a congressional subcommittee was making outrageous demands for EPA documents, and was summarily and arrogantly rebuffed by the clerk of the House of Representatives.

The White House staff looked at these matters only as they had an impact on desired goals or undertakings. For example, the War Powers Resolution was dealt with only as to the degree to which it affected aid to the Nicaraguan Contras, or the Grenada invasion, or the Beirut situation. The White House never confronted that act for what it was—an unworkable effort by Congress to inject itself into the conduct of foreign policy. It never has worked, never will work, and is unconstitutional in part and probably in whole.

Similarly, in the dispute concerning the EPA documents, the president asserted executive privilege, but that is where White House involvement ended. The White House was glad to consider that a DOJ matter, and so we wrestled it to the ground. Not once, so far as I know, and despite our continuing efforts, did the White House consider this to be what it was, an invasion of presidential power.

❖　❖　❖

Departments and agencies throughout the executive branch were continually seeking increased law-enforcement authorities. There was no systematic and comprehensive process within the executive branch for considering such authorities at inception or coordinating them when granted. The case-by-case approach could result in a government of relatively independent and specialized "mini-police forces."

In a letter dated June 7, 1983, I urged the White House to devise a procedure that provided for coordination of this function while respecting the legitimate revisions of other executive branch agencies.

At the time, there were as many as one hundred federal organizations involved in some aspect of criminal law enforcement. There were eight current proposals (of which the Justice Department was aware) in various stages of consideration to grant additional law-enforcement authorities through legislation. These involved such authorities as the power to arrest, to carry firearms, to execute search warrants, to serve subpoenas, to administer oaths, and to pay informants, among others.

Many regulatory compliance offices have developed into national networks of field offices with investigators who consider themselves to be in the criminal investigation business. In addition, the number of security forces with protection responsibilities has also grown.

This increased expansion into law enforcement was a result of increased regulatory and investigative functions: for example, Commerce's Export Trading Act regulatory authority, EPA's toxic-waste responsibility, and even Agriculture's tick-investigation activities. In addition, the Inspector General Act of 1978 established a new set of actors who were involved in the full range of law-enforcement activities.

The increasing concern for security results in requests for numerous law-enforcement authorities, either through formal legislation or through deputization as U.S. marshals. The pattern was evident. Once an organization embarked upon its function, it often hired people with some type of law-enforcement background, and they began to seek additional law-enforcement powers. The department could only expect this trend to continue.

Such a state of affairs raised the following concerns:

- Increased likelihood of unexamined and uncoordinated law-enforcement activites in federal investigations

- Considerable variation in training, recruitment, and supervisory practices

- Lack of evaluation and oversight of non-DOJ law-enforcement programs and personnel

- Lack of appropriate information exchange

- Possible misuse of sensitive investigation techniques—undercover operations, for example—which may lead to congressional limitations of proper use of such techniques by the FBI and other Department of Justice investigators

- Increased risk of federal liability exposure

- Increased threat to civil liberties

- Diversion of limited federal law-enforcement funding to single-purpose agencies at the expense of general-purpose law enforcement

We proposed that an executive order be issued to the departments and agencies to direct that requests for additional law-enforcement activities be provided for consideration to DOJ before being submitted through the normal OMB legislative clearance process.

Nothing came of it.

In other less prominent matters, we had to do battle as best we could. For example, OMB unilaterally decided to support a provision in the Paperwork Reduction Act amendments of 1984 that would require that written deliberative exchanges between OMB and any rule-making agency generated in the regulatory review process be placed in the public record. Clearly, the deliberative process within the government must be preserved for candid and robust exchange of viewpoints, rather than stylized and ritualistic public posturing. The practical effect of doing otherwise constitutes a major erosion of presidential power.

So here once again we had to do battle not with the other branches but within our own branch as well.

So, too, with the Special Prosecutors Act, another blatant and (one continues to hope) unconstitutional effort to interfere in an important and basic executive function—taking care that the laws be executed. As stated elsewhere, it is bad legislation on the merits and an effort by Congress to invade executive terrain. But not once to my knowledge did the White House so view it or express opposition.

When it was amended for the worse and extended, as of January 1, 1988, the president signed it—over my strong opposition. His White House staff urged this course because of "image problems" stemming from pending special prosecutor cases, and the near certainty of an override. Neither was, in my opinion, sufficient basis to extend a bad law, and one that so significantly impinged on executive power. Harry Truman vetoed the Taft-Hartley Act in

1947 knowing it would be overriden—and he emerged a stronger president because of it.

The difficulty we had with numerous other issues (I have already detailed the legislative veto, but there are many others) shows an almost total disregard for the concept of presidential power. That this was the case, however, is not so much a fault as it is a commentary on how things are handled in Washington. So much time and effort is consumed on specific issues of impending urgency that it is almost impossible to stand back and look at the large issues, to say nothing of doing something about them.

We at DOJ, however, could at least take comfort in the fact that we constantly hammered away at this principle.

Still another device utilized by the Congress to limit presidential power was the attack on the pocket veto.

Historically, presidents had, in effect, vetoed a bill by not signing it between sessions of Congress as well as between Congresses. Under the Constitution, the president has ten days to sign or veto a bill and return it to Congress. If Congress is between sessions, or has adjourned at the end of a term before the ten days expires, the president can veto it merely by not signing it.

Increasingly, while I was in office, litigants would contend that the president could not "pocket veto" a bill except between Congresses. That is, they claimed that he could not do so during an adjournment between sessions of the same Congress (known as an intersession veto) or during an adjournment while Congress is still in session (intrasession veto.) They took this position despite the fact that the pocket veto has been used more than 1,000 times.

In August 1984, the United States Court of Appeals for the District of Columbia Circuit sustained that position in a two to one vote. On appeal, the Supreme Court dismissed the case as moot. As a result, the question is still unanswered.

Some judges have not been at all bashful at intruding themselves into the province of the executive. Mention has been made elsewhere of judges who want to run the Immigration Service or displace the AG and determine who should appoint special prosecutors. Other judges have run school systems, sewer projects, and prisons.

The tendency for judges to involve themselves in executive-branch functions continues to grow. The temptation to throw in a little politics is also ever-present. Judge Harold Greene, for example, wanted to act as AG in May 1984 when he issued an order directing me to appoint a special prosecutor in the "Debategate" matter, the Carter briefing-papers issue. Judge Greene's action was a highly improper effort to invade the executive's sole province, and it was, as it should have been, promptly reversed by a unanimous court of appeals.

Similarly, Judge Stanley Weigel in California issued an order directing me to invoke the same act to determine whether U.S. activity in Nicaragua violated the Neutrality Act. That was similarly improper, and was similarly overruled on appeal. He was inspired by the request of the majority of Democrats on the House Judiciary Committee (who are also not known as being above politics).

Judge Gerhard Gesell once ordered me to conduct "at least a preliminary inquiry" into totally unsupported allegations of high-level government misconduct in connection with the killings of five people at an anti–Ku Klux Klan rally in Greensboro, North Carolina, in 1979. On appeal, he too was overruled.

All these attempts were the result of not understanding how the act was supposed to operate—plus a desire to muscle into the executive function.

A federal judge in Chicago directed the federal government to turn over $17 million of the secretary of education's discretionary funds to the local school board, to formulate a plan to provide $103 million a year, and to seek the additional funding from Congress. That was another outrageous intervention, and it too was quickly reversed.

More recently, a federal judge in Kansas City actually imposed an increased state income tax to help fund his earlier school-desegregation orders. This, too, was overruled on appeal.

The fact remains, however, that the White House failed to respond to a continuing barrage of congressional and judicial assaults on its power and prerogatives. The president did not unsheath the various weapons given him by the Constitution, and thus a usurpatious Congress continued its efforts to usurp.

14

RESIGNING
DOES NOT
COME EASILY

ONE WOULD THINK THAT RESIGNING FROM OFFICE would be a relatively benign event. Not so. The media and the columnists—the latter with their requisite cynicism—just *knew* there had to be a clandestine motive. The true reason—the simple fact that we felt it was time to return to private life—was not enough for them. For many days we heard on television and the radio and read in the press all the *real* reasons why we were leaving:

- I'd had a falling out with the president and/or his staff and "couldn't take it any more."

- Jean hated Washington and wanted to get out. (Actually, she loved life in the city.)

- *I* hated Washington and wanted to get out.

- I'd been involved in a scandal and had to get out before it broke.

- Running the Department of Justice was too much for me, and I had to get out.

- I hadn't been running it all along, and thus would not be missed.

- The Troika at the White House had never gotten along with one another; Baker and Deaver wanted Meese out, and the only way was for him to be appointed attorney general. Thus, I was either cajoled into leaving or simply pushed out the door.

*The attorney general's entrance at the Department of Justice building.
Department of Justice photograph.*

❖   ❖   ❖

Fortunately, when one leaves office the media becomes benign. I
remember a farewell party at which I sat next to Jane Weinberger,
the wife of the secretary of defense, who gave me a preview of
what it would be like once I had left office. I had told her I was
glad that for the first time in four years I would finally be able to
speak my mind without the constraints imposed by public office.

"Yes," she replied, "but then no one will give a damn what you
say."

Some time later, after I'd been out of office for quite a while, I
was at another dinner party and happened to be seated next to
Katherine Graham, publisher of the *Washington Post*. I told her that

in California I now had the best of all possible worlds: I subscribed to the *Post*, and received it ten days late.

❖　❖　❖

In January 1984 I announced my intention to resign, and the next two months (while my successor was going through the confirmation process) saw a round of farewell parties given for us by the many good friends we had made in Washington. Ten days before we were set to move back to California, trouble developed in the confirmation process and the Special Prosecutors Act came into play, which meant that it could well be 1985 before my successor was confirmed.

At first I thought this wouldn't affect my plans, but I soon saw it would. The president had made his nomination and would stand by it. But if I left, the president would have to make an interim appointment, and I didn't think the public would put up with an acting attorney general for what might well be an entire year. The pressures became enormous, and I saw no other choice but to agree to stay on, which I did.

Of course that ruined all the speculation as to why I had *really* left. It required reconnecting with people we had already said goodbye to several times. One close Justice Department colleague quipped that the new motto for my office was "Forgotten but not gone." A year later, when at last I did leave office, I said, in my farewell address to the Department of Justice employees, who had just given me a standing ovation, "I hope not too much of that applause is from relief that this day has finally arrived. It is purely a rumor that the movie *The Long Goodbye* is a Department of Justice documentary."

❖　❖　❖

High-level government service is a privilege, and serving as attorney general has particular meaning. It is not an overstatement to

The attorney general bids his employees farewell at a reception in February 1985. From the left: Smith; Ron Blunt, counselor to the attorney general; Myra Tankersley; Bill Webster, director of the FBI; Lee Colwell, assistant director of the FBI; Chief Justice Warren Burger; Dick Hauser, deputy counsel to the president. Official Department of Justice photograph.

say that the Department of Justice has an impact on more of our citizens than any other department of the government. Seeing that our laws are faithfully executed, selecting judges who will be in office for life, having the power to investigate and indict, maintaining the highest ethical standards, and protecting domestic stability and national security—all of these are awesome responsibilities.

The Department of Justice is a remarkable institution. It could not be created; it is the result of long years of growth. Populated by able and dedicated people, both career employees and appointees, it serves the people well. It was my honor to have headed this very special organization for more than four years.

At the end of my farewell address, as I concluded my tenure as attorney general of the United States, I said:

> It is remarkable the extent to which a nation's history is marked out by its laws, and the extent to which the greatest of nations and peoples are remembered in their laws. We trace our moral lineage to the Ten Commandments. The civilizing influence of Greece flowed from her laws. The greatness of Rome, by which we are still influenced, rested not with her engineers, whose roads and aqueducts still stand throughout Europe, nor with the military prowess by which she was defended, but with the laws by which she was governed.
>
> The linkage of history and law is neither casual nor coincidental, for history is humanity's record, and humanity is not an abstraction: it is people, individuals rendered unique, separate and distinct by the God who made them, and by the fears, desires and dreams that drive them. The law honors their distinctiveness and protects them in it, acknowledging rights and then strengthening those rights. Each step builds upon a previous one, and we see in our own Bill of Rights an extension and elaboration and a perfecting of those more exclusive rights given in the Magna Carta. . . .
>
> With all of this as prelude, we see in our own nation a history written in law. Our founding documents are legal contracts, which at the same time codified our rights, and created means for their further refinement. We in the Department of Justice are both the stewards of that history and protectors not merely of the law, but of what the law itself protects—the rights of the American people.

And thus ended the Washington adventure.

—Epilogue—
Ronald Reagan:
A Thirty-Year
Reminiscence

THE FIRST TIME I HEARD THE TERM "KITCHEN CABINET" it had nothing to do with Ronald Reagan. The term was used in the early 1950s to described the small group of people that ran the speakers bureau of the Los Angeles County Republican Central Committee. As a young lawyer living and working in Southern California, I had started to become more interested, or, rather, reinterested, in politics (which for me automatically meant Republican party politics, for I'd always felt as if I had been *born* a Republican) and I became heavily involved in speaking and debating at the time of the first Eisenhower vs. Stevenson campaign.

The term "kitchen cabinet" popped up again fully a dozen years later, this time in reference to the nascent political career of Ronald Reagan. For some reason, writers on the subject—even longtime Reagan observers such as Lou Cannon—cannot get straight who was and who was not in Reagan's original kitchen cabinet.

One reason for this failing may be that the term was not used until quite some time *after* the group was organized and functioning, and then seldom by the group itself. In fact, at first the group had no name at all. It was simply a group of friends that became an executive committee, a group of friends that just may be unique in the annals of U.S. political history because the group, or at least its nucleus, has been with Ronald Reagan ever since it came together.

In the beginning, the group consisted of three main figures.

Although I would come aboard almost immediately, I was not one of them. Those three men who made up the nucleus of what would *later* be called the kitchen cabinet, and who persuaded Ronald Reagan to run for governor of California in 1966, were Holmes Tuttle, Henry Salvatori, and A.C. ("Cy") Rubel, who died less than a year later.

If anyone can take credit for Ronald Reagan's eventually becoming president of the United States, other than the Reagans themselves, it would be those three men—because they promised to provide for him the two things he could not do without, a political organization *and* the funds (not simply the fund-raising) for his race for governor.

Today, many people who did not become executive committee members until much later, or not at all, are mentioned in print as having been part of the founding group. But of the original ten people who were present at the creation, there remain only three who have been with Ronald Reagan ever since—Holmes Tuttle, Jacquelin ("Jack") Hume, and me.

There are any number of other misconceptions about the early work of the kitchen cabinet. One is that we had our collective eye on the presidency from the very beginning. That simply is not true. In 1966, all we thought about was our first obstacle, the Republican *primary* for governor of California, for getting past it was going to be a pretty sizable trick.

Another point that has to be kept in mind is that at the beginning Ronald Reagan was looked at as a curiosity, albeit a glamorous curiosity, having come out of Hollywood. I can remember that when *Life* magazine ran an article of a couple of pages on him at that time, the other candidates were furious at *Life* for giving him all that free publicity. In light of what happened, they should have saved their energy for campaigning against Reagan, who eventually won the governorship with a record one million votes!

People also have the idea that at some point in those early days we all sat down with the governor and hammered out a manifesto that listed all the salient points of the doctrine to be known as "Reaganism." Sorry, but that didn't happen either. True, "The Speech," Reagan's now-famous nationally televised exhortation to vote for Barry Goldwater given at the 1964 Republican National

Convention, contains all the elements. But it was not chiseled in stone just for that occasion. We all basically knew what the conservative philosophy encompassed because we shared it, and had felt it evolve in ourselves and our own political beliefs. After all, we were still reacting to almost two decades of FDR and his policies.

The most important thing we had going for us, and we all knew it, was the personality, the simple human magnetism, of Ronald Reagan. He was more than just somebody or something—an actor!—new on the scene. He was really quite different from anyone anybody had seen before.

❖   ❖   ❖

The first of D.C.'s infamous "layers," which I mentioned earlier, is "perception"—how things *seem to be* as distinguished from how they are. From the beginning, the perception of Ronald Reagan has been one of a positive, charismatic, principled leader with a strong political belief that it was his determination, and destiny, to implement—a person impervious to the usual political influences and one whom the voters could trust. That was the perception of the man in the street, the voter, and that explains why Ronald Reagan has been elected overwhelmingly each of the four times he has been a candidate for public office.

Many of the intelligentsia, the press, even the businessmen did not see him that way, however. Their perception was of an actor who could project these qualities, but who was a shell behind the façade, one who would collapse if separated from his cue cards or deprived of his script.

On January 21, 1981, one day after the inauguration that followed a landslide victory, the *Washington Post*'s David Broder wrote, "Realistically it is unlikely he will have either the ambition or energy to seek a second term at age 73."

Ronald Reagan was consistently underrated by many, but he had a quality somehow overlooked in political measurements. It was that, separated from political viewpoints, people just plain *liked* him. He was a phenomenon in politics, but the pundits simply could not comprehend this. The Mary McGrorys of the world never have understood, and as a result have continued to react with sputter and vituperation.

This quality manifested itself early. When Reagan was first elected governor, Jesse Unruh was the most powerful and experienced legislator in California. He could not wait for this *actor* to arrive in the real world of Sacramento, where he could be separated from his cue cards. Jesse probably never knew what hit him, but suddenly he was the *second* most powerful political force in the state, and a rather distant second at that.

During the 1966 primary election campaign for governor, the wily old pro Governor Pat Brown never took Reagan seriously. He was sure that the Republican nominee would be George Christopher, the mayor of San Francisco. Accordingly—and not having a serious competitor in the Democratic primary—he directed his whole campaign at Christopher. When Reagan won an overwhelming victory in the primary, Brown was wholly unprepared. His campaign then lashed out with an effort to portray Reagan as a "right-wing extremist." When that did not sell, he resorted to other tactics, perhaps best typified by his television ad in which a father tells his daughter, with utmost seriousness, "Remember, it was an actor who killed Abraham Lincoln." The result was a historic landslide victory for Reagan.

Businessmen were not much more politically astute. Indeed, businessmen as a group are surprisingly naive in political matters. Not many months after the 1976 Republican National Convention, when Reagan had narrowly lost the nomination to an incumbent Republican president, but had nevertheless been received by acclamation, I got a call from the CEO of a major corporation requesting that I arrange for Reagan to have lunch with him and a few others to discuss the future of the Republican party. I did so.

During the luncheon, the CEO pointed out the difficulties the Republican party faced now that the Democrats had taken over the White House, the need to recover from the Watergate debacle, and the challenge that we faced for 1980. Then, to my surprise, he suggested that for Reagan to continue as an active candidate for presidency would "muddy the waters" and confuse the situation for the more viable candidates. He therefore urged that he not run, but use his considerable talents to support other candidates.

At this time, Reagan was busy making speeches around the country, not just for political purposes, but simply to make a living. He knew how enthusiastic his audiences were both for his philosophy and program, and for himself personally. In the many conversations that I would have with him when he returned from these trips he would relate (in his modest way) how enthusiastic and contagious his receptions were.

He therefore, without any rancor or resentment, told this CEO firmly that he had no intention of becoming politically inactive, to say nothing of agreeing to withdraw as a future candidate at this early stage.

So, too, with the press. After it became clear that Reagan was going to win the Republican nomination, I was invited to meet with the editorial board of the *Los Angeles Times*. Although not so stated, it was clear that the principal inquiry was whether Reagan was smart enough to become president, an interesting subject considering the fact that he had twice been governor of the state in which the *Times* had been the principal newspaper. In essence, my response was that there were a number of (admittedly) smart candidates running for this high office, and Reagan had outdistanced them all.

Since Reagan was smart enough to accomplish this, perhaps the question should be directed to some of the other candidates.

And so on.

❖   ❖   ❖

My relationship with Ronald Reagan took on new dimensions after 1968, when he named me to the Board of Regents of the University of California. This was two years after I had started handling his personal legal affairs.

In the mid-1960s, the regents meetings were not just the site of heated dicussions—they were a battleground!

It is hard to recreate those days in prose, but they were a

fractious and scary time. The meetings rotated from campus to campus within the huge UC system, and it seemed that every place we went we were accosted by malcontents. Simply trying to walk into the meeting hall was an ordeal, what with being pushed and jostled by angry crowds of students and other demonstrators (which often included dissident faculty members and outsiders).

In those days, a regents meeting was always a front-page story. We might have debated a ten-year plan for the medical school, but the headline would be about the rocks thrown through the windows of the meeting hall. Today, all that most people can recall from that general period was the so-called free speech movement— ironically, the principles of free speech were rarely honored by the demonstrators who were demanding that right for themselves.

One of my curious claims to fame during that period had to do with black activist and self-proclaimed Communist Angela Davis, whose dismissal from the faculty caused an immense furor. I happen to be the person responsible for her dismissal. I had left a regents meeting to make a five-minute phone call—had it taken ten minutes, the world might never have heard of Miss Davis— and when I came back to the room, I learned they were about to reappoint her as a visiting lecturer.

I had no strong feelings about her either way, but I asked a lawyer's question. "Wait a minute," I said. "Don't we have a bylaw that says a faculty member can't be a member of the Communist party? If it is still on the books, we should enforce it; if it is still on the books and we don't like it, we should repeal it. But we shouldn't just ignore it." With that, the discussion began anew as to how to treat Ms. Davis, which also happened to be the beginning of her rise to prominence.

❖   ❖   ❖

Even Ronald Reagan, ordinarily a most even-tempered man, was bothered by the often-outrageous actions and speech of some of the demonstrators (not to mention some of the other regents).

As chairman of the Board of Regents, I sat right next to him, and it was not uncommon for me to have to restrain him, to help him fight the urge to respond in kind. From time to time his Irish temper would rise, and I would have to put my hand on his arm to make sure he stayed seated. But once, while I was looking the other way, that temper rose and boiled over.

A demonstrator had said something particularly vile and untruthful, and Ronald Reagan shot out of his seat and went after the man, all the way across the room. By the time I could catch up, the future president of the United States had grabbed the fellow by his lapels and was giving him one hell of a good shaking. I managed to pull the governor away, and got him back to the table.

The next day, I scanned the papers and checked the news broadcasts until I was convinced, to my great relief, that because of the crowd no one from the media had witnessed the confrontation and seen Ronald Reagan taking matters—and the demonstrator—into his own hands.

❖   ❖   ❖

I have probably attended many more political conventions than most people, but perhaps the most interesting convention in which I was personally involved was the 1976 Republican National Convention. It was held in Kansas City, and Ronald Reagan contended against a sitting, although unelected, Republican president, Gerald Ford. It is fascinating to speculate how history would have been changed had events been different during that convention.

In an early campaign strategy meeting held in the spring of 1976 at the Los Angeles Club in Los Angeles, at which Reagan and Holmes Tuttle were among the attendees, the discussion drifted back to the 1966 Republican primary for governor. At that time it had been decided by the Reagan campaign that if he won the primary he would immediately embrace his opponent, George Christopher, and bring his campaign people into our organization. The purpose was to unify the party and create the strongest possible effect going into the final election. That is exactly what happened.

It was now decided to approach the Ford campaign people to achieve the same result, whoever was nominated in Kansas City. The Ford campaign agreed, and it was arranged that the winner would visit the loser in the latter's quarters on Wednesday night after the voting.

Somewhere along the line, however, the Reagan campaign staff (presumably John Sears) had imposed two conditions on this meeting: first, that it would be between the candidates alone with no staff present; and second, that the question of who was to be the candidate for vice president would not be discussed. (Why this latter condition was included after the vote on the president is hard to understand, particularly since if the candidate were Ronald Reagan he had already announced that his running mate would be Senator Richard Schweiker of Pennsylvania.)

And that is what happened. President Ford visited Reagan in his suite at the Alameda Plaza in Kansas City, and no mention was made of the vice presidency. But some of us were convinced that if Reagan were asked by President Ford to be the vice presidential candidate, he would accept. All presidential candidates have to disclaim interest in the vice presidency until after the balloting for president is concluded. I know that for a long time Reagan was not interested. But now, at his age, the odds were strong that this might be his final political effort. If a Democrat won, he would undoubtedly be in for eight years. If Ford won, he and his new VP would overshadow whatever base Reagan could maintain for another four years.

Since the indications were that Reagan would accept, several of us, particularly Justin Dart, made a feverish effort that night and early the next day to contact President Ford, or his campaign managers, before he made his decision on a VP candidate. But neither Dart nor others were able to get through to urge that he, Ford, ask Reagan to accept the vice presidential nomination. The reason seemed to be that Ford and his people were closeted, not to be disturbed and, in the meantime, Ford had settled on Senator Robert Dole.

The election that November was very close. Ronald Reagan was then very popular across the nation, as was so well proved four years later. It is easy to speculate that if Ford had asked Reagan to be his vice president, Ford would have won in 1976. The fact that he and his people were incommunicado during that crucial period may well have changed history.

❖   ❖   ❖

The question of just how good a president Ronald Reagan was is one that citizens and scholars alike will debate for years and years to come. Yet that is not the question that I find the most interesting. The question that truly intrigues me is: What made Ronald Reagan the president he was—and the man he is?

Over the years, as we progressed from what I call "shoulder-rubbing acquaintances" to social friends, I have had literally thousands of opportunities to observe Ronald Reagan in action. And I *still* cannot pinpoint exactly what it is that makes him so special, nor do I know anyone else who can pinpoint it. Yet I am sure he has more of "it" than anyone else I have ever met. Whatever this quality is, it is the secret to his incredible success.

Here are some of the main impressions I have formed over the years. First of all, Ronald Reagan requires more knowing than any man I have ever known. He is not the kind of person that you meet today and consider a bosom buddy tomorrow. A lot of osmosis is required.

Yet he is anything but standoffish. He is outgoing, he is warm, he is delightful, attentive, and sensitive. He cares about the impression he is making. All of those things. But he does not have that Irish hail-fellow-well-met quality I often saw in others back in Boston or in the halls of Congress.

In most cases, you can tell exactly what your relationship is with someone. But with Ronald Reagan that is very difficult to do. I don't think he has a best friend, as the term is generally understood. Nancy Reagan clearly does have a best friend and I think she fulfills that need in him—or plays that role. At the same time, he is very generous, and great fun to be with. He likes to be out there on the golf course, likes to have fun with the boys and do all the things one associates with adult males having a good time. He is the same whether his wife is with him or not.

In fact, he is the same now as he was when I first met him twenty-five years ago. That he has not changed a bit is, in my opinion, another very interesting thing about him. You expect some changes after a person has been president of the United States for eight years, but he is the same person now as he was then.

That quality—call it "X" or Quark or the Z factor or *something*— gives him a commanding presence, and an amazing strength of personality.

❖   ❖   ❖

Ronald Reagan's irrepressible sense of humor traveled with him to Washington—and it traveled well.

The Pension Building in D.C. is a cavernous structure with huge pillars that support a many-storied inside space. Every year, NBC presents its "Christmas in Washington" program in that space. In 1981, a current issue was where the MX missiles should be based. At the Christmas program, I had a seat near the president. He came in, sat down, glanced at the huge columns, and said, "Now I know where to base those MX missiles."

One night Jean and I were having dinner alone with the president and Nancy. We'd had a round of drinks, and the president suggested we have another. Checking her watch, Nancy said that we didn't have time. The president put his arm around Jean's shoulder and commented, "Here I am supposed to be the most powerful person in the Western world, and I can't even have a second drink before dinner."

He is also attentive. One night a large reception was held in the state dining room. As is customary, it ended with a receiving line at the end of which stood the president and the first lady, greeting the guests. It was a long line, and Jean and I decided that, seeing as we'd done it so many times before, they didn't need two more hands to shake, and so we did not go through the line.

The next morning there was a regularly scheduled meeting of all ninety-four U.S. Attorneys with the president. It too was in the state dining room. I had presented the president, and as he passed me on the way to the podium he whispered, "Where were you and Jean in the receiving line last night?" It was the one time we had *not* gone through a receiving line—and the last.

❖   ❖   ❖

Howard Baker, Ronald Reagan's third chief of staff, shared that sense of humor, which I am sure enlivened oval office discussions during his tenure. On one of those magnificent Washington days, I was meeting with Baker in his Capitol office when he was still majority leader. We were looking west down the Mall toward the Washington and Lincoln memorials. I remarked to him, "That has to be the best view in all of Washington." Without hesitation, he rejoined, "The second best!" Once a presidential candidate, I guess, always a presidential candidate.

A secretary who worked in the west wing during both the Carter and Reagan administrations once commented about how easy it was to tell the difference between a Carter cabinet meeting and a Reagan cabinet meeting. In the former case, somberness always prevailed. In the latter case, laughter almost always began and punctuated the meetings, and was almost a sure sign when the meeting was breaking up, so pervasive was the Reagan humor.

But many of those meetings were dull—particularly Stockman's budget presentations and those involving economic projections and assessments. Michael Deaver created a stir when he commented that from time to time the president dozed off. Naturally, the press picked that up and used it extensively, particularly to bolster their picture of the Reagan governing style as being "hands-off." (Actually, the president made a point of being attentive—even through some awfully dull presentations when most of us would have liked to doze off. He made a point of paying attention according to the presenter's status on the ladder—in other words, the lower down he or she was, the *more* the president made a point of paying attention. As I have said, he is a kind man.)

In this case, Deaver provided unneeded and inaccurate ammunition to the media—which of course made the most of it.

❖   ❖   ❖

There has been much comment about the president's hands-off style of governing. With respect to his basic philosophical principles and action, matters of policy or rightness, he was hands-*on* all the way. Examples of this are the air traffic controllers' strike and the invasion of Grenada. In cases such as these, it was Ronald Reagan who knew what the decision had to be, and he directed its implementation. Such decisions were his decisions, and came from deep within him. In each case he was aware of the consequences and risks—and the trauma.

PATCO, the air traffic controllers' union, was one of the few unions that supported him in the election, and if the strike materialized he knew that many members would lose their jobs. But he also knew what was in the public interest, and in each case was strongly supported by the public. (At a speech to the American Bar Association, when I mentioned the administration's action in responding to the strike, I received a standing ovation—the first I can remember from *that* group!) Other examples of action such as this are innumerable—the sale of the AWACs to Saudi Arabia, the strike against Qaddafi in Libya, the capture of the airborne *Achille Lauro* terrorists, and so on.

❖   ❖   ❖

Because he has a genuinely soft heart, discharging someone, anyone, did not come easily to the president. As early as his first year as governor, one of his principal aides had committed what the kitchen cabinet considered to be a major indiscretion—of a magnitude that we thought required termination.

Everyone there agreed that a discharge was necessary, including Nancy. We all gathered one night in his living room with him and Nancy. Reagan listened, but said little. And no termination took place. His decision, however, turned out to be correct. The aide learned from his mistake and became a valued asset, during both the Reagan governorship and his presidency. Furthermore, the fact that it is difficult for him does not mean that he will not do so. He *did*, for example, in the cases of Secretary of State Al Haig, Richard Allen, James Watt, and Donald Regan, among others.

❖   ❖   ❖

Ronald Reagan is such an innately fine person that he feels that if he is asked a question, even if on the run, it would be impolite not to respond. This trait has made famous the likes of Sam Donaldson, the ABC White House reporter who fires off questions at the drop of a helicopter. It has also upset some well-laid plans.

Doing battle with drug traffickers is a difficult and dangerous business, and those DEA, FBI, and Customs agents, or members of the Coast Guard and others who engage in it, are not recognized or appreciated as much as they should be. It is important that the public be aware of what is happening in this arena.

We had just concluded a major drug bust in Florida, and it coincided with a presidential visit to that state. We arranged to have the president view the results and congratulate those who had participated. We assembled everything that had been seized in a hangar-sized warehouse. That included large tables of cocaine in plastic packages, stacks of hundreds of thousands of dollars in cash, arms of all kinds, boats, and an airplane.

The president delivered his remarks, and then I escorted him around the warehouse, followed, of course, by the whole White House press corps. Just as we were passing the table laden with piles of $100 and $1,000 bills, Donaldson yelled out to the president, "Do you support moving the effective date of the 1982 tax decrease from July back to January?" To my dismay, the president answered the questions, and of course his answers were what dominated the news. The whole drug story was eclipsed.

The tangles with the media were endless and, as I have said, very much part of life in D.C. One day I had finished briefing the president on the progress in our program against organized crime, our utilization (for the first time in any degree) of the RICO statute, and our international efforts. That was followed by a press conference in the White House press room.

At that time I was asked a wholly unrelated question—about how the president could accept support from a union that had an official with a criminal record. Quite facetiously, I responded that if they were going to apply that test, the president could not do business with Congress.

That was reported in a way that created the impression that I had said that leaders of Congress had criminal records. Of course that brought down the wrath of the congressional leaders who ranted in public, in addition to burning up the telephone lines. (It was one of the few times I received a call from Senator Robert Byrd, then the minority leader.) When I explained my remarks, the calls subsided—and in one or two cases the callers reacted with a trace of humor.

It was not entirely a laughing matter, though, because several congressmen had recently been investigated, indicted, and convicted of various offenses—most notably in the Abscam cases. (Actually, from 1977 to 1984, fourteen members of Congress were convicted of crimes.)

❖   ❖   ❖

Finally, let me end this account of my longtime friendship and relationship with my client, the only one who became the president of the United States, with a brief description of a trip that the six of us—Nancy and Ron, Mary Jane and Charlie Wick, Jean and I—made to London and Paris not long after Ronald Reagan had reverted to his original status as just plain citizen.

In London, Prime Minister Margaret Thatcher, always a warm ally of President Reagan's, received us with genuine friendship and affection. There was a series of gatherings and receptions, both public and private, culminating in a marvelous formal dinner. President Reagan was installed by Her Majesty Queen Elizabeth II as an Honorary Knight, Grand Cross Order of the Bath.

It was much the same in Paris, where President Reagan was greeted with great warmth and respect, and became one of the twelve foreign associate members of the Academy of Moral and Political Sciences of the Institute of France.

At each event, there was an outpouring of real affection for Ronald Reagan from all the British and French people we encountered. Of course, it included Nancy and the rest of us, but the reception given the president was especially warm. We had known for decades that we Americans loved him, but it was wonderful to see evidence of that same emotion across the Atlantic.

Through it all, Ronald Reagan was simply himself, smiling, gracious, charming, and natural. Once again it struck me that the man drew people to him by some special magnetism that is given to few others.

As I have already said, I felt it an honor to have served Ronald Reagan as his first attorney general; let me end by saying it was also an honor simply to have known him.

An Appreciation

William French Smith was a fascinating and unique individual. Those of us who served President Reagan by working for Bill Smith in the Department of Justice shared an extraordinary experience in public service. Because of Bill's modesty and self-deprecating personal style, his approach and contributions to government service have never been fully understood or properly reported. Characteristically, Bill has overlooked many of his finest professional qualities in his own book.

Although President Reagan and his first attorney general came from very different backgrounds, they had much in common. Above all, both men brought strong convictions and firmly held principles to public office. They articulated those views with clarity and forcefulness and surrounded themselves with individuals who they felt could implement their principles in the complex federal establishment.

In the first few months of his tenure, Bill Smith devoted considerable time and energy to the selection of the persons in whom he would entrust the implementation of his and the president's goals. Most important, once he brought together his team, he guided and led that team with keen attention, support, and a style that encouraged a remarkably free, robust and open environment for dialogue, debate, and predecisional disagreement. The process was stimulating, and inspired confidence in the decisions produced and loyalty in the decision-makers.

At 8:45 every morning Bill conducted a "senior staff" meeting to review issues, plan objectives, and coordinate the operations of the department. This meeting included the deputy attorney gen-

251

eral, the associate attorney general, the solicitor general, the assistant attorneys general in charge of the Offices of Legal Counsel, Legislative Affairs, and Legal Policy, as well as the counselor, the . Public Affairs head, and Myra Tankersley. At 12:30 P.M. every working day Bill had lunch in the attorney general's dining room; all the presidential appointees and certain other senior policy people were welcome, and encouraged, to join him. These lunches quickly became a second daily senior staff meeting. Luncheon conversation was less structured than that of the morning meeting. The exchanges included more personal sharing of experiences and ideas. Together, these two daily meetings and Bill's deeply ingrained insistence on open and free debate became fundamental to an operating style that stimulated and nurtured candid yet constructive professional exchanges in a setting that bonded a diverse group into a closely knit team. The camaraderie of the "Smith team" became well known and was respected throughout the executive branch. Particularly within the Department of Justice, at the senior level and among the career professionals, there was a strong sense that the attorney general had assembled an energetic, open, resourceful, and cohesive force.

Bill never fought for headlines and publicity. He enjoyed the substance of the work, was a voracious reader, heavy questioner, and methodical student of briefing books. Bill was intellectually stimulated and aggressively curious. He sought the views of others and encouraged free debate before him on issues being wrestled with by the department. Bill enjoyed managing his team and the constant challenge of the job. He found reward and satisfaction in work well done. He took visible pride in the successes of his team. He was supportive and reassuring in times of difficulty. As one of his colleagues put it, the enduring legacy of Bill Smith is that he now provides the standard by which those of us who served with him will hereafter measure ourselves.

ROBERT A. MCCONNELL
THEODORE B. OLSON
KENNETH W. STARR
Washington, D.C.
July 1991

INDEX